\

3 PRESIDENTS
2 ACCIDENTS

More MO41 UFO Crash Data and Surprises

Paul Blake Smith

W & B Publishers
USA

W & B Publishers

For information:
W & B Publishers
9001 Ridge Hill Street
Kernersville, NC 27284

www.a-argusbooks.com

ISBN:9781942981930

Book Cover designed by Dubya

Printed in the United States of America

3 PRESIDENTS, 2 ACCIDENTS:

More MO41 UFO Crash Data and Surprises

TABLE OF CONTENTS

PREFACE

.My first book, "*MO41, The Bombshell Before Roswell: The Case for a Missouri 1941 UFO Crash,*" from Argus Publishing, was researched for more than four years. I had gathered so much material, in fact, that I was not able to put it all into one edition. Additionally, after the book went to press, I collected still more data, new information that was at times quite startling and needed to be aired to help bolster the case for a genuine extraterrestrial event. So for these reasons, I now offer a "sequel" of sorts, a follow-up publication that will help flesh out the initial claims, facts, and reasonable speculation within the original premise's publication, which came out in February of 2016. Then also hopefully tell a fuller, more supported, and more understandable nonfiction narrative, via two different approaches, to help prove the case. And it also adds some fascinating new side stories and factoids to the drama, laced throughout "*3 Presidents, 2 Accidents: More MO41 UFO Crash Data and Surprises.*"

This book represents the next step in the investigation, but it also taps me out, so to speak. I have no further information to present on the MO41 event, it's all laid out herein. And as is the case with all aspects of this amazing saga, strong circumstantial evidence without tangible proof of the ET tragedy and its aftermath is the rule of thumb. But I hope for the open-minded reader, the overall case has been effectively made.

For those who are new to this startling saga, and missed out on "*MO41*," we'll begin with a summary of that book within the Introduction. It could also serve as a helpful refresher course for those who have read the original material but may not own a copy, or have forgotten parts of it. A few fresh tidbits of information are sprinkled into that encapsulating rehash as well.

Within Section One, Chapter One, we'll take a closer look at the night of the MO41 UFO accident, in relation to an eyewitness to its "Ground Zero," plus Washington figures like the First Couple and the director of the FBI, along with a traveling top general. In Chapter Two we see what the President Franklin Roosevelt was up to in his Oval Office in the week after the ET crash, according to existing records, when military/government intelligence reports, photographs, and opinions were readied by and for advisors who came strolling in. In Chapter Three we'll uncover the stunning connections and coincidences in the secret and sometimes mystical world of hardcore Freemasons, seemingly filling every level of power during the early '40s, from Cape Girardeau citizens on up following the Army-recovered spaceship crash. Missouri's Grand Master Mason, future president Harry S Truman, figures repeatedly and prominently here. Chapter Four delves into the distinct possibility that none other than John F. Kennedy might well have found out about the celestial affair, in '41 or a bit later.

In Section Two, we'll go on the road to do some first-person exploring in a "quest for proof" and discover some surprising new information and allegations. Chapter Five encapsulates the year 2013's trips by the author across the state of Missouri to his old hometown and its surrounding countryside, searching for more data. It relates how people and places who popped up now and then in the April 1941 UFO case began to figure again during World War II in

Cape Girardeau, some in surprising fashion. Chapter Six airs a peek at nearby Chaffee, Missouri, the other town closest to the MO41 crash site, within neighboring Scott County; does it hold a memorial clue to the crash? Chapter Seven reveals some juicy recollections from a longtime Cape citizen who learned about the MO41 event back when it happened, albeit from second and third-hand sources. We'll also examine a Russian UFO crash and some stunning old ET footage recently revealed. In Chapter Eight we'll take a look at enticing and previously untold allegations and recommendations that have arisen since the publication of the initial *"MO41"* book, including a possible "Secondary Crash Site" from "that night." Plus, we'll ponder the tale of *another* UFO landing – this time safely - in the same Cape Girardeau SCS neighborhood just a few years later.

In a two-part Section Three we'll examine Accident #2, a surprisingly under-reported but dramatic episode from perhaps America's most discouraging era ever: January of 1942, the early dark days of the nation's involvement in World War II, when almost everything that could go wrong, did go wrong following Pearl Harbor's attack. President Roosevelt's biggest Hollywood supporter, actress Carole Lombard Gable, literally went down in flames, in a shocking tragedy that stunned and saddened millions of people worldwide. Were aliens to blame for this aerial disaster? And was it related somehow to MO41?

And finally in a special "Bonus Chapter" we'll discover how FDR's tragic death and secret autopsy was handled by some of the same men who manipulated JFK's sudden and suspicious demise and autopsy. Their bullet-wounded bodies, their caskets, their Secret Service agents, their transportation to Bethesda Naval Hospital, their possible ties to the handling of MO41… was it all just a coincidence, or a conspiracy?

And of course after that comes a Post Script with still more data, plus all the Chapter Source Notes & Trivia that went into the making of the book, revealing or backing up the references, research, rumors, and remarks herein.

A quick reminder is placed here for the reader: *almost all records from 1941 are long gone, and so are all of the eyewitnesses to the events described.* Even their offspring are deceased. Physical evidence was scooped up and hauled away seven decades ago. And so many people involved were either sworn not to speak of the extraterrestrial affair, or were just plain afraid to, warned or not by their own representational democratic government and military. The blockbuster or "bombshell" drama is now over 75 years old. But sometimes-staggering clues and nuggets of truth keep shining through the haze of seven decades, and are presented here with reasonable conjecture and logical - not outlandish - speculation.

A substantial purpose behind the first book and this new publication has been to draw very serious media and cultural attention to the 1941 Cape Girardeau saga, which has been sadly but amazingly overlooked in the annals of UFO research and history. To gain the spotlight for not just two enjoyable, intriguing, and enlightening "*MO41*" tomes, but to also entice more professional, seasoned investigators to dig deeper into the case. To have these more experienced and polished researchers uncover more within the chambers of government *and* rows of farm crops that I cannot unearth. If this happens – and is done well - my work will be done, my goals accomplished, and I'll be very pleased overall, whether I am included in the process or not.

I believe that the overall narrative herein adds up to what may well be the greatest real-life story with the most amazing impact in United States history. {Yes, this author really believes it all actually happened.} For now, I seem to be nearly the only voice speaking out on this stunning but still largely-hidden event. Someone with great political power needs to pick up the ball and run with it from this point. All I know is that poor ol' me did what he could without fumbling, or getting blitzed and driven into the ground. Perhaps in the future, I'll be on the sidelines of this exciting case, cheering it on, satisfied with my own past contribution should it be out of my hands.

Overall I wish to add that I sincerely hope that readers around the world will have enjoyed what I have written and have learned plenty of new *stuff*; I sure did while writing it! I was repeatedly surprised by our nation's modus operandi in the 1940s, and also by my own hometown's past and its most exhilarating claims to fame. May you thus be inspired to dig into the great mysteries of life within the framework of your own lifetimes. Cheers…

.. Paul Blake Smith
... Summer, 2016

INTRODUCTION

A Summary of "*MO41*"

"...1939, two years before a captured UFO..."

Let's review what information was originally covered on the April 1941 alien occurrence in Cape Girardeau, Missouri, as explored in the original 2016 nonfiction book *"MO41, The Bombshell Before Roswell: The Case for a Missouri 1941 UFO Crash,"* from Argus Publishing.

MO41 **CHAPTER ONE**: A 52-year-old Christian pastor, Reverend William Huffman, told his family at close to midnight one night in mid-April 1941 that he had been called out to "an airplane crash" reputed to be just outside the city. The accident site was in a farmer's field, perhaps "twelve to thirteen" miles or so away from his simple house on North Main Street in Cape Girardeau, Missouri (population 20,000 then, 40,000 now). The minister was escorted to the tragic scene by a police associate who was not in uniform. Once there, William viewed flames and smoldering smoke in a field, metallic wreckage, and bodies lying on the ground. He was stunned when it turned out the airship was circular and obviously not of earthly origin, with small grey alien bodies – two dead, one barely alive at first - stretched out in the grass not far away, where flames had been tamped down. Bits of metal from the crashed craft were strewn around the field, being inspected by a crowd of local citizens, including the farm's workers, the Cape Girardeau police and fire department first-responders, and apparently some military men in uniform and an FBI man (local field agent Arlin Jones, most likely). The firefighters, most likely led by dedicated Chief Carl Lewis, were dousing the flames, having been alerted first by someone on the farm property, having witnessed the crash just after sunset. This citizen in turn dashed inside and used a telephone to call the local operator, who patched him through to the Cape Girardeau police and fire departments, which shared the same downtown building.

As William walked up to the sole live alien, still on his back, his breathing shallow, apparently unable to take in our oxygen-rich atmosphere. The weirdly grey-skinned, hairless, bulbous-headed entity evidently died as Reverend Huffman watched, helpless. As people pawed and jawed at the site, William said some prayers for the departed, these rather creepy lifeless extraterrestrials that he thought he heard someone say were physically pulled from the crash and laid out side-by-side together.

.As the flashlights and lanterns and car headlights filled the night air, William watched a pair of photographers snap pictures now and then of the amazing scene. One shutterbug – quite possibly local newspaperman Garland Fronabarger, age 36 - had two local men pick up a dead ET body and pose with it, taking a photo with a small box camera, kept in his shirt pocket. This was not the larger, more professional camera the unnamed gentleman utilized to record the scene. Each of the identical, skinny humanoids were about four feet tall at most, with surprisingly long, thin arms and legs, and either greatly wrinkly, crinkly skin, or they had on silvery-grey flight suits of some sort. Their heads were similar, all three balloonish, with huge black eyes. Each had only four digits, three fingers and one thumb, each noticeably longer than a human being's. There seemed to be no space helmets, oxygen tanks, gloves, shoes, or weapons of any kind in the debris. And perhaps oddest of all, none of the trio of cadavers showed any sign of injury or burns, despite the traumatic crash and blaze. Just how exactly did they die?

.To better understand the crash-landing, Pastor Huffman stepped over to the motionless aircraft, blown apart in at least one section. He peered into the ship's "flight deck," or "cockpit," and noticed at least two small seats, as if for children, which the aliens rather resembled, compared to human beings. There was a strange, unidentifiable writing on a metal band around the interior of the craft, rather like Egyptian hieroglyphics. William didn't know what the symbols meant but he did recognize some knobs or switches or dials of some kind on a type of dashboard or control center within the ship. It was not a large spacecraft, but perfectly circular and smooth on the outside, minus the blown-apart section. Obviously the shrapnel on the ground came from the exploded "very shiny" vehicle's chassis, now in shards that folks at the scene would pick up and inspect, curious and emboldened since no other aliens seemed to be around to rescue or revive their fallen comrades.

.William Huffman and the others puzzled over the finds until bright lights suddenly filled the site. It was the United States Army that had moved in, taking over. Uniformed soldiers – perhaps armed? – surrounded the site and hemmed in the crowd, showing great authority over the situation. Everyone present was told they could not take away any part of this accident scene: no debris, no photographs, no notes, no evidence of any kind. They were to put back on the ground anything they had planned to take home as proof. They were to turn over all record of the event, and told in no uncertain terms "This did not happen, you didn't see anything." The soldiers then took Reverend Huffman over to one side, away from the crowd, and let him know he was to be silent for his own good, to never speak of the alien crash to anyone, at any time. Perhaps for the good of the country, or for "national security," all were most likely told the same thing: *keep silent, forever.* Someone who was in a position of great authority had obviously ruled on the matter and demanded security at all costs. William was then free to go. He was driven home by his police associate friend. This mystery Cape man might well have been Pastor Huffman's across-the-street neighbor on N. Main, Justice of the Peace Milton Cobb, age 47. His house had a clear view of William's and Milton would have known the obscure evangelist and church fundraiser at Red Star Baptist Tabernacle was home that night.

.When William arrived home he was rather visibly ashen and shaken. He gathered his concerned family in the modest living room – minus his heavily pregnant daughter-in-law, who gave birth May 3rd of '41 – and nervously told them just what had happened. The reverend had quickly violated his secrecy oath, but he was only human, bursting to tell what he had just been through. His loved ones were eager to hear about it, hopeful that he was all right. William's redheaded wife Floy; his married 24-year-old son William Guy Huffman II; and his younger son Wayne, age 22; they all listened intently to every startling word, perhaps stunned beyond belief. Reverend Huffman was definitely not the type to lie or drink or drug himself, or to make up tall tales or distort reality for some reason. That made the revelations all the more shocking. Huffman told his brood he would speak of it just this once and never again, and when he finished, somewhat unburdened, went off to bed. He lived up to his word and never again uttered a peep – evidently to both his family and other Cape

Girardeau citizens – for the rest of his life. However, his wife Floy finally did when she spoke up while ill with cancer in 1984, as absorbed and carefully noted by her daughter, William's granddaughter, Charlette Huffman Mann. She in turn wrote a letter with details to a UFO investigator in the early 1990s, and the story was researched by a few different parties as the new century emerged. In wrapping up the story, Mrs. Mann mentioned how her grandfather became a changed man after the shocking experience, becoming a little quieter but more open-minded to the great mysteries of life. He died in 1959, never going public with what he saw and knew.

.Someone who allegedly backed up Pastor Huffman's story was Phillip Reynolds, the grandson of a Cape fireman who was said to be at the scene of the crash, dousing the flames and inspecting the physical remains of the downed ship and its dead crew. Walter Reynolds supposedly told his family as he was dying of Stage Four cancer that the former Cape minister's wild story *is true*. Walter should know, he saw everything for himself, including some of the cleanup by the Army soldiers who assumed command. The fireman got into trouble with the enlistees when he was nabbed trying to slip a piece of the metallic debris into his pocket. The soldiers made him give back the evidence and then ejected him from the site. Later, in the event's aftermath, Mr. Reynolds said his telephone was allegedly tapped and he was being watched around town. Evidently someone – the FBI? The Army? The police? – was worried he might take revenge on being booted by spilling his guts to others, including the press.

.Linda L. Wallace is the daughter of a former Sikeston flight training school's air "line maintenance" crewman who well may have been part of the military attachment that traveled to the impact site and commandeered the wreckage the night of the crash. Linda found surviving family members pretty tight-lipped about it all, so she searched old records from Sikeston (1941 population, 7,000). 1941 law enforcement, fire department, newspaper, and airport paper trails were all sadly long gone, and Linda also sadly found almost all of her father's Army buddies were either passed away or going into retirement homes far away. She did find a suspicious-sounding Sikeston newspaper article from the summer of '41 that mentioned how odd it was that all visitors to the airbase were now being stopped by an armed guard and screened carefully before being allowed in. Linda also discovered that Cape Girardeau County's sheriff, Rueben Schade, was the brother of Sikeston army unit's "purchasing agent," Ben Schade. It is logical to conclude that one of these two men tipped off the other about the crash early on that evening, keeping in mind that Reverend Huffman stated he saw uniformed military men already at the accident scene when he arrived. Responding briefly to the MO41 tale in the 1990s, Ruben and Ben's surviving brother, Clarence, confirmed that he had indeed heard "long ago" about the ET crash and bodies, but that he was skeptical as to the story's veracity, since he wasn't called to the site to see for himself.

.In another interesting twist of fate, Charles B. Root was the captain of the aerial training school. He had transferred to the Sikeston base within the past year from his position amongst high-ranking officers and officials in Washington D.C. If an Army order came down for secrecy, citing "national security" at the crash site as Huffman alleged, issued by the soldiers who arrived in an organized manner, then it is logical to speculate that Captain Root was the one who called Army high-ranking officials in the nation's capitol for instructions, which came quickly. He had the connections and the pull. Perhaps he did so before driving to the site, just after being informed by one of the Schade brothers as to the true serious nature of the crash and its staggering implications.

.Charlette Mann provided the original and best details of the amazing saga as she began giving a limited number of interviews in the late 1990s. She recalled that as a little girl, around the years 1953-'54, she would see her father, W. Guy Huffman II, take out a photograph at family dinner parties and even utter a few words about the spaceship accident from over a decade earlier. The snapshot was of one of the aliens, propped up between two men at the site, looking very foreign, mysterious, and downright creepy. The picture frightened, fascinated, and fixated little Charlette, who never forgot its details. The huge ET head, the seemingly crinkled grey skin, the big black eyes, the little slits for a mouth, with no ears or hair... it was stunning to think such a creature was actually real. Charlette nor her surviving older sister couldn't produce the snapshot as proof positive of her tale thanks to the actions of one man, a Kansas-born and bred fellow named Walter W. Fisk. This neighbor in 1953 supposedly stole the picture and never brought it back.

MO41 **CHAPTER TWO**: About two weeks after the "MO41" crash incident, as we'll call it for short, the cameraman from the farm crowd who snapped the picture of the held-up dead ET came forward. This unnamed photographer – again, quite possibly G.D. Fronabarger - looked up William Huffman at his Cape address in late April '41 and while appearing "very frightened" handed him a copy of the tantalizing snapshot. He then left the Huffman home quickly, fearful of being seen or overheard in his act of defiance of never discussing the MO41 case, or having evidence taken from the scene (it was kept in his shirt pocket that night). There was an air of mistrust and perhaps paranoia in Cape Girardeau, for those who had been to the UFO accident site and knew the truth. Would the Army, the FBI, or Cape cops check up on citizens, to see if they had been whispering the tale to others? Would there be reprisals of any kind?

Preacher Huffman couldn't bring himself to destroy or toss out the photo copy, but he simply gave it to his son, Guy, and he apparently tucked it away in a box or a drawer for the remainder of the decade. After World War II broke out, William and Floy's younger son Wayne went into the Army. He tragically lost his life in battle in Europe in 1944 and was buried there. It was thus easier for the Huffmans to pack up and leave Cape that year, for a new church and new life together in Oklahoma. Later they moved to a small town in Kansas, where Guy ran his own furniture store. His family chipped in to assist him, and that's when they met a supposed insurance agent from across the street, in Walter Fisk. When invited to a Huffman dinner party in '53, the subject of life beyond earth came up, so naturally Guy retrieved the amazing MO41 photograph to get worldly Walter's opinion. Charlette Huffman Mann recalled for researchers being at the dinner table, even what they had to eat that evening. It just so happened that their guest, Mr. Fisk, was once in the army, then in the navy, and later it was discovered he was in military intelligence. A government *spy* who knew photography so well that in the 1950s he became a professional photographer for a U.S. news agency. Guy didn't tell Walter much about the alien image, nor the MO41 event, but Fisk said he needed to take the photograph home "to study" and then bring it back. He never did. In fact, he skipped town with it soon thereafter, even apparently leaving his insurance job behind. An interesting nugget of information was uncovered by Linda Wallace when learning of a newspaper report from the 1990s on how U.S. military/government intelligence over a period of decades utilized insurance companies for mining insider data on Americans. In effect, spying on private citizens. Was veteran Fisk a part of that operation during the Depression?

Walter Fisk had ghosted the scene, but not before Charlette Huffman, then eleven years old, saw the shocking picture he swiped "about twenty times." Its extraterrestrial subject matter haunted her, with its big black soulless eyes, huge head, and skinny arms, propped up by the two Cape Girardeau men. The alien seemed to have "crinkled skin." It was just downright creepy, but always unforgettable. It also matched perfectly with a description of recovered alien bodies in a recently-unearthed U.S. Army *Special Operations Manual*" from 1954, quite unbeknownst to Mrs. Mann.

.In learning more about Walter Wayne Fisk, researchers like Linda Wallace found out his espionage past, and that he was still alive in the 1990s, living very near Kirtland Air Force Base, Manzano Storage Facility, and Sandia National Laboratories in Albuquerque, New Mexico. Those are three sites long suspected of secretly harboring crashed UFOs. Fisk proved an evasive and grumpy interview, refusing to admit to three different researchers much about the Huffman photograph (although he did remember Floy as "Red" due to her hair color). The former veteran asserted he was once a news photographer working at the White House in Washington D.C. in the 1960s, and yet he also spent time at the State Department there, where he claimed he once took a snapshot of a UFO from one of their windows! Walter also claimed to have been a few other things in life, professions that sounded very dubious, changing his allegations at times as if he was fibbing and trying to throw off investigators on his trail. In the summer of 2012, W. W. Fisk died at age ninety at an Albuquerque veteran's hospital leaving behind no clues, cooperation, or confessions.

.Charlette Mann also described reading recently uncovered documents regarding a 1947 UFO crash in Roswell, New Mexico. This was called "The White Hot Intelligence Assessment," written by the staff of Army Air Force General Nathan R. Twining, intended for a handful of top government officials to read, including President Harry S Truman in '47. In this typed document, the strange recent recoveries from the New Mexico desert floor were "deemed extraterrestrial in nature" when compared to "artifacts – (redacted) - discovery of 1941." The words "from the Missouri" fits the blacked-out redaction space perfectly. It was an electrifying statement in the leaked, once-classified Top Secret report, one that was backed up by a further remark in typed print. This second revelation referred to the MO41 materials as *"the recovery case of 1941,"* startlingly. Another big impact confirmation! The report's statement complained that this '41 recovery "did not lead to a unified intelligence effort" to "exploit technological gains" minus its connection to "The Manhattan Project." That was the creation of the atomic bomb, which the document alludes to as having been aided by alien technology recovered and copied from the Cape Girardeau, Missouri, accident. What a huge story if true!

.The stunning documented remarks on the '41 technology the government got its hands on in private, out of the public eye, brought to mind the alleged statement by a scientist working in a lab setting in the early 1960s. According to an eyewitness, this physicist, Dr. Otto Krause, once spoke candidly about the atomic bomb and its components, which included technology "taken *from an aerial crash in Missouri in 1941.*" The vehicle was described as *extraterrestrial in nature*, he went on to explain. This advanced propulsion device with atomic properties copied from the MO41 hardware was considered more Top Secret than the atom bomb itself, Krause supposedly added.

.On top of all of this, a retired American intelligence agent named Thomas Cantwheel typed up a letter at the end of his life and sent it to a UFO researcher. This document summarized major intelligence secrets he learned in the field of applying recovered extraterrestrial technology into top secret government projects as the 1940s melted into the '50s and beyond. *"There was an aerodyne recovered in Southwest Missouri in 1941,"* Cantwheel mentioned almost casually in his near-deathbed statement. Cantwheel had cancer and was in his early nineties, but his letter of confession was quite lucid and cogent, and once again it mentioned MO41. We can forgive an ill old man looking back five decades for slightly misstating that the site for the alien crash in Missouri was "south*west*" instead of the "southeast," near Cape Girardeau, as we know is the case. But once again we have yet more circumstantial evidence that *some* people high up in American government, or working in association with the government and the military, knew that three people from another world crash-landed their spaceship in April of '41 and that the great secret was hushed from public scrutiny for decades.

MO41 **CHAPTER THREE:** Valuable clues to the actual crash site for the MO41 affair began to surface after the year 2000 on the internet. In fact, they didn't really come to the fore until after 2012, when the national discussion forum *"Topix"* sprouted a few lengthy threads on the alien incident as several Cape Girardeau County and Scott County citizens chimed in on what was the true landing site in '41. One source who called himself "Just Wondering" typed up some helpful but still mysteriously obscured communications within this *Topix* site, stating that the MO41 crash was quite real, very alien, and hushed up at the time… yet those who were involved may have done something about it years later. That is, first responders.

"Those great men" got together and funded a kind of memorial of some sort, which was left in place to this day, indicating their reverence and respect for those who died in the crash. And that this alleged object or marker is still to be found in Scott County, perhaps in or near the city of Chaffee, yet it means nothing to the younger generation that see it today. It was put up "by the generation after" the fine gentlemen who were involved in responding to the flame-filled accident, as presumably a memorial to the three dead alien creatures.

.Not only does there allegedly exist an unspecified MO41 memorial, but a person – as of 2013 – that lives near Chaffee who "owns a piece of the wreckage," our internet friend "Just Wondering" asserted. This unidentified man relays that the alien accident was always referred to as "the Cape Girardeau crash" instead, just to "throw off investigations," amazingly. So whomever possesses this ET grand prize doesn't want to give it up or gain publicity, that we can glean from the *Topix* assertions of "J.W." Another tantalizing and exciting remark, yet frustrating to all in the end as no more info was displayed to back up or explain the online posting.

.Responding to this and other typed statements by others wanting to know more about MO41, a person calling himself "All Souls" produced information that titillated *Topix* even further. "All Souls" stated that his own grandparents "owned and farmed the land where the crash occurred," and apparently spoke of it just a bit over the decades, intriguing the source so much he returned to the area to investigate. The grandparents – and evidently their offspring – didn't want to talk about it, still fearful of government reprisal. They had supposedly sold the farm just after World War II and moved away from the region. "All Souls" went to Cape Girardeau and began his own search. He found the right area and interviewed locals, which led him to an elderly farmer who had purchased the property in the postwar years and continued to farm it. The aging gent told the *Topix* poster that at one point he decided to install a cistern, or water tank, to collect rain water. When the farmer dug into the ground, he found bits of strange metal imbedded in the soil. He collected the weird shrapnel and found some of it marked or embedded with odd symbols he could not recognize. The debris could not be really bent or mangled, nor sliced with special farm metal cutters. This amazing physical proof from MO41 was alleged to have been stored in the farmer's barn for decades, then just a few years ago it became so decrepit it was torn down. What became of the UFO debris "All Souls" did not know, and the old farmer would not reveal.

.Other *Topix* statements – whether they are true or not – passed along rumors and assertions that the MO41 crash did indeed occur in between Chaffee and another small town in Scott County, just south of Cape Girardeau. All of the local villages in those days had mostly a few volunteer amateur firefighters and little equipment, thus if an area farmer or his employee had reacted to the crash outside his farmhouse door with a call for help, he might naturally have selected nearby Cape Girardeau's firefighting team first.

MO41 **CHAPTER FOUR**: Sikeston born and raised but currently living in Ohio, not too far from Dayton's Wright-Patterson Air Force Base – the source of countless rumors as a holding and inspection site for recovered crashed alien airships and corpses – Linda L. Wallace put together what family narratives and media clues on MO41 she could assemble. The resulting early 2014 e-book called "*Covert Retrieval*" produced some interesting sidebars and hints on the Scott County angle of the accident saga.

.Linda's father was in 1941 rather a technical wiz at the Parks Air College at Sikeston Airport and worked in conjunction with the conjoined Missouri Institute of Aeronautics, teaching young Army enlistees of the "309th Flying Training Detachment" to properly maintain their planes. He was a "line maintenance" crew member, but in fact more of an "aviation operations expert," not quite in the Army at the time, but close. The Wallace family patriarch also knew a lot about various flight technologies and communications, and after the crash was evidently the subject of silly rumors involving MO41, which he may have helped recover and inspect. By early May, his lovely fiancé – Linda's mother – came back to Sikeston after finishing her college experience. When she arrived she heard gossip that speculated that her man was somehow responsible for the crash-landing of an otherworldly aircraft, thanks to his expert manipulation of a mirrored device in field communications for military members, called a "heliograph." Other rumored tales of a recent downed circular ship and some dead "little people" taken to the Sikeston airport were fairly prevalent that spring. But Linda's dad (now deceased) wasn't talking over his lifetime, and Linda's mom decades later evidently knew more than she was willing to discuss, frustratingly.

.After Pearl Harbor, Linda's once fun-loving father was now in the Army for sure, and transferred to Chicago for "advanced training." Linda's mom suspected from the start this move had something to do with the alien accident, but couldn't prove it. The patriarch had landed in the middle of Army Counter Intelligence Corps training centers and secret work on the atomic bomb, going on inside a covert metallurgical laboratory at Chicago University. When he came back to Sikeston, the matriarch found him a changed man, much quieter and pleased to curl up alone with a book on Albert Einstein's scientific equations for time and space. Interestingly, Einstein was mentioned in a later-leaked FDR memo as possibly having knowledge of the crash technology and may well have been imported for his opinion of the alien ship's atomic know-how. He also co-authored a mid-1940s report on the impact projected alien contact with mankind in the future, found within leaked documents around the turn of the century. Albert Einstein died without a public comment on it all, in 1955.

.In doing some research, Linda found a surviving crew member from her father's day, an elderly man in a nursing home who fondly recalled her dad. He was the same man who was reported by some to have told folks in the 1940s, "I picked up the bodies" from an alien accident. Linda asked the elderly veteran about this but he clammed up immediately. Other small leads here and there, tidbits of information, were interesting for Linda but were always just out of reach. A check of Sikeston newspaper files, along with law enforcement and firefighting records, proved fruitless. All paper records of 1940s events had been tossed out, replaced by modern computer files. Linda did find one newspaper with edition copies left from '41, and through that discovered the eerie fact that many unusual "accidents" and "suicides" in the region took place in the months after the otherworldly accident. Even those in the MIA/PAC community in Sikeston spoke at times in private circles about the mysterious rash of sudden deaths, including one man who was said by the newspaper article at the time "working on a government project" before he was found hanged in his own barn. It was scary to ponder then, and to this day.

.Linda talked to a few Scott County residents who did remember hearing fragments of the '41 tale, and also of a meteorite that whizzed through the region a few years later. She found a man, born in Cape Girardeau, whose grandparents were area farm employees in '41 and knew of a mysterious aerial crash incident, but the family moved afterwards to Minnesota, in '43. There they would ask each other questions about the mysterious event, the unidentified man learned, but then the story faded from family lore as the decades went by. But another person – a young girl back in 1941 – told Linda a more detailed saga, perhaps partly from memory and also from family lore…

.The little girl in '41 was with her parents when they stopped at a small store in a rural "crossroads community" in Scott County. There they heard the story of a crashed object not too far away, so the family jumped back in the car to go see what everyone was excited about. They arrived at the site – in broad daylight – and joined a crowd of onlookers who stared at what the now older woman remembered as "three boulders." They were metallic in appearance, in three big chunks, evidently. Military men in uniforms, a few in suits, arrived on the scene with a big flatbed truck, keeping the crowd at bay. That is, until they noticed the little girls' father, who was a strapping farmer with plenty of muscle. He was asked to help load what they thought would be the heavy foreign object onto the back of the unusual truck. Instead, all were surprised at the lightweight nature of the item being recovered. The father's help wasn't really needed after all, but after touching the "boulders" he later needed several hand-washings in the family's kitchen sink to rid of a nasty stench. This was a particularly strong memory. The old woman's recall to Linda Wallace did not specifically mention a circular aircraft and dead aliens, and the mentioned possible site for this event was far too south in Scott County to have fallen within the "twelve or thirteen miles from Cape" that Reverend Huffman asserted. Needless to say, the little girl at the time of the unusual happenings could have missed or merged or mangled some memories when telling author Wallace her recall about the case so many decades later.

.Perhaps it was around this time that a very large airplane landed at the PAC/MIA base at the Sikeston airport. Linda had another relative who was affiliated with the facility who recalled to her that this big cargo-like plane landed and was at one point surrounded by armed, uniformed men, as if they were protecting something very valuable and secret.

.In other parts of her kindle book, Linda Wallace summed up some UFO reports and circumstances that the military was rumored to have been involved in, both regarding MO41 and other tales. She delved into the history of Air Force General Hap Arnold, who left the military after World War II to join the RAND Corporation – and their effort to create "a world-circling spaceship." Now where did they get *that* idea? Linda also discovered that General George Marshall – said to have been a part of the recovery and storage process of MO41 – hired plenty of outside intelligence agents for his CIC to keep a better what on this country in the immediate weeks and months after April 1941. Counter Intelligence Corps' ranks swelled greatly in the aftermath of the extraterrestrial event near Cape Girardeau. Marshall and Arnold were close friends, and over the war years had plenty of contact. Arnold was also good friends with Oliver Parks, who ran the PAC schools in the Midwest. After the war, Hap Arnold was also seen frequently at Wright Field in Ohio, where the 1941 Sikeston air training captain, Charles Berton Root, ended up – right smack dab in the middle of the Wright's "Air Material Command," which has long been strongly rumored as the program and site of recovered alien vehicular wreckage and examination. Root also was stationed back in the Washington D.C. area after WWII, as well as becoming Deputy Chief of Staff at AMC within the Wright Field set-up, and his second-in-command at Sikeston's MIA, Ralph Rockwood, also ended up at Wright. Other "coincidences" and strange UFO-related occurrences are further detailed in the pages of Linda

Wallace's kindle book, *"Covert Retrieval,"* still recommended if available for anyone interested in MO41 and beyond.

MO41 **CHAPTER FIVE**: The Reverend Turner Hamilton Holt was a Greenwich, Ohio, pastor who was a cousin to President Roosevelt's United States Secretary of State, Cordell Hull, still in office in 1941. Turner went to Washington at some point during the Depression era and came back a bit rattled and shaken himself (sounding so very much like Reverend William Guy Huffman). Hull died in 1955 and a few years later, Holt passed away from leukemia. It wasn't until they reached their sunset years that Preacher Holt's two daughters in 1999 spoke up with a shocking account that compares very favorably with MO41, and should be examined seriously by all interested in this saga.

.Once when in D.C., Turner told his daughters later (separately), he met with Cordell Hull, who took him to the U.S. Capitol Building. Once on the exterior steps, Cordell swore Turner to silence about what they were going to go see. The two trooped inside the building where Hull worked for many years as a congressman, and still traveled to on occasion in order to testify as a cabinet member. Hull led Holt down deep into the structure's sub-basement, and finally over to a kind of storage room. They entered and turned on the lights. Inside was the most astounding sight of Turner's life.

.When looking around, Turner recalled he laid eyes on a round, grayish-silver, metallic spaceship, cut into sections. It lay on the floor, looking damaged, some of it covered by a wrap or tarp, near shrapnel pieces from it. Nearby were "three glass jars," the sister said in a 2009 interview with Grant Cameron, not the "four" they originally stated in the past. Inside each was a small grey alien creature, uninjured but dead, floating in some formaldehyde. The description the two daughters recalled of what their father imparted to them matches perfectly with what W.G. Huffman claimed to his family. These spooky humanoids were big-headed with big eyes that were shut, long thin arms and legs, and three-fingered with one thumb per hand.

."These are creatures from another world," Cordell supposedly told Turner, then invited his cousin to lift up one end of the crippled spaceship. Turner said he expected it to be heavy, but instead it was quite lightweight. Before they departed, Hull supposedly said that the Roosevelt administration could not tell the public about the startling artifacts as "it would start a panic." The two men discussed the amazing size of the heads of the beings, Turner recalled; this unusual feature really riveted his focus.

.Evangelist Holt later broke his oath of silence when he told the story to his oldest daughter, said to have been close to twenty years old at the time. This translates into sometime in 1941, happily for our story. The other daughter was not told until some years later, being too young and immature at the time of the incident to fully understand and appreciate its impact.

.In backtracking a bit, the Linda Wallace e-book recounted the author's conversation with a family member who told her where the UFO crash materials went after they left southeast Missouri. "It was placed in a dungeon," was all the source would grudgingly say. A *dungeon*? What seems ridiculous now sounds perfectly accurate. The sub-basement of the U.S. Capitol Building could have been quite an apt description for this.

.Could such a wild idea be really possible? Could a crashed alien ship have been taken to the most famous building in America, where hundreds of congressmen and visitors work every day? Back in the spring of 1941, the alien artifacts needed a secure home, if even a mere temporary one until something more long-term could be worked out. Recall that Turner said the lightweight airship was broken down into sections, not nearly-intact as Pastor Huffman said he saw at the crash site. It seems obvious that the ship was taken apart, perhaps even cut by an acetylene blowtorch or industrial-strength cutting devices, then wrapped up in blankets or a tarp, and hauled down the freight elevator of the Capitol Building, possibly by Army soldiers in uniform or civilian attire. The items were locked up in the storeroom far below the offices and workspaces of the congress, and only a select few people were likely informed on the subject, obviously including Secretary Hull. If Cordell truly showed his trusted cousin Turner the objects, it was probably after hours, to get a clergyman's honest opinion and spiritual or Bible-based reactions.

.Although one of Turner's daughters has now passed on, the other continued to tell the tale, but the story has not changed and there is little that can be added to it. It fits with the Missouri reports and would make sense when one realizes President Roosevelt would have wanted the MO41 recoveries kept locked up from the public and the press, and guarded in a site no one would possibly think of as a repository for the otherworldly treasures. With no CIA, or DIA, or NSA, or Pentagon in those days, the selection of the storeroom many floors below the basement level of the Capitol makes more and more sense. The U.S. Army always kept a special liaison office under the Capitol, as likely did the State Department, and the Vice President (Henry Wallace) had his official office in the building too. What is more, if FDR wanted to see the artifacts for himself, he could simply take a short ride down the street from the White House, and enter under the guise of visiting important political figures, if spotted and asked about his presence in the congressional home.

.One final note of great irony: on the morning of Saturday, April 12th, 1941 – thought to be the most likely date for MO41 – the Cape Girardeau newspaper printed on the front page a syndicated news photo of a body being transported out and away from the U.S. Capitol Building. It was of a recently-deceased U.S. senator, his body having lain in state for viewing in the rotunda, showing the world again that the grand building was quite used to storing and displaying corpses.

MO41 CHAPTER SIX: In searching for documented proof of the MO41 affair, one can turn to some leaked memorandums once issued by President Roosevelt at his Oval Office desk, during WWII. These documents were carefully vetted for authenticity by Ryan S. Wood and his father, a retired scientist, Dr. Robert Wood. The memos were once in the possession of General George Marshall's trusted intel operative, Thomas Cantwheel, which he leaked in the 1990s before his death. Cantwheel was once a member of Marshall's elite "Counter Intelligence Corps" and its special "Interplanetary Phenomena Unit," the team that was designed to scoop up and examine any physical evidence of "non-terrestrial" visitation to Earth – at least within American borders. Roswell, New Mexico, in the summer of '47 might have been one of their first big tests to retrieve alien materials, after all that the IPU learned from studying the Cape Girardeau affair in '41.

.The first memo was stamped "Top Secret" and was dated February 27th of 1942. This was a directive for FDR's Chief of Staff, General George Marshall, to allow more scientific access to "the materials in possession of the Army that may be of great significance toward the development of a super-weapon of war." Another reference in the memo refers to Dr. Vannevar Bush, head of the president's scientific research team in the late 1930s and the new "Office of Scientific Research and Development" as of mid-1941, and into the new wartime decade. The memo states that Bush was leading the effort into understanding "the celestial devices" to "find practical uses for the atomic secrets learned" within their engines and propulsion system. This was a reference to at the very least the crash-landed Cape Girardeau find (and perhaps another discovered ET craft), which FDR also referenced as "this new wonder."

.A similar authenticated FDR memo, issued from his Oval Office as "Double Top Secret" on February 22nd, 1944, was sent to "THE SPECIAL COMMITTEE ON NON-TERRESTRIAL SCIENCE AND TECHNOLOGY." The important, later-leaked document urged this small group to go forward with a program "put forward by Dr. Bush and Professor Einstein" in studying what was obviously the recovered MO41 materials. *Alien hardware.* Inspected by *Albert Einstein?* Plus, President Roosevelt agreed "that the application of non-terrestrial know-how in atomic energy" be applied in the scientific group's ongoing efforts to perfect "a super-weapon of war." *The atom bomb* (of which Bush and Einstein were familiar). So here again we see that FDR wanted the atomic propulsion system within the crashed spaceship copied and applied towards a reliable and worthy nuclear bomb – and likely other atom-splitting technologies being developed - to be used as soon as possible on Nazi Germany and/or Imperial Japan as the war raged. In the memorandum's closing paragraph, the chief executive lauded the Special Committee on "coming to grips with the reality that our planet is not the only one harboring intelligent life in the universe."

In a 1971 book, *"Einstein: The Life and Times,"* by Ronald Clark, it is noted with curiosity that in the midst of WWII Vannevar Bush responded to Albert Einstein's eagerness to take part in the American war effort through scientific advancement by placing him "on a committee where it seemed to me that his particular skills would be most likely to be of service." The author noted this mysterious, unspecified committee work was never learned, yet around this time Einstein told a friend - in August of '43 - that he had "closer relations with the Navy and Office of Scientific Research and Development in Washington." As mentioned, the OSRD group was Dr. Bush's pet, and an offshoot of that organization undoubtedly produced the "Non-Terrestrial Science and Technology Committee," the one that Roosevelt referenced "Professor Einstein" being a substantial part of in early 1944. The information and sources here dovetail neatly.

.Another memo was unearthed and authenticated, involving Dr. Van Bush's response to these issues, but not for Franklin Roosevelt – who had died suddenly in April of 1945 – but to his successor, President Harry S Truman. Bush told Truman he was still working on various answers to questions Roosevelt proposed on the "non-terrestrial sciences" that the MO41 finds yielded. Apparently part of all of the above memorandums seemed to deal with the notion of possibly creating a new aircraft or space vehicle that could deliver weaponry, based on flight technology gleaned from the MO41 alien technology.

.An interesting support to the notion that secretly, behind the scenes, was the surprise findings of a pair of British spies during World War II. William Stephenson was the head of a British Security Coordination effort to pry into American secrets in the 1940s. He and one of his top agents, Roald Dahl, hobnobbed with top Roosevelt administration officials, including Vice President Henry Wallace and U.S. wartime intelligence chief William Donovan, an old and trusted friend of Franklin D. Roosevelt. One of the biggest of all secrets learned was that – most surprisingly – *President Roosevelt had a space program in mind!* As discovered and reported by Dahl in late 1944, the plan by FDR and his top scientific advisors was to create a spaceship to fly at least to the moon, land pilots there and have them plant a U.S. flag while exploring the surface. Then presumably to have these brave pioneers get back in the craft and fly back to America, where they would set down safely. To alert British intelligence upper echelon to this amazing and noble presidential plan, Dahl filed a report with Stephenson, at the spy network's headquarters at Rockefeller Center in New York City. Apparently this remarkable information was generally laughed at. Then, flash-forward to July of 1969. That's when Stephenson cabled Roald Dahl to remind him of FDR's spaceship-to-the-moon proposal when the entire world watched as American astronauts did just that, landing on the moon and planting the American flag to "claim it" for the United States while exploring there. Stephenson congratulated Dahl, he had been right all along! But one must ask: *where and how did FDR come up with the idea of a flying airship that could burst through the earth's gravitational field and make it to the moon, set down, and then return safely with pilots intact?* It almost certainly *had* to stem from the recovered Cape Girardeau alien ship, and its technological application into a planned "S craft," as detailed by Thomas Cantwheel in his summation letter, typed in the late 1990s before he passed away. This was a top secret project that tried to apply retrieved alien technology into a manmade vehicle that was tested in the New Mexico desert from 1945 to 1947. The results back then were not good, with many accidents and some pilot fatalities.

.It must be pointed out here that Roald Dahl went on to write the popular book (turned into the classic movie) *"Charlie and the Chocolate Factory."* In this early '60s story, the lead characters ride in a flying glass and steel elevator, which lands safely near little Charlie Bucket's home and picks up his family, to take them into space. In a little-known sequel, *"Charlie and the Great Glass Elevator,"* author Dahl wrote of young Charlie and Willie Wonka, the elevator/spacecraft's inventor, flying into space, only to run into extraterrestrials, overcome them, and come back down to terra firma where they land safely and are hosted at the White House by a chair-bound "President Lancelot R. Gilligrass" (sounding very much like "Franklin D. Roos-e-velt."). Spaceships and aliens and an FDR-like president, fascinated by it all... where oh where did Roald Dahl get his high-flown ideas?

.In October 1941 the U.S. government ran a geographical survey of the Cape Girardeau area, with fly-over photography that can still be seen to this day. In another odd October '41 incident, a "crashed" UFO was evidently discovered in the Carolinas. This was precisely where General G. C. Marshall was staging Army maneuvers, testing his top soldiers in war situations. A soldier's mother passed along later a big secret from "the Carolina Maneuvers," which matches well with MO41. As if it was Marshall's attempt to carefully train and educate his top men on what to do about a non-terrestrial aerial accident, just as he was training them on how to handle battle conditions in the training exercises. Could this be why Dr. Van Bush was complaining to President Roosevelt he couldn't get unfettered access to the MO41 artifacts for proper, sustained scientific research, resulting in the '42 memo from FDR to GCM? .

.In a fascinating side note, an esteemed physicist, Dr. Rolf Alexander, stated in an interview years after the fact that he met with George Marshall in 1951, in Mexico City, and asked the former Secretary of State and U.S. General/Chief of Staff at that time about UFOs. Marshall surprised scientist Alexander – if not outright shocked him – by admitting candidly that some UFO sightings were real, and that extraterrestrial beings had crash-landed their scout vehicles on American soil in three incidences to that point. We can certainly hypothesize reasonably that MO41 was the first, and Roswell, New Mexico, was the second crash, but the third remains speculation. Possibly it was in the mountains near Los Angeles in February of '42. In each case, George told Rolf, the recovered ETs apparently seemed outwardly fine but succumbed due to their inability to breathe out atmosphere, causing them to "incinerate from within." *Quite like what witnesses described in that Cape Girardeau farm field.*

.Two more documents from the desk of President Roosevelt in the 1940s need to be explored herein. The first FDR issued five weeks after the eye-popping Missouri occurrence, on May 20th, 1941. It was a decree to create the "Office of Civil Defense." Roosevelt had been planning for weeks and finally issued the public goal of creating watchdogs in each American community to keep an eye on the skies. Civil Defense volunteers were to scan the skies and keep an eye out for foreign aircraft, reporting them to the military, along with any fires or suspicious activities they might encounter. Within this document lay the makings for FDR's all new "Civil Air Patrol," which once again would allow American citizens to take to the skies and keep a close lookout for any unusual airships, helping the military to control our airspace. Coincidence?

.On May 27th, 1941, the handicapped president took to the national airwaves in a major radio speech that drew diplomats from all over North and South America, and also the second highest radio audience in his administration's tenure. FDR backed up his week-old civilian defense act. In the broadcast, the Commander-in-Chief described yet another Oval Office document he had just authored. "I have tonight issued a proclamation that an unlimited national emergency and requires strengthening our defenses to the extreme limit of our national power and authority." All this was supposedly due to a "war for global domination" going on... and yet *America had not been attacked or even threatened by another country*. "We are placing our military forces into strategic positions. We will not hesitate to use our armed forces to repel attack," the president dramatically announced. President Roosevelt would have originally issued this order a few weeks earlier, just after MO41, but ill health had cost him time and effort; he was sick in bed for weeks in May with intestinal problems and anemia, requiring secret blood transfusions. Certainly the spring of '41 was a most tenuous but telling time!

MO41 **CHAPTER SEVEN**: The entire MO41 affair was first brought forward via a letter written by Charlette Huffman Mann. She sent it to UFO researcher Raymond Fowler in 1991. Ray looked into the matter and then forwarded it to a more well-known investigator named Leonard Stringfield, a former U.S. Air Force officer. He explained what he could on the Cape crash in one chapter within his rather obscure 1991 book *"UFO Crash/Retrievals, The Inner Sanctum, Status Report VI."* This intrigued another researcher, Dr. Stanton Friedman, who traveled to Cape Girardeau to look into loose ends of the story. So did Ryan S. Wood, who wrote an early public report (that contained some small factual errors), printed within a 2001 MUFON issue of *"UFO Journal."* Some general backing for the story was provided for MUFON by Dr. Robert Sarbacher, a government source with apparent insider knowledge of crashed UFOs. Dr. Robert Wood, PhD, Ryan's hardworking engineer father, also helped out by way of authenticating documents uncovered by researcher Timothy Cooper, who received the Thomas Cantwheel letters and old FDR memorandums, kept from his days of working for George Marshall in the Army's

CIC and special "Interplanetary Phenomena Unit" and also the CIA. Tim Cooper then asked his father, retired Air Force aerial investigator Master Sergeant Harry Cooper about the dumbfounding Missouri crash claims. According to Ryan Wood, *the retired military officer told his son Timothy that the MO41 allegation was quite accurate and valid.*

.Also digging into the story was "*Earthfiles*" internet and radio host Linda Moulton Howe, who chipped in with helpful information on Dr. Otto Krause, and his 1962 remark about an aerial crash in Missouri yielding valuable atomic know-how for American weapons technology, considered "more Top Secret than the atom bomb itself." This was mainly derived from a "neutronic propulsion device" in the ET technology. Linda passed along other tidbits and tales of MO41 in the late 1990s and early 2000s in the Art Bell national radio show "*Coast To Coast A.M.*," helping the story gain more notoriety and momentum.

.Through all of this, Charlette Mann privately provided as much information as she could, with the original William Huffman recollection unchanged or distorted. She gave only occasional interviews on camera, one with Ryan Wood and another for an East Texas television station in 2008. That was the same year Cape Girardeau's CBS affiliate, KFVS-TV, also ran a two-part story on MO41, being of great interest to the area.

.Ryan Wood kept the ball rolling. He included the Cape Girardeau crash in his fascinating 2005 book on UFO crashes around the world, called "*Majik: Eyes Only.*" He also teamed up with his father, plus Tim Cooper, Stan Friedman, fellow UFO researcher/authors Jim Marrs and Timothy Good, and a TV producer/director, to feature MO41 within the SyFy Channel special program "*The Secret,*" which aired a number of times due to its popularity, first in 2003. A recreation of the nighttime 1941 crash scene was shown briefly in the documentary. As British researcher Tim Good told viewers within the cable TV special, "I believe this whole business got started during World War II. My feeling is that the Missouri incident of 1941… {sic} did indeed occur." And the educated, cultured, and worldly Mr. Good doesn't endorse just any rumor or claim, either.

.Speaking of highly educated and cultured men who believed in the '41 UFO affair, the famous nuclear physicist, Dr. Edward Teller, was evidently aware of the situation as well. In the 1980s, Teller wrote a letter to President Ronald Reagan, mentioning the year, "1939, which was two years before a captured UFO, and Pearl Harbor." Obviously this was a reference to MO41, and can be seen to this day within Ryan Wood's marvelous document website, majesticdocuments.com. With this one statement, we can reasonably conclude three things: first, Teller was aware of the Missouri crashed UFO and that it was "captured" by the American military. Second, we can conceive that President Reagan was also already familiar with the MO41 recovery as Teller did not bother to explain the extraordinary case he mentioned, almost casually, in the letter's sentence. And third, Dr. Teller may have either seen the crash recovery, or some files pertaining to it, especially regarding its ET atomic engine makeup, in order to help apply this advanced knowledge to America's refinement of the atom bomb, since Edward was after all a nuclear physicist who worked on such programs. {And fourth, as president Ronald Reagan flew to Cape Girardeau, visited privately with backers in town, and later issued UFO/ET references in a few public speeches, in his second term in office.}

.The MO41 story got picked up on as the years passed, mentioned in more book chapters, and in more newspaper articles. On websites, podcasts, and in blogs. It was explored in YouTube videos and on Wikipedia, at least for a while. Phillip Reynolds stepped forward in 2012 with what he knew about his grandfather, the late Walter Reynolds, evidently the Cape Girardeau fireman who confessed his part in the aerial crash first response. This was examined in the website BeforeItsNews.com. The popular web publication About.com asked their resident expert, Billy Booth, about the Cape Girardeau affair, and after his own research he concluded: "I personally feel the crash occurred." The online forum *Topix*, as previously mentioned, also began an uptick in helpful comments and clues on the subject as the years passed. In 2014, another cable channel – History – explored some of MO41 within its MUFON series "*Hangar 1*," claiming that some of the alien technology from the crash was taken to Purdue University for intense study, something no one had mentioned before in their investigations.

.And as 2014 passed, researcher Linda L. Wallace offered kindle readers a peek at her new e-book on the Sikeston end of the tale, with the insightful "*Covert Retrieval*," plus her updated website seekingmoinfo.com with tantalizing tidbits for computer surfers.

.All in all, the staggering story has grown slowly but surely into the public consciousness, although not quite in a mainstream manner. But one thing is certain: no one has ever seriously looked into the claims and facts in this case and decided it's a lie, or a hoax, or a great distortion of the truth. On the contrary, they find in the end it's *real*, and worthy of more investigations.

MO41 **BONUS CHAPTER**: Various sources on various Internet posting sites have chipped in with their second-hand stories on how they learned President Franklin Roosevelt actually shot himself, while on vacation in Warm

Springs, Georgia. The date of the great chief executive's death has always been recorded accurately: April 12th, 1945 – the fourth anniversary of the MO41 tragedy near Cape Girardeau. But the official circumstances of FDR's demise have always been accepted by historians and news people without any proof or documentation when it was simply declared by the president's aides. For the world to believe, the official story was that Roosevelt grabbed the back or side of his head and suffered a cerebral hemorrhage, or a major stroke, which left him near death. He was allegedly carried to his bedroom in "The Little White House" in Georgia (his vacation retreat), where he labored to breath, unresponsive for over an hour. Finally, FDR succumbed. Yet according to so many accounts passed along within online forums, Mr. Roosevelt was said to have in reality *pulled a .45 caliber pistol from under his "lap robe" and pulled the trigger*, when almost no one was around, just a few assistants in another room or outside of his "Little White House" vacation cottage. Internet forum posters from around the country contributed stories passed along to them from sources in the FBI; the Marines; Bethesda Naval Hospital; FDR insiders; the Secret Service; a D.C. mortuary; and "an attending pathologist at FDR's autopsy, removing the bullet" from his skull. All tales agreed that depressed president had in fact committed suicide by handgun, knowing full well that his end was near anyway.

.Other relatives and persons known to FDR had already committed suicide, or tried to, as of April '45, including cousin Kermit Roosevelt, who had shot himself in the head over a year earlier, a fact the Roosevelt family kept covered up for decades. Even Missy LeHand, the president's secretary, tried to kill herself, and that was while *in* the White House. Sudden violent death was going around the world as the war raged on, and suicide was not uncommon, but still stigmatized and not openly discussed, nor its clinical depression causes treated well in that era. FDR's

Secretary of the Navy, James Forrestal, and Roosevelt's Under-Secretary of State, Sumner Welles, also went on to attempt suicide. Additionally, Lucy Mercer - the president's girlfriend who was present in the Georgia cottage that fateful day - may have told her sister of what really happened in FDR's death; in November of 1947 this sister also pulled out a handgun and shot herself in the head.

.If Roosevelt actually committed suicide, why did the president wait until the 12th? He arrived in Georgia on March 29th and had all the time in the world during the next two full weeks to undertake the fatal act. Did it have to do with the April 12th, 1941, alien crash anniversary date?

.Presidential aide Daisy Suckley wrote in her diary that during previous evenings before the president's death, he rather strangely spoke about the subjects of ghosts and reincarnation! Obviously the survival of the soul after the demise of one's physical body, and haunting spirits, that was the topic that was foremost on Roosevelt's mind. He *knew* his end was near, either through natural causes or suicide. This even extended back to his January inauguration, when son Jimmy stated later that his thin, frail father spoke of death, his will, and his funeral arrangements, just after he was sworn in on the portico of the White House, instead of the Capitol Building.

.By ending his own life, there is no question the very ill FDR put himself out of his misery. He had experienced a long string of health problems, some of them very serious. Everyone around the president knew his health was failing, his color and vitality were fading, and his chances of substantial recovery or revitalization were nearly gone. Several months before, he had made sure to place Missouri's tenacious senator, Harry S Truman, on the presidential ticket for the '44 election, knowing it was quite possible Franklin would either resign for health reasons before his term was up, or that it was possible Roosevelt would die in office. As we have seen, Truman almost had to have been briefed on the MO41 matter, and like FDR was a hardcore Freemason. {Another sign that Roosevelt in fact shot himself was that he was given no Masonic funeral service; Freemasons don't permit that ceremonial procedure if a member commits suicide.}

.In removing himself from the White House to Georgia, Roosevelt spared the nation the embarrassment and disgrace of a suicide in the executive mansion. He evidently had a general game-plan to make his exit from this world as early as one year previously, in April of 1944, when a secretary noted in her diary that Roosevelt asked her to bring her a loaded handgun, while they were on a vacation in coastal South Carolina. Again, while away from Eleanor, the family, friends, and most aides, and the White House. Now in April of '45, Franklin pulled the trigger on his plan, quite literally it would seem.

.When FDR was declared dead, his body was quietly attended to by Georgian morticians, and the upper part of his head was kept strangely wrapped, so that any bullet hole in his skull could be obscured to the few that were allowed to see the body. But was it kept in its casket after the morticians finished at 5:45 the next morning? By 9:15, First Lady Eleanor ordered the casket kept closed, even to family members, and it was taken under heavy guard the next morning to a train in Warm Springs. From there it was transferred on a long slow ride to Washington D.C. There was to be no "lying in state" in the U.S. Capitol Building, thanks to Mrs. Roosevelt's strange-at-the-time decision to avoid that experience. {Later, James Roosevelt was going through his father's papers and found a four-page, handwritten document by FDR in 1937 specifying that the president *did* want to at least have a service with his casket present within the U.S. Capitol Building's rotunda, handled by the Army with no speakers, just silent prayers and short hymns.} Although the presidential coffin was brought into the White House, its lid remained firmly shut at all times (minus a few minutes alone for Eleanor in the East Room, with guards turned away). Next it was taken to Hyde Park, New York, where the president was laid to rest in a rather simple private ceremony, although newsreel cameras and still photographers were allowed to record the service respectfully. Again, *no one* was allowed to open the coffin to see the president in death, leading one to wonder if the body of the great man was actually in its casket until the very end, his interment. Was the public hoodwinked, to cover a secret cranial autopsy after a hushed-up suicide? And did any of this macabre matter have to do with what took place four years earlier in Missouri?

SECTION I:

National Data – Washington D.C.

Extended Background Research

CHAPTER ONE

Saturday Night Fervor

... "A new sense of urgency of air defense"

A sudden explosion with a fireball wafting upwards. That's what damaged part of a farm family's crop and compound, as well as a typically quiet Saturday evening in Cape Girardeau, Missouri, the sleepy small town on the muddy Mississippi River. It was April 12th, 1941, unusually warm and windy that day. By sunset conditions were seemingly calming down... but then factors heated up beyond most men's imagination. One person enjoying the unseasonable outdoors apparently saw just about everything that shocking night, but he could not have foreseen how this sudden impact would soon impact the lives of three American presidents (and possibly the deaths of two of them). Perhaps all of United States history would turn on this cosmic dime.

As the sun sank out of the moonlit country sky, farmhand Rusty Blevins (pseudonym) walked a little slower than usual, tired from the long day's farm chores... until this abrupt and traumatic event on his boss's land. It naturally jolted him with great shock and horror. Evidently an airplane of some sort had just come hurtling down and crashed right outside the farmyard, with its resulting fire lighting up the area in a dramatic flash. Flames leaped up around the wreckage and glinting shrapnel. "There must be passengers and crew in a terrible state, perhaps some dead and others barely alive," Rusty likely thought in a daze. He shook himself alert; ran at top speed into the nearby farmhouse; and searched for the property owner's living room black telephone. Young Mr. Blevins was evidently nearly the only person at home at the time, with the farm's operators away in town to celebrate the festive Easter weekend, with religious services planned all over town early the next morning.

The stunned farm employee could barely think straight as he grabbed the phone. He tried to calm himself, then shakily rang up a Cape Girardeau telephone company operator.

."*Operator! This is an emergency!* There's been a plane crash on our farm, outside of Cape!" The telephone switchboard operator quickly patched Rusty through to the downtown Cape Girardeau Fire Department, where a desk sergeant – possibly a policeman - answered. Nearby, a few off-duty cops and firemen were likely chatting, smoking, playing cards, or even having Saturday evening dinner. Some were upstairs, relaxing in the private quarters, accessible by a staircase, an iconic silver pole close by to slide down. The Cape police and the fire department shared the same building, the same emergencies, and often the same problems, stemming from upset local citizens, seeking action for their dilemmas. And this one was a doozy. It galvanized the handful of men into action, and fast.

.Frantic Rusty relayed his bare-bones facts to the calm sergeant: a plane crash on his employer's farm, with a fireball turning into flames just outside his window... The downed airliner must have lost its way to or from one of the two nearby local airports… that was all he knew. "Can you send some help right away, to put out the fire and save our house and barn? There's gonna be victims on the ground!" Rusty gave the address, perhaps some general directions, and hung up. He needed no further thinking or hesitation. Blevins was determined to do the right thing: run right out to the crash scene and see if he could save some lives. It painfully promised to be a very gruesome task; there was sure to be blood, broken bodies, and cries for help in the wreckage.

.Rusty raced outside, into the flame-and-debris-filled field, and stopped to stare in amazement. *This is weird! There are no bodies, no suitcases or parts of luggage, and no blood anywhere. The airplane seemed as round as can be, not a cylindrical vessel with wings, struts, propellers, or exhaust vents.*

The silvery-grey wreckage was clearly damaged with glistening metallic shrapnel all around, yes, but this was nothing like what young Mr. Blevins expected. He peered into the substantial hole in the disrupted disc, which lay in the dirt with mysterious figures visible inside. *Something, or someone, was moving, at the weird controls. They seemed like children!* Thin and bigheaded children, less than four feet in height. Two weren't really moving. Were they dead, or just unconscious? A third was moving about lamely but clearly alive, limbs stirring.

.Rusty dodged the flames and decided to take action. He realized that if he waited for professional help that was on its way, it might be too late. Blevins *had* to get into this weird airship and pull the little children to safety. In the distance, he could hear other people, the shouts and footsteps of a few neighbors running to the crash scene to offer help. And then, sirens. The firemen he called, maybe a medical staff, and some cops, he was sure of it. But adrenaline-filled Rusty Blevins could barely notice any of

this. He stood staring intently at these three little people...
and yet not human beings at all. Not children. Not even...
from this planet? *What in the name of God?!* These were
otherworldly creatures, illuminated by the flames, unlike
anything he'd ever seen before! Or ever heard or read of.
Rusty's mind must have frozen for a sec, completely
shocked amidst the sunset's afterglow and frightening
flames all around him. He'd never forget this macabre
night, that was for sure.

Farmhand Rusty Blevins kept quiet for over fifty years on
this stunning memory, and only spoke to a precious few
around the turn of the new century, but those fleeting few
minutes on the farm back in the spring of 1941... it was the
most amazing experience in his long personal history. In
Missouri history. In American history. And maybe, just
maybe, in all of *human* history. Should he contact the
Army? Or the FBI? Or even the president in Washington?

The time has come to see what government records are left
today to help prove this astonishing case. Of course,
through the last seven decades of government secrecy and
denials on UFOs and alien visitation, the idea of finding
"smoking gun proof" left in any files is fairly ludicrous. For
instance, the White House in the Great Depression did not
keep any telephone records, and any classified memos and
briefings were long ago expunged from the official papers
left for academics and historians to sift through. Explosive
matters of national security or top secret subjects would not
be left around for the public to peruse. So finding any meat
left on the bone for modern investigators to pick through
has been tough. However, not all hope is lost...

The official White House schedule of then-President
Franklin Delano Roosevelt (1882-1945) has gone up in
cyberspace. That is, a worldwide internet website
nowadays displays as many digitized and approved pages
as possible of the great man's presidential daily office logs.

Mostly his White House appointments, kept by his faithful staff. A careful search for clues within these logs in the month of April 1941gives us detectable clues, although certainly there are no explicit documented references on what bewildered Rusty Blevins was experiencing on the ground in Missouri. His Saturday night was bizarre, FDR's was seemingly banal. But clues are there for us if we look hard enough.

.Before we commence to fathom these logs, we must keep in mind that Franklin Roosevelt was very bound by his disability (polio) and the heavy burden of governing the nation during the Great Depression. The president stayed at the White House a great deal in the early spring of 1941. Ushers, stenographers, and an appointment secretary would record who arrived at the White House to see the famous man, and when they left. There was a busy but not hectic pace to the leader's schedule. Times of meetings were often recorded, along with which room of the presidential manor the chief executive received his guests in. Set plans could be rearranged according to events and breaking news. A few months earlier, for example, schedules were quickly altered when gorgeous movie star Carole Lombard – a very public supporter of President Roosevelt – and her mega-popular husband, actor Clark Gable, stopped by the White House for a visit with ensuing chit-chat with the First Couple.

The digitized logs even show us today when Mr. Roosevelt was wheeled by an aide to a doctor's office within the executive mansion, and when he retired to his private bed chamber upstairs every night. Usually this was around 10:30 to 11:15 p.m., depending on how much business or company was present to entertain and how physically fit the popular Commander-in-Chief felt. Due to his disability, there was no "sneaking off" somewhere, where aides and security agents could not find the famous handicapped man.

If it had been a long day and/or he was feeling particularly under the weather, Franklin Roosevelt might be wheeled upstairs by a valet in an elevator to the privacy of his bedroom and shut himself off even *earlier* than 10:30. He would often read books or briefing papers there; spoke privately on one of the two telephones on his bedside table; had a smoke and/or a snack; listened to music or radio programs; or attended to still other matters upon being alone. Usually this activity took place after his valet helped him out of his chair or braces, out of his suit, and into his pajamas. This was FDR's private time, warm in his safe, secluded bed chamber, thus his activities and specific sleep times were not recorded. Franklin often conversed with close friend Harry Hopkins (1890-1946) at his bedside when it was about time to turn in, both men in their "jammies." Harry bedded down in a guest room not far away, single and bored at the time. When home, First Lady Eleanor Roosevelt (1884-1962) always slept in a bedroom across the hall; on this Saturday night she was in Boston, eager to return by a planned aerial flight to D.C.

.According to Eleanor Roosevelt's own newspaper journal remarks, the First Couple were planning on attending as usual the special Knights Templar sunrise services at Arlington National Cemetery around dawn the next Easter morning. It was to be conducted by this small group affiliated with the Freemasons, which meant a lot to deeply Masonic Franklin, although Eleanor wrote in her daily newspaper column that she too had enjoyed the uplifting program in the past and was looking forward to experiencing it again. It was rather a pleasant tradition for the Episcopalian Roosevelt family when in Washington to get up extra early, get dressed, and be driven across town to honor Easter's true meaning with this exclusive group at dawn. Naturally this would likely have meant that an earlier bedtime Saturday night for both would have been logically in order, but this obviously was not done.

.On the night of Saturday, April 12th, official records reveal that FDR was home with little to do, save only entertaining a few companions at the White House. Yet *something* important was evidently perking him up pretty good. Existing logs show the chief executive did not make his way upstairs to his bedroom until 12:10 Sunday a.m. – already Easter morning, the 13th - and from there, who knows what he did? Why was the president up so very late, instead of going to bed early as was his original plan?

.The president's Saturday evening dinner guests at 7:15 were his usual sidekick Harry, whom he lunched with just five hours earlier, and probably with presidential physician Dr. Ross McIntyre (1889-1959), whom he had just been treated by in his White House medical office, minutes ago. Some occasional White House visitors were back again on this night; Littleton Hambley (age 54) and his wife, Elizabeth Suckley Hambley (age 47) enjoyed FDR's meal, too. Elizabeth - or "Poppy" - was the sister of FDR's personal aide, Margaret "Daisy" Suckley (1891-1991), who was likely also present at the dinner table (while simply listed in logs as "household" in attendance). Littleton was a United States Army officer, it should be noted. If phone calls came in that night from various Army officials and War Department personnel, bringing MO41 to the attention of the president, Littleton Hambley might well have fielded some of them personally at times, so trusted as he was by the president. Or at least he may well have been consulted about the validity of the news and its sources as the shocking and perhaps alarming reports rolled in.

.While simple farmhand Rusty Blevins dealt with a feverish influx of strangers, neighbors, and first responders to his boss's farm near Cape Girardeau, the Army was quickly alerted in the area. {There was a National Guard Armory across town, for instance.} And since the reports were of such an unusual nature, phone calls to higher ups in the military were probably patched through pronto. Dazzled Blevins had gotten his wish: the Cape fire department was currently doing its level best to fight the flames and search for injured or dead passengers as he watched, still stunned. But these courageous men also called in cops; the FBI; trusted soldiers; the press, utilizing big flash cameras; and likely the county coroner and/or medical examiner. Plus undoubtedly doctors and nurses from the two hospitals. They scrambled to first find medical bags and an ambulance but rushed in valiantly amidst parked vehicles, curious neighbors, and farm implements here and there. It was a madhouse on the farm, really, as complete darkness set in, the afterglow of sunset long gone.

.Back on the East Coast, an odd, perhaps telling incident happened to the president's wife on this unusual Saturday night. According to her own daily columns, Eleanor Roosevelt was ready to fly back from Boston but suddenly her flight was cancelled. *Who would possibly cancel the First Lady's airliner trip to D.C.? And why?* Even if there was a weather delay, a commercial flight for the most famous and powerful woman in the world would merely sit in Logan Airport and wait as long as possible for the storm to pass in order to take her and her party (and other passengers) south to Washington. Or if there were mechanical difficulties, Mrs. Roosevelt and company would simply be transferred to another available commercial airplane. Or perhaps she would charter a private flight home. But instead, for some unexplained reason, Eleanor's party was forced to leave the airport in the dark with their luggage; drive in a car across the city; make their way through a bustling Boston train station; and buy tickets, forcing them to wait in line like many others as the next available train arrived for boarding. It must have seemed like madness as well.

The legendary First Lady wearily settled into her train car likely after midnight and stayed on the ground all the way back to Washington, not arriving in D.C. until around 8:00 the next morning, according to the White House logs and her newspaper column, "*My Day.*" We can therefore presume her scheduled flight was to leave at a pretty late hour, just as she departed Philadelphia by plane at 11:25 p.m. the night before.

.Obviously the logical, speculative answer for the cancellation of the First Lady's late flight and her complicated ground-only travel arrangements was the fear by the president - and/or his top military or administrative advisors - that perhaps *the skies over America that night were not safe.* Franklin was rightfully worried about his wife, that in theory she might be the victim of some sort of aerial attack by vengeful "non-terrestrials" in our airspace. The reports of three dead aliens on the ground, with an advanced spacecraft, near Cape Girardeau, may well have created conditions of great trepidation by the president and his staff, in ordering his wife to stick to the train, even if it took all night long to arduously travel home - which it did. If FDR cancelled *all* flights in the country, it would have set off an unprecedented controversy, a very newsworthy story inspiring genuine panic. There were evidently no reports coming in that Saturday night of other crashes or brushes with other "flying discs," or mysterious aerial assaults, in order to justify such a national shutdown, as seen in 2001 just after the 9-11 airplane attacks (one of which was begun after takeoff at Boston's Logan Airport.)

.Eleanor Roosevelt made it home likely weary, but had only a few hours rest at the White House. Even that was complicated by the loud squeals of excited small children and young parents in the building and out on the grounds, due to a morning Easter egg hunt on the lawn. This planned annual event was a shadow of what would take place the following day. First, thanks to Eleanor's lengthy train trip, the wife of Vice President Henry Wallace (1888-1965) had to step in and host the Sunday morning events in the grass outside. Ilo Wallace (1895-1965) handled the get-together but the following "Easter Monday" was a monumental White House event that dwarfed it in every way. On April 14th there were as many as 53,000 people(!) on the grounds, likely to this day the largest crowd in the history of the White House. "Grown-Ups Outnumber Children," newspaper headlines described later, with folks listening attentively to Franklin giving a brief address from a portico balcony. Then Eleanor supervised as best she could another, this time very crowded, Easter "egg roll" in the grass, where European refugees were allowed to take part. The rest of that bustling Monday the president saw only a few visitors in his office, understandably. MO41 data discussions would have to wait, partly because of the enormous crowd right outside and partly because Army Intelligence reports and photos undoubtedly had to be developed.

In returning to Sunday morning, April 13th, at close to eleven o'clock a.m. the First Couple were finally ready to be driven to a D.C. church service, saying nothing to the press or the public about the previous night's events. Likely Eleanor was never told a thing about the blockbuster secret, but Franklin's mind had to have been abuzz with many intriguing, or even frightening, theories and worries. MO41 seemed huge, and yet... there was nothing FDR could do, really. Except wait and be ready for any other out-of-this-world news.

.Reporters and photographers duly recorded the First Couple as they calmly arrived by limousine and later departed a stately Washington house of worship on a fine, sunny April Easter Sunday. Before leaving, the Roosevelts calmly posed for pictures and newsreel images, all smiles on the front steps of St. Thomas Episcopal Church in Washington. To aid his deception of appearing to be healthy and able to walk, cheerful Franklin stood and made some brief remarks, tightly gripping a sturdy son's arm, then cheerfully donning a top hat for the convertible limo ride home. The First Couple would part company not long after, as Eleanor was off to California to attend the marriage ceremony of son James to a Beverly Hills woman on Tuesday. Where Franklin went the rest of Sunday remains mostly a mystery, but two men were more than likely nearby: his ubiquitous pals Mr. Hopkins and Dr. McIntyre. Both *probably* already knew about the nearly unbelievable "new wonder" being quietly handled in southeastern Missouri that very afternoon. They were the commander-in-chief's two closest and dearest friends, seeing him for hours every day.

.Almost all White House employees traditionally had Sundays off and the press was always assured that anything really newsworthy would not be addressed until Monday morning. Reporters knew they had the day to themselves, with the White House press office closed. Easter Sunday was thus a fantastic opportunity for FDR to quietly handle the MO41 matter without publicity or annoying nosiness by nearly anyone in town. The president supposedly lent some time to a book author in the middle of the afternoon, with little else on the record of substance.

On the surface, April of 1941 may have seemed a lazy, quiet period, but contemporary historians note that this was the month where behind the scenes Mr. Roosevelt was significantly stepping up secretive efforts to help the British fight the bloodthirsty Nazi military machine, following the success of his generous Lend-Lease Act, passed in March. FDR had a nation of 130 million people to govern, working around a growing $57 billion national debt in 1941. But with the opening of more defense plants to provide military hardware, the United States economy was slowly perking up. In war-ravaged England, however, April 11th and 12th were days that lived in infamy, as it turned out. Hitler's air force had dropped wave after wave of special incendiary bombs on the city of Bristol, reducing much of it to a pile of burning rubble. "The Good Friday Raids," as they became known, are recalled today with a cold shudder, for the death and destruction they brought. The fiery blitz had only made the British people more determined to fight back and win, but things looked pretty bleak that spring. The American president wanted desperately to aid friend Winston Churchill (1874-1965), the Prime Minister of Great Britain, in fending off Adolph Hitler's ruthless offensive forces, in the oceans especially. Aggressive Nazi naval vessels were at times threatening American shipping. FDR knew that Hitler would, if he could, squash the British and soon turn his ravenous war machine on the United States; the sooner Roosevelt could stop Hitler the better, short of openly declaring war. Private presidential orders were issued that spring to American ship captains to relay all information on German vessels sighted in the Atlantic to English ships and military sources. U.S.-made war supplies were being shipped directly to the British military in North Africa. American vessels prowled around further from "national waters" into more dangerous territory. FDR knew this would be very provocative to the aggressive German military and even Churchill recalled later he candidly told his cabinet that summer: "Everything was done to force an incident that could lead to war."

It was a dangerous game the American commander-in-chief was playing, mostly without much fanfare, during "The Battle of Britain." Yes, April of 1941 was the month things grew more serious, and December was of course the month the powder keg blew. There was already open warfare around the globe, and machinations afoot to expand it. *Was this reason alone for alien beings to arrive on Earth for a closer look?* Perhaps one could view it today as if visiting extraterrestrial beings were seated on the fifty yard line at an action-packed seesaw football game, with "long bombs," "ground assaults," and "the blitz" being utilized every play, nearly every day.

.As mentioned President Roosevelt did not reach the privacy of his third floor White House quarters that Saturday evening, April 12th, until after midnight, evidently absorbed or troubled by late events. Unfortunately, the FDR Presidential Library does not possess White House telephone records for 1941, or for most other years of his administration. Likely all Secret Service records from this era are long gone as well. But assuredly the "time window" for mind-numbing phoned updates on the Midwest's alien situation is there, wide open, as we shall see...

.According to Charlette Huffman Mann, her grandfather first learned about the farm crash incident generally "around nine" p.m., Central Time, perhaps a bit before. Reverend William G. Huffman (1888-1959) likely arrived on the macabre scene around nine-thirty, or just after. According to his granddaughter's recollection, William said he noticed that *a few men in military uniforms were already there.* Once he said some prayers over the dead nonhuman bodies and peeked inside their busted spaceship, the evangelist soon found a contingent of newly-arrived U.S. Army soldiers closing in, hustling him away from the scene, warning him to silence. Therefore, military personnel were obviously made aware of the incredible, galvanizing situation a good deal earlier in the evening. They after all required time to assemble men and materials and vehicles in order to zip to the site. It can therefore be estimated that the crash took place likely between 7:15 and 8:15 that evening, as reported by beleaguered Rusty

Blevins. Some first responders - including Cape Girardeau County Sheriff Ruben Schade (1905-1986) and his Sikeston-based Army-employed brother, Ben (1910-1974) – had to have realized the otherworldly nature of the strange event and sounded the first military alarm perhaps by 8:30 or so, Central Time. Urgent calls to the military then went out, likely first to the Sikeston airport's MIA training base, and from there up the Army chain of command. This would have been about 8:30 to 9:15 that night, it can be guesstimated, and from a police source phoning William "around nine" we can tell the Cape cops back at the downtown station house were not quite yet made aware at this point the extraterrestrial nature of the crash.

All of this was took place about 9:30 to 10:15 p.m., Eastern Time, at the White House, which probably was not notified of anything at that point. Such amazing matters had to go through proper channels first, it would stand to reason.

.It seems logical to conclude that urgent phone calls quickly went higher on the military ladder until likely the Army's top man was contacted, Chief of Staff George C. Marshall (1880-1959). He was probably located while in Mississippi and notified in this 9:30 to 10:15 p.m. timeframe (Central Time, for him). Perhaps even the Secretary of War in Washington D.C., Henry Stimson (1867-1950) was contacted as well. In theory, either of them *could* have ordered the crash site sealed *without* the Commander-in-Chief's knowledge. Stimson might have taken charge had Marshall been in the air, leaving Mississippi for Georgia that evening, perhaps turning back when notified, to better grasp the situation (he was due at Fort Benning). It also seems pretty unlikely Stimson or Marshall would *not* have recorded the evening event's stunning secret information in any diary, for national security reasons, it should be added. They were seemingly pretty busy on the phone, wondering if we as a race or as a nation were about to be invaded by a very foreign power. They were of a military mindset: protective, curious, and courageous in their approaches to problem solving. They needed all the data they could get to make the best decisions.

.Back at the White House, President Roosevelt had finished eating his dinner by this time and was surrounded by friendly holiday company, relaxing quietly while perhaps mixing drinks, as he was fond of doing. At some point, Stimson and/or Marshall knew, FDR needed to be briefed, and then during the growing fervor for answers and clarity that Saturday night, he would need to be asked "*Just exactly what do we do now?*"

.The dazzling story was likely working its way up to the handicapped president by maybe 9:45 to 10:30 p.m. Eastern Time, let us speculate reasonably. These emergency-level calls were eventually patched through by White House switchboard operators to the telephones in the dining and living quarters, likely answered first by aides Harry Hopkins or Daisy Suckley, the dinner guests. There was no centralized Pentagon headquarters in those days (it was still under construction), but various War Department offices and Army bases in the D.C. area, sites that would have needed and fielded dispatches and updates, calls and command decisions by the commander-in-chief, FDR knew all too well.

.Therefore, it can be reasonably estimated that President Roosevelt was most likely called by his trusted General Marshall, or possibly by Secretary Stimson, headquartered a few blocks away, by 10:15 p.m. Eastern Time, 9:15 Central, as fairly feasible speculation. Hence, *FDR could easily have spent much of the next two or more hours that night involved in hushed phone conversations*, trying to find out from high grade officers and government officials if the stunning information flowing in was just a silly joke, a drunken prank, an honest mistake, or the creepiest real-life jolt of his lifetime (to that point). After moving upstairs to his bedroom at 12:10 a.m., the president might well have continued to place and receive calls on his two private bedroom telephones, preferring the comfort of his bed and the privacy of his personal quarters for top secret conversations. And after all, who could sleep after hearing *this* bombshell news?

.Then there's the distinct possibility that amidst all of this F. D. Roosevelt - and/or an aide (Hambley?) - conducted a flurry of calls in tracking down and contacting his *en transit* wife, protectively cancelling her late Boston-to-Washington flight, forcing her to take the train home instead. "For critical security reasons I can't explain, you *must* stay on the ground," would have been his order.

.The remaining records for George Marshall's workload for that specific day show precious little. There just isn't much available overall, mostly since *if* the much-decorated general and his chief executive truly communicated on top secret alien matters, such highly classified proof would not be carelessly left behind for historians to inspect and reveal. George's personal record of his daily activities is nearly blank for this day, merely stating that on Saturday he was "on duty 12:15 to 6:00 p.m." (Central Time), likely written that morning as a general plan. On a typed itinerary of his trip, it obvious George abruptly stopped that Saturday evening and tellingly doesn't appear to have filled out the rest of his scheduled tour's planned events! Much like speculation for Eleanor Roosevelt possibly being grounded from flight that same night, could George C. Marshall have been given the same no-fly order?

.According to the existing records on this series of quick stops and visits - by airplane, to various Army camps - Marshall was scheduled to fly on April 12th at 5:00 p.m. Central Time from Camp Shelby, Mississippi (or from nearby Esler Field, in the Hattiesburg area) to as mentioned Fort Benning in Georgia, to cap a very busy Saturday. But there are no leftover records or remarks at all about such a trip. In other words, it was either uncharacteristic sloppy record-keeping, or proof that something very important came up. Quite possibly General Marshall stayed in Mississippi under orders and only left Sunday morning in daylight hours, when it appeared as though all was reasonably safe and clear in our skies, with no conceived alien invasion or assault was evidenced being undertaken.

.Before he departed Washington on the Army camp tour, Marshall wrote a friend that he would be traveling only with "Colonel Ward and two pilots." So it's not as if the general was lacking a trusty pilot, a competent aide, and a reliable vehicle to move around the country with. If a problem arose, a snap of his fingers could have produced personnel and planes, so something pretty big *must* have come up, it is again safe to assume.

.GCM evidently did not jot down a thing, nor did an aide or secretary, for that Saturday night or entire Easter Sunday. If someone did, it was certainly scrubbed from Marshall's later-released files. All we know for sure is that at some point on Monday, April 14th, he was back at his office in D.C.'s War Department building, dictating memos for his secretary to type up and mail, many of them nearly identical thank you notes to the camp commanders and their wives from the military outposts he recently toured. The copies of these thank-you notes can be found online today in the digitized Marshall website. *But there are no thank-you copies for the leaders of either Camp Shelby or Fort Benning,* further reinforcing the notion that Marshall ducked out abruptly and didn't complete his carefully mapped-out Sunday itinerary.

.It is logical that the famous general spent Saturday night in the Shelby/Hattiesburg area, possibly still at the base itself, fielding shocking phone calls full of details and updates on the ongoing MO41 Army recovery operation, and keeping in touch with FDR at the White House. Then George left Mississippi the next morning after ascertaining the skies were safe, especially since many airports in America – such as in Cape Girardeau and Sikeston – were not lit, so night travel to some destinations simply wasn't possible.

.Experienced Army personnel with at least one ranking officer in charge probably needed to covertly review the rural Missouri accident site's remaining situation *in the light of day* - probably Sunday the 13th - to make sure most everything was carefully picked up and whisked away, with any leftover eyewitnesses or new visitors hushed up or perhaps even threatened. From the early post-midnight hours on, the Easter "day after" would likely have been *the* big day of Army recovery, initial scrutiny, and transportation of the cosmic artifacts.

.Although he could have sent most any underling to do the roving camp scrutiny job, the Army's chief personally attended to most important matters, even setting out a grueling schedule for himself, with many flights and bumpy car trips and tough walking tours of bases in Texas, Oklahoma, Louisiana, and Mississippi. The sixty year old Marshall obviously investigated critical situations for himself, and MO41 was likely no different. If George took over the MO41 recovery materials on Easter Sunday, it would have been a top secret under-the-radar expedition that likely took up nearly the entire day, hence why GCM's April 13th schedule was left blank, and why he could not complete his camp inspection tour. *Somebody* in great power and authority in the U.S. Army naturally had to have trusted to handle the sensitive, secretive MO41 project.

.A specific military directive possibly involving George Marshall was issued on that Saturday, April 12th, and it might have everything to do with the MO41 news, if it was genuinely sent out late in the day. Or, if this order went out earlier that afternoon, it is mere coincidence, a thoughtful but fretful reaction to ruthless Axis air assaults overseas. The precise hour's timing is unknown, but the rather urgent-sounding directive was all about *American fliers keeping their skies safe from hostile and/or unidentified aircraft*. And also establishing an American air warning system, to sound the alarm when our airspace had been violated. According to a web page entitled "*The Army Air Forces in World War II*," an official order came down that Saturday for the four major American military forces to organize a bomber and interceptor command, in order "to create offensive and defensive task forces" that would give "a new sense of urgency of air defense." This would include "an aircraft warning system in addition to primary function of interception."

.General Marshall's top military aide was the highly respected Army officer Orlando Ward (a Missourian, incidentally). Ward (1891-1972) had also returned to D.C., for he sent George's Assistant Chief of Staff Twaddle an office memorandum on Monday, April 14th, records show. This was rather unusual, as the memo issued George Marshall's thoughts on a subject now most critical to him, and yet it wasn't specifically stated as "dictated by" or even "signed by" or "initialed by" the stern general. Almost as if it was received by Ward from Marshall over the phone. The subject matter was described as "urgent" in another memorandum sent reinforcing it all a few weeks later. Anyway, this is what the G. C. Marshall mind-set was all about: *the Army brass needed to quickly create and study mobile anti-aircraft defense.* Admittedly, anti-tank needs were also mentioned in this directive; Marshall's obvious main desire was to somehow pierce strongly armored vehicles of all kinds in a quick, moveable manner. The creation of this new and/or improved metal-busting technology was urged to be completed before 1941 was out, that's how crucial this matter was now to General Marshall.

Defending American citizens and servicemen from enemy airships, that was definitely the key objective for George Marshall by sometime Monday, the facts show. Sunday was his "missing day," where GCM seems to have fallen off the radar that Easter. But he made sure to show up for at least *some* work in his office on Monday, and start relating orders to his secretary that in theory could have been understandable military reactions to MO41.

.Much of the established mundane material that was typed up on that April 14th by Marshall's office secretary or stenographer appears to have been about an hour's worth of dictation and typing. That is, the notes to various people regarding military and hospitality matters relating to the camp tour. But what else could have been going on at some point that Monday inside the War Department workplace? If the Missouri events and objects were genuinely taken charge of by GCM, then he likely dictated some key points for his most trusted office assistant to put into a secret report. This likely would have been typed with carbon copies for the elite brass that Marshall would meet with the following day, in FDR's Oval Office. The president and critical cabinet secretaries, they would probably need a classified, fact-filled, MO41 run-down. Just exactly what happened and what precisely had been recovered and specifically where it was now being stored. Any photographs taken would need to be carefully developed, with copies of them made in a controlled darkroom, readied to accompany such a blockbuster report. Perhaps even bits of actual recovered spacecraft debris were literally sitting on the general's desk, for him to toy with as he issued the account to be typed up.

.Easter Sunday was overall a fairly quiet day for the civilized world. The pope in Rome issued his usual message of peace, broadcast on radio. Japan and the Soviet Union signed an ill-fated neutrality pact. Famous astronomer and cosmology author Annie J. Cannon - one of the most famous scientific minds of her day, cataloguing more stars than anyone – spent her final hours alive on planet earth. She died in Massachusetts on that Sunday the 13th at age 77.

.Back at the White House hours earlier, on that previous, momentous Saturday night… first hearing the mind-boggling news that an unconventional alien spaceship had crashed outside sleepy Cape Girardeau and that three little grey-toned interplanetary men inside it had abruptly died this was likely felt at first by the president to be either a terrific prank or a terrific shock. Mr. Roosevelt might have reached for his usual pack of cigarettes and a little wine, or stronger drink, to help carefully digest each astounding update as it came in. He was probably understandably skeptical at first, then gradually fathomed this incredible claim was no gag, and that some definite directives for the soldiers at the Missouri scene were necessary. Thus, Roosevelt would have been quite awake until after midnight and was likely charged up with curiosity and excitement, questions and commands. Even his valet would have been shielded from hearing what was being discussed in private, in the president's bedroom, alone. In all likelihood he shared these scraps of otherworldly news with his trusted friend Harry Hopkins, who may not have been all that trustworthy, in the end (suspected of being a secret communist spy for the Soviet government)..

.Yes, by now it was April 13th and even *this* is rather spooky and remarkable for President Roosevelt. He loathed and feared most anything that had to do with the number 13, making FDR a classic "triskaidephobe." That is a person who is so superstitious he or she will go to extra lengths to avoid doing most anything that has to do with, or adds up to, the number 13. One academic's study of Franklin D. Roosevelt states he "might have been our most superstitious president. He was scared to death of the number 13." For example, if FDR hosted a dinner party with a total of thirteen tallied in advance, Franklin added another person at the table. He would refuse to leave on trips on the 13th, and leave on at 11:55 p.m. on the 12th, or possibly even push the journey off to the 14th. Roosevelt considered any personal actions on the 13th of any month a little risky and bad luck. Thus not moving to his quarters and then at some point finally to sleep on April 13th was a definite no-no, indicating again a *very* serious matter was going on at the time, requiring his undivided time and attention. But as he eventually lay in bed that night (or early morning hours), closing his eyes... the strange, spooky descriptions of the dead grey extraterrestrial visitors from Cape Girardeau had to have been dancing in his head. It may have been Easter, but it now felt like Halloween. No one in the country understood that better than Rusty Blevins, since his quiet Cape Girardeau evening at home – or at his boss's home – had turned into a cosmic nightmare.

."For reasons of national security," farmhand Blevins was informed with great emphasis and severity, this stunning Saturday night must never be discussed again. *Ever*. It was a closed subject. This theme was drummed into Rusty's head by members of the United States Army, gathered on his employer's land with flames doused and evidence culled, but he was hardly alone. Everyone present, including kindly Pastor Huffman, had been told this repeatedly. Scowling faces and pointed fingers in his chest likely became another memorable sight this unforgettable night. Keep your mouth *shut* if you know what's good for you. Youthful Rusty did as he was told, but eventually talked late in life.

.Across D.C., the stodgy Director of the Federal Bureau of Investigations, John Edgar Hoover, was also likely made aware of the incredible crash on this very Saturday night. Alarm bells might have gone off, in a sense, via calls to his FBI office and/or suburban residence, as the evening wore on. According to records unearthed by one UFO investigator, Mr. Hoover privately became very intrigued with the cosmic subject while publicly claiming "the bureau has no interest in such matters." In fact, documents show that over 1,600 FBI reports on UFOs were filed, resulting in *thousands* of pages of inside information on the many bureau investigations that were going on over possible alien spacecraft sightings. Hoover seemed in reality concerned, nearly *obsessed*.

.Add to this situation the fact that following Hoover's 1972 death, many more sizzling, sensitive files and other embarrassing reports were systematically destroyed upon the late director's standing orders. They were rounded up from FBI headquarters at 935 Pennsylvania Avenue (down the street from FDR's White House), and from Hoover's "Personal and Confidential" office files. Even after lugging, scrubbing, or burning, some of the most stunning material from the bureau's filing cabinets, many nuggets of priceless FBI research remained. Not everything controversial was destroyed, it is quite apparent, although plenty of what was left was unfortunately redacted and withheld for many years before its eventual release, or intentional leaking, to the American public. We can still pick up some historic clues, happily.

.On March 7th, 1941, a St. Louis FBI field office agent named G. B. Norris announced to the press the opening of a satellite agency office on March 11th downriver, in Cape Girardeau, the city's first. There would be one FBI agent in charge of this new office, in precisely which Cape office building the FBI had not finalized yet. A month or so later,

Mr. Arlin E. Jones of the FBI moved to Cape Girardeau with his wife Katherine, and they settled into a home on Broadway. "Resident Agent Arlin" also worked on Broadway, out of a small office within the town's U.S. Post Office, which in itself was small and outdated. Plans for a new postal headquarters were in the works that very April '41, aided by Senator Harry Truman, and presumably Arlin would get himself a new office too.

.In the run-up to Agent Jones taking over in Cape, Agent Norris was accompanied by his fellow St. Louis-based agent, John R. Bush, in discussing with a reporter from *The Southeast Missourian* the FBI need to coordinate and exchange information in southeast Missouri with local police and sheriff's offices. The overall FBI purpose for opening the Cape Girardeau branch was stated to have been to "investigate sabotage and espionage," supposedly mostly due to the recent vengeful damaging of some manufacturing equipment by disgruntled laborers in a few Cape area factories, or at least rumors thereof. Sudden and shocking initial news of an airplane crash in the region that mid-April might well have brought both Norris and Bush, along with Jones, quickly to the accident site, for fear of possible sabotage or deliberate intent.

.A March 12th, 1941, article in *The Southeast Missourian* quoted Agent Bush as reiterating in another public speech - this one held in Cape Girardeau County - *that the feds had been conducting surveillance and ongoing investigative operations,* supposedly involving anti-American agents and saboteurs in seemingly sleepy southeastern Missouri. "A few well organized spy rings have been found, and some convictions had," one source put it at the time, within the article. Stings had been undertaken, and arrests had been made. This may seem detached from MO41, but it is a clear indication that Hoover's G-men had been very busy in the area in busting more than one group of spies. Who could operate "spy rings" in southeastern Missouri? One possible answer would lie within Cape Girardeau's substantial German-American community. There were so many Germanic citizens in Cape that a mid-town church held a weekly service in the German language. Of course, being of German descent was hardly a crime, but if this ethnic group was becoming riddled here and there with pro-Nazi sentiment and spies, deliberate sabotage and stealing, then there was a problem that would have required more than just the Cape police force. Hence, the FBI was operating in the area, undoubtedly with phone taps, tails, and interrogations.

Thus it is clear that Hoover's active agents, field operatives, police contacts, and helpful informants were established and active in the Cape Girardeau area that spring of '41, making connections, absorbing facts and rumors, and working undercover even *before* MO41 took place. These sources were undoubtedly still around as of April 12th, able to dig into the UFO crash story, either that very night or in the immediate aftermath. It is thus very conceivable that Director Hoover knew all about what happened regarding MO41, within, say, *hours*. Hoover might even have been in touch with FDR *that night*, in feverishly coordinating a response, investigating the scene, and hushing the eyewitnesses, it was all so extraordinary and shocking. The U.S. government was stumbling into unknown territory, with no precedence to rely upon as a framework for proper procedure. MO41 was truly "America's First."

Within all of this intelligence angle of the MO41 activities comes yet another reason for the federal government to have kept the lid clamped down tight on news about an alien spaceship crash and recovery. *The shocking news could not be allowed to reach the ears of pro-Nazi representatives and espionage experts in Cape Girardeau, to be funneled back to Adolph Hitler's Nazi regime in Germany.* President Roosevelt would have rightly worried about losing the secret advantages of this possible "non-terrestrial science and technology" recovered by and for the U.S. military and its defense systems. If the captured ET material had advanced metals, weapons, defense, and/or flight propulsion systems worth replicating then the Nazi war machine rampaging in Europe must not suspect a thing, nor make an attempt to find out more within D.C. circles. Thus FDR would have strongly encouraged Hoover to infiltrate, spy on, expose, and arrest pro-dictatorship representatives in the southeastern Missouri region and keep a close eye on Cape Girardeau citizens in particular. It was for the overall good of the nation. Security was vital.

.It seems a very good bet that the new Cape Girardeau area FBI agent, Arlin Jones, was quickly notified by cops sometime that eventful extraterrestrial evening, for a perceived "airplane crash" might possibly have involved anti-American sabotage. However, by the dark hours of the night when the police and fire departments - and Reverend Huffman and medical personnel - were all notified by phone, was anyone actually *in* the FBI satellite office to take the emergency call? If it truly was a Saturday night during Passover/Easter weekend the city's office was likely closed. Could Arlin have been phoned at his Broadway home instead? After all, a police source called an obscure part-time pastor/fundraiser; surely one of the *first* phone calls they placed was to track down Agent Jones - if he was in town.

.If Arlin E. Jones was eventually flagged down and arrived late, the Cape field office agent might have even missed much of the affair. If a "fed" like Agent Jones *did* make the scene on time, the stunned "G-man" probably would have had any notes or debris promptly taken away by the all-encompassing and deliberately intimidating Army. Even the policemen on the scene were hushed up, supposedly. But this does not mean that a later call was placed to FBI officials, or a detailed report didn't wind up on Hoover's D.C. desk, especially by any law enforcement officer looking to score points with stern Edgar.

.Certainly news of this magnitude would have at least warranted a phone call that night to Washington FBI headquarters, if not being patched in to Hoover himself at home at some point. Perhaps images of rewards for service in the face of Army hostility danced in the head of any Cape Girardeau FBI representative. And why not? After all, Cape cop Marshall Morton had recently been accepted at FBI training headquarters in Virginia in the months after the Cape Girardeau alien crash, along with a second Cape officer later named Fritz Schneider. These were two respected men on the 1941 CGPD force and were likely responders at the scene. The March 7th, 1941, Cape newspaper article made clear local law enforcement candidates *would* be sought for the FBI academy, a month *before* MO41, but the issue still smacks of the duo's possible inside MO41 cooperation with knowledgeable FBI agents, to have ultimately been selected above all other law officers. Officers Morton and Schneider a decade later would be named co-Chiefs of Police in Cape Girardeau, an unprecedented arrangement, strangely enough. Another payoff for their cooperation and public silence on the UFO crash? Could, as alleged, local fireman Walter Reynolds really have been "watched," perhaps shadowed by co-workers, Cape cops, the military, or federal agents, as he supposedly claimed on his deathbed? Or genuinely suffered his phone being tapped in 1941 Cape Girardeau? Did he start talking too much and give local anti-American spies *reason* to stalk him? If so, the top suspect in such skullduggery would have been an FBI agent, acting upon the direct orders of J. Edgar Hoover, who liked to control the game of espionage to his advantage whenever possible, perhaps feeling a *competition* with FDR. Brazenly bugging telephones was a fairly old federal bureau practice

.A 1993 Anthony Summers biography of J. Edgar Hoover revealed that indeed the FBI had been illegally wiretapping American citizens as far back as the 1930s, so much so that in 1941 a special new file index was created to keep track of them all. Over 13,000 individuals were recorded at that time to have been electronically tracked by the feds - some of them by order of tap-happy President F. D. Roosevelt himself - and more of the same was to come in the decades ahead, no matter who was president. FDR evidently gave his first official go-ahead for covert phone-tapping by spy-master Hoover on most any "person of interest" back in May of 1940, thus making Mr. Reynolds' startling claim about April of 1941 more plausible. {One of Roosevelt's sons wrote years later that he was rather taken aback then by his famous father's growing, disturbing habit of reading FBI summaries of tapped phone calls ordered for his political enemies and friends alike, including private sex life details and political machinations and general insights that often gave FDR the inside story and the upper hand.}

.For Franklin Delano Roosevelt back at the White House, dealing with the implications of the incredible issue beyond that staggering Saturday night was something he'd very privately handle in the next week and occasionally in the coming four years. Perhaps he was on the phone to J. Edgar Hoover that night, exchanging incredulous information, or at least in the days to come. Franklin would certainly go on to discuss it with the proper "upper echelon" of his administration, but not for a day or two, his schedule was already so filled in advance. And when he *did* get to the heart of the matter it could happily be done so most discreetly and conveniently, within the confines of previously-arranged meetings behind his legendary office's doors…

CHAPTER TWO

Days Later: FDR's Oval Office Logs

.... *"3:39 - Motoring"*

Although "Easter Monday," April 14th, White House records show a bit of a slow day for President Roosevelt - perhaps thanks to the huge, noisy crowd outside - big wheels in the administration began rolling into his Oval Office on Tuesday and Wednesday. A few men named expressly or indirectly in top secret government documents regarding ET crashes leaked several decades later "just happened" to be the popular commander-in-chief's welcomed guests in the wake of the great Cape Girardeau incident.

.At noon or so on Tuesday, April 15th, Secretary of State Cordell Hull (1871-1955) arrived at the White House for a briefing of an unspecified nature. He attended a busy, high-level conference in the president's office with Roosevelt; Secretary of War Henry Stimson; the Secretary of the Navy; the Chief of Staff of the Army, George Marshall; Treasury Secretary Henry Morganthau; and FDR's most trusted friend and aide, the nearly omnipresent Harry Hopkins. Something quite major and critical needed to be disseminated and discussed in private, of that we can be certain. *This was the highest circle of power in the entire country. Something mighty big was up.* Marshall's only note on this meeting which has since surfaced was that it centered around "strategy." The confab required forty-five minutes of FDR's daily schedule, at the least.

Hull was in charge of handling foreign affairs, and what could be more "foreign" than the MO41 affair's unexpected "visitors"? FDR wasn't a huge fan of Hull's, and in fact behind Cordell's back made fun of his lisp and somewhat imperious approach, preferring to deal with his underling, Under-Secretary Sumner Welles (1892-1961). So a *very* important matter of both State and military affairs with national security concerns was to be discussed in great privacy without notation, of that we can be certain.

.As mentioned in "*MO41, The Bombshell Before Roswell,*" the initial "safe deposit" for the alien materials was most likely a special storeroom several floors down below the U.S. Capitol Building, where it is known now that Secretary Hull once showed off the otherworldly items to his visiting cousin, Turner Holt. Three aliens kept in "three glass jars," Holt's daughters' confessed, along with a silvery-gray spaceship, cut up in sections, kept inside this dungeon-like storage site. In an interesting twist of fate, Cordell Hull seems to be the only person in this 1941 saga *not* to have been buried in a cemetery; instead, he insisted that upon death his body would also be placed down inside a Washington building's basement! Perhaps since no person can have their remains entombed permanently under the Capitol Building, Cordell and his wife managed the next best thing. They were interred in a crypt below D.C.'s stately National Cathedral in 1955. If Secretary Hull had this rather unusual entombment in mind for his own dead body someday all along, then it starts to become clearer why the extraterrestrial materials were "buried" in similar fashion in Washington in 1941, where he was a major player on the governmental scene. It would be a safe and secure site, this well-guarded below-decks Capitol Hill vault, especially if the non-terrestrial race from outer space sent more representatives to retrieve it all someday, by either diplomacy or force. A possible vengeful "alien invasion" from the skies might seem silly today, but at the time it might well have been a cause for genuine concern, especially among the protective military men involved in safeguarding the big secret.

.In mid-June of '41, working without supervision from Mr. Hull, War Secretary Stimson and General Marshall got together to formulate plans for the creation of the all new "Army Air Force," officially announced not long thereafter, to be headed by GCM's pal, General Hap Arnold. This special division of the army's air power would take precedence over the old "Army Air Corps," and try to do a better job of patrolling the skies during America's neutrality prior to its entrance into World War II. *What was suddenly so important going on in the skies that a whole new revamped branch of the Army needed to be concocted that spring,* in order to better explore and guard a peacetime nation's airspace? Perhaps MO41 was a partial reason, and a very valid one at that.

It is speculative, yes, but reasonable to believe that General Marshall laid out top secret, heart-stopping Army intelligence photos and hurriedly-typed reports for the elite group that Tuesday in the somber Oval Office. This probably included classified, jaw-dropping images and descriptions of the recovered alien bodies and their ship, plus updated briefs on the handling of the situation on the ground by the army, at Missouri locations. Many riveting questions and critical issues *had* to be brought up and resolved. For example, how the materials were eventually flown to Washington, and the disposition of it all from there; i.e., where was it currently being stored, and how safe was it? How secure was the Cape Girardeau farm's crash site, and for that matter southeastern Missouri and the entire nation, really? Were people talking? Was there proper and effective security on the ground there, around Missouri towns like Cape, Chaffee, and Sikeston, ensuring all gossip was squelched? Did anyone in the local or national press know? In those days there were all many radio stations eager for a scoop, and newspapers, who were fed by three main sources: United Press International; the Associated Press; and the International News Service. They'd practically *kill* for this amazing story, one would think. Would the administration need to apply high-level pressure on any loose-lipped reporters or overzealous citizens who were getting close to the truth? Would a cover story need to be concocted?

.Beyond these more immediate security questions lay deeper, more profound issues. Would humans absconding with these weird, foreign bodies and ship wreckage be considered by an alien culture be undertaking an outrageous act of war? Should the government and the military go on "stand-by," a high alert for any more aerial incursions or touchdowns from another planet? Were there any other crashes reported in America in the past week, or anywhere else in the world? Should the Roosevelt team literally *bury* or burn the evidence forever, or just hide it for secret study? Or should they instead openly display it to the world eventually with a bold, exciting public announcement and newsreel cameras? Should the vice president and congressional leaders at least be informed of any aspect of this, once they got back from holiday recess? Or should everyone in that Oval Office simply wait patiently in silence and generally do nothing for a while?

.In the 1947 "White Hot Intelligence Estimate," Air Force General Nathan R. Twining (1897-1982) issued his report for President Truman and his top aides on the Roswell,

New Mexico, UFO recoveries. The Twining report mentions "the Missouri recovery of 1941" and also a typical military response to finding such foreign bodies and craft wreckage. The document states clearly (with emphasis added): "There are questions that remain unanswered, such as: *What forces face us? What kind of defense do we have? Where do they come from and what kind of weapons do they possess? Where can we stage our forces in advance? How wide a front? How many craft can we expect?*" All of these same questions and more were likely brought up initially on the Saturday night of the April 1941 UFO crash. And probably then again within FDR's Tuesday office confab. Outside it was a fine April afternoon days later, just as the cherry blossoms and spring flowers were coming up so beautifully in peaceful, unaware Washington D.C. But inside the white-painted home/office, great uneasiness and perhaps outright fear grew.

Keep in mind that America was not at war with Nazi Germany or Imperial Japan in April of 1941, or even on the brink. If these top U.S. military personnel were just going over simple briefings and reports, suggestions and questions on upgrading our national defenses, then what possible need was there for such a series of brass-and-braid, face-to-face consultations with the busy president in the White House? Couldn't they have decided such matters in their own conferences and then through quick memos and calls to and from the president?

.These high-level White House national defense meetings took place just three to four days after what was likely the crash date; in light of MO41 information we know of, and the military mind-set of readiness for war, the get-togethers make perfect sense. *The wild notion that we might be invaded at any time by a hostile or angered alien race that just lost an advance "scout ship" and three crewmen - just before an oncoming onslaught, perhaps? - must have weighed heavily on the military leaders present,* used to thinking in such strategic defense terms, weapons ideology, and conspiratorial war theories.

.That something major was brewing is even clearer when we consider Oval Office visitors on Wednesday the 16th. First, the president welcomed aforementioned Undersecretary of State Welles, a longtime political ally and trusted close friend of the president. {As if to prove this, Sumner Welles's personal papers still reside in the FDR Presidential Library in Hyde Park, New York.} This uneasy balance of towering State Department figures led to friction between the two erudite gentlemen and their busy office staffs, a sticky situation that was not resolved until Welles' resignation in a cloud of scandal in 1943. If Hull knew about the alien affair that spring of '41, Welles would more than likely need to know too. If nothing else, Roosevelt would want to tell his old pal Sumner, a fellow wealthy New Yorker, just to have someone close and trusted to confide in. To bounce information and ideas off of, in the privacy of his closed-door office. The State Department, after all, dealt at all levels with foreign nations, governments, cultures, languages, and races. Sumner was briefed for fifteen minutes, the logs show, then two more familiar names to us arrived at the chief executive's door. For serious and alert UFO observers, there is a bit of a bombshell in the Oval Office records next…

.Arriving on FDR's business doorstep was none other than Dr. Vannevar Bush (1890-1974), alongside the president's personal physician, Dr. Ross McIntyre. The scientist and the admiral. The nuclear bomb administrator and the ears-nose-and-throat doc. The odd couple stayed to quietly conference with President Roosevelt on matters until 12:45. *Their presence together is a red flag, a beacon to UFO investigators, a virtual smoking gun.* There was something remarkably important for Bush to review in person, obviously; a simple telephone call on the matter from the president was insufficient, as was a brief note.

.As noted earlier, Dr. Vannevar Bush was a highly respected scientist, engineer, and academic who was heading advanced "defensive technology" science research and development projects for FDR, toiling in very lofty East Coast intelligentsia circles in the 1930s and '40s. He was among the most very trusted and educated scientific minds in the nation, perhaps the world, and he "hung out with" the same, on committees, at conferences, and socially. A fine administrator with a wife and two young sons to care for, busy Dr. Bush also became head of the newly-created "Office of Scientific Research & Development," appointed by FDR at its origination in June of '41. He was also part of aviation technology studies. Van's input and opinion of the unique, highly-advanced technology involved in any alien spacecraft recovered would be a complete natural. And once again, the name "Dr. Vannevar Bush" – the Massachusetts Mason - turns up in UFO/ET documents dated from the next several years, and of course in the memorandums explored in the previous chapters. This may have been Van's very first taste of the subject, that Wednesday morning, briefed across the desk from the somber president.

.By Dr. Bush's side, observing the president closely as always, was Dr. McIntyre, the Surgeon General of the Navy. Vice Admiral McIntyre was a very experienced man in his field and a trusted presidential confidante. Ross knew where all of the Roosevelt health secrets lay, and would fib and fudge the truth to the public on such matters to aid the president when necessary. FDR was once a Navy Undersecretary, and felt a kinship with the sea that Dr. McIntyre shared. The kindly, dedicated physician saw Roosevelt all the time, practically living and working daily out of the White House. He'd even see FDR later that very afternoon, as he did at that hour nearly every day. Ross would at times would go on trips with Franklin, and greeted almost every morning by checking up on his famous friend's general well-being. So why bring him in *now*, in a more formal office setting? And strangely paired with the imminent technology scientist Bush? The answer is quite simple

.According to Ryan Wood's research, the Naval Surgeon General's office went on to play a major role in handling the bodies of recovered "Non-Terrestrial Biological Entities" in the years after the MO41 incident. Thus, on this cheerful spring morning, Franklin Delano Roosevelt was briefing two key alien advisors at once about something so grand and sensitive it required their personal attention in great privacy, face-to-face. As Ryan Wood succinctly put it: "Bush covered the Technology, and McIntyre covered the Biology." The alien spaceship, and the grey bodies. The hardware and the software. The components and the corpses, both would need intense scrutiny by top, qualified, respected minds. Thus both greatly skilled and trusted men with existing security clearances had a terrific need to learn as much as they could about MO41. They likely pored over that afternoon the spellbinding Army reports on the weird "little people" and their busted spacecraft and whistled with amazement and excitement, providing they had not already been informed prior to the meeting. That they were called in together on this day in mid-April '41 now makes perfect sense. If there were typed reports and photos to fathom, it was likely done at this time with trembling hands. There was much to digest and discuss. *This was exhilarating history!* Unlike any other assignment in humankind's existence.

.For Dr. Bush, there was probably a discussion of the power plant and/or energy propulsion system of the downed craft, and the need to study it at length to see precisely how it worked. As we've seen from the leaked memos and other sources, Vannevar was soon to explore the "atomic secrets" hidden within the ship's internal drive and come to some dramatic success in transferring its components into a highly classified propulsion device utilized within American defense technology. Specifically, something called "The Manhattan Project."

.For Dr. McIntyre, there was probably a dialogue of the eerie bodies to scientifically dissect and inspect at a covert autopsy, perhaps at the Bethesda Naval Hospital, just outside D.C., to the north. The grey, pliable corpses were naturally to be sliced open and explored, every inch, every organ, every detail, to fathom the differences between man and alien, for the human race to learn as much as possible. Thereby perhaps harnessing any advances found for mankind's future medical science gains, as well as understanding non-terrestrial civilization. Autopsy photos, film, tissue samples, slides, records of heights, weights, densities, etc., all would need to be very cautiously undertaken, stored, and guarded in controlled conditions by qualified medical support personnel.

.This was heady stuff, for all three high-level men to hash out in the Oval Office and beyond, between themselves and their staffs and the Army controller of MO41, George Marshall. Great secrecy would be necessary, so the subject was at least for the time being nearly off limits to everyone they knew, minus those key working personnel. Bush and McIntyre could not even go home and tell their families or friends, at least not now. The duo would presumably be working soon with military people who FDR and GCM trusted, at least for the immediate future, setting up times and days to view the physical materials in private, and then with extensive laboratory and pathology tools. Spies, snoops, loose lips, press scoops… they had to be avoided at all costs in the coming process.

.President Roosevelt had authorized the government's atomic bomb research program, undertaken by top U.S. scientists and repatriated newcomers, back in October of 1939. Van Bush was a prominent person in this sensitive and delicate research, in coordinating information, and in reporting back to the president when he felt circumstances required it. But he and others worked at a very deliberate, slow pace as the next few years went by. Progress in developing a working atom bomb was glacial and frustrating for all, especially impatient Roosevelt. The incredible recovery in April 1941 of the Cape Girardeau farm's downed spaceship and all the fascinating technology it held may well have galvanized and energized Bush and friends' efforts to polish and finish a workable manmade bomb. *Something* quite substantial took place that infused the U.S. process with sudden optimism; Dr. Bush and Vice President Wallace met with FDR at the White House on October 9th, 1941, and suddenly there was a new outlook on the program. Partly thanks to a recent private British report that helped understand uranium's content and potential, Bush unexpectedly announced to Roosevelt that an atomic bomb was not only possible but that it could be accomplished within two years' time. Roosevelt quickly gave Bush the go-ahead to proceed with design studies, experiments, construction, and testing of the American detonation device, with resources and funding provided via congress (mostly in secret). Put simply, by December of '41 FDR wanted the atom bomb built, even if he had to steal and copy the alien technology necessary to complete the weapon. In fact, he wanted the Cape Girardeau recovery weaponized in every possible way, as quickly as possible, to win the war.

.The list of top honchos for Franklin D. Roosevelt to consult with in the White House on April 16th hardly stops there. The very first visitor in the Oval Office that Wednesday morning was in actuality an old political crony and top party organizer of the day, Edward J. Flynn (1891-1953), of New York City. Flynn was the Chairman of the Democratic National Committee, a very powerful post in those days. Back in '41, American presidential candidates didn't have to canvass and campaign for votes in state primaries around the nation nearly as often or as intensely as they do today; they were often picked by delegates at national conventions or at times simply selected by a handful of powerful party bosses in private back-room meetings. Flynn was one of the top power brokers in the country, based out of New York City, the head man on the Democratic Party totem pole. He was a trusted friend of New York-based FDR, and might well have been informed about the amazing Missouri discovery on that particular Wednesday morning. After all, it was Flynn who was instrumental in agreeing that Roosevelt would make a good president to promote in the Democratic ranks back in the early 1930s, and it was Flynn who helped guide FDR to an unprecedented third term just a few months before, in the 1940 presidential campaign. Now perhaps Ed was being rewarded for his confidentiality and loyalty with the ultimate inside scoop, possibly the biggest stunner of his life.

.Ed Flynn served as the Democrat's official party chairman until 1943, but he remained a highly influential power player for some time to come. For instance, according to historians, Ed personally sat down with President Roosevelt in the summer of 1944 and carefully went over the short list of strong candidates available to replace quirky Vice President Henry Wallace, whom party bosses grew to feel had drifted simply too far to the left to stay on as the nation's number two leader. Roosevelt and Flynn studied and bantered back and forth at length this list of eligible names, and strangely kept coming back again and again to Missouri congressman Harry S Truman (1884-1972), a hardcore Democrat *who did not even receive FDR's backing in his 1940 state primary election.* Franklin put his money on Loyd Stark, Missouri's Democratic governor, to win the primary for the U.S. senate in the summer of '40, to be rid of Truman for good. The two diverse men's contact was little to none, their relationship next to zero as of April 1941. According to biographers, even on a personal level Roosevelt previously didn't really much care for Senator Truman, and HST privately felt the same way about the president! They were both in favor of New Deal policies and principles, however, and were brother Freemasons, yet there was evidently precious little contact or affection between the two Democrats. Roosevelt was more of an entitled, wealthy aristocrat, while ex-farmer and store clerk Truman was a humble and often debt-ridden "man of the people." For some reason - and we can logically guess why now - after April of '41 FDR warmed up to HST. They shared a common knowledge, perhaps even a quiet bond.

Both President Roosevelt and Ed Flynn agreed in mid-'44 – and likely well before that - that the feisty Missouri politico would be the ideal candidate to run on the next ticket as vice president. {As researcher Linda L. Wallace discovered, a *New York Times* article from July of 1944 stated the convention change from Vice President Wallace to new V.P. nominee Harry Truman "was by no means unexpected" and "had been planned that way by dominant leaders." Most likely Flynn and FDR.}

Who was amongst the very first people to meet with new President Harry Truman in his Oval Office two days after FDR died? Ed Flynn. This took place right after Chief Executive Truman had lunch with Harry Hopkins. The day before, Friday the 13th in April '45, Harry first met in that famous White House office with General Marshall, Secretary of War Henry Stimson, and James Forrestal, along with the Secretary of State (Cordell Hull's replacement), all familiar names in the MO41 affair, as we have seen. And where was President Truman's first trip out of 1600 Pennsylvania Avenue that first day? Straight back to the cross-town Capitol Building, downstairs, for "lunch"!

.{April of 1941, that was the point when and where Harry S Truman later disclosed to close friends and biographers that he initially became quite friendly and very respectful on Capitol Hill to committee witness George C. Marshall, who of course later became Truman's trusted Secretary of State. Could GCM at this point have taken the famous congressional Missourian into his confidence about what crash-landed in his own home state? And perhaps also the other senator from Missouri, Bennett C. Clark (1890-1954)? No, actually he and Roosevelt nearly despised each other, at least on political issues. Little is known about Senator Clark's activities in those immediate days after MO41, nor Missouri's Republican governor, Forrest C. Donnell (1884-1980). Both powerful Missouri men weren't exactly FDR fans, for sure.}

.F. D. Roosevelt was a political animal, and so was party boss Ed Flynn. They wanted every advantage they could think of to keep their party's leaders and followers in line and in power over Republicans in the 1940s. Whatever it took, they needed to know about it and exploit it for political gain. This may well have included a least a brief thumbnail sketch for Flynn on MO41. Ed's visit took a half-hour, unless he stayed as a guest for the FDR meeting next with Undersecretary Welles, all three men being long-time Empire State wealthy citizens, political allies, and quite well acquainted socially. But it's not just what took place in the afternoon inside the White House, but *outside* it, that may raise the most glaring and suspicious red flag of all in the April '41 presidential logs...

.On the afternoon of Wednesday, April 16th, 1941, with lunch out of the way, the satiated chief executive called in his most elite and highest-ranking military advisors. Their Oval Office meeting at 2:00 was strictly "off" as the meeting log shows, a very rare reference. "That means '*off the record*,' which means it was quite classified," researcher Ryan Wood explained. Extremely serious, high-level stuff was going on.

Some in attendance for this critical Wednesday pow-wow probably had to have flown in special, indicating they had been alerted days in advance. It might have been about something other than MO41, but that does not preclude its introduction and discussion that afternoon. Certainly the ongoing war in Europe and North Africa was discussed, and a secret memo from attendee George C. Marshall to Secretary of War Henry Stimson described this fact later that very afternoon. It was unusually dictated by Marshall, but not read or signed by the great military man; it was also strangely hand-delivered that day across town to Stimson's home. What else this private summary mentioned being discussed with FDR we'll apparently never know (but part of it is now available to the public at the digitized George Marshall Foundation online database).

.The president and his top military men and advisors talked in the Oval Office for a while. The brass and braid likely asked and answered questions as best they could, and followed executive commands and decisions. MO41 was of course a matter of "national security," to be kept to themselves, if further discussed at all. There would be no note taking allowed. The assembled men took their professions - and their eventual retirement pensions - quite seriously. It was in their best interests to go along with the plan of general silence and quiet, covert actions on the extraordinary physical evidence for alien visitation.

.The talk went on and on, likely with brief periods of silence as the men read and tried to digest the information in any reports handed out, and perhaps the images in any photographs or ship shrapnel introduced. This was juicy, critical, riveting stuff. Then for some strange reason, the president oddly felt the urge to leave the entire building. *Why?* Because he wanted to go for a ride in his car! What was so incredibly important on this day of high level meetings that the wheelchair-bound president needed to break with his top military advisors, leave the White House entirely, and be driven somewhere? And *where* did he go?

.According to the appointment logs, at "3:39" FDR went "motoring." Strange! The president was out of the White House until 4:20 (although the incomplete, odd "2" in this scribbled time-slot might have been an entirely different number, say, a "4:40"). If it was indeed 4:20 when the president came back from his drive, he was therefore gone only forty minutes. And if he was back at 4:*40*, he was only gone one hour. How far could he possibly go in that brief time? Not far, obviously.

.It is glaring that something very unusual was up, something President Roosevelt just *had* to go check on in person. A car was brought around by the Secret Service, although likely not with great fanfare or decoration. Perhaps it was even unmarked, with no U.S. flag flying on its grill. The chief executive was wheeled out to it by his loyal valet and helped into the back seat. His special wheelchair was placed in the trunk, as per usual. Who knows how many of the top brass went with him, within the president's limo or in other vehicles. But off they went, with a specific nearby destination in mind. Exactly *where* was not allowed into the White House records, *which is suspicious in itself*, but it obviously had to be somewhere pretty important, to break into all of these high-level meetings.

.It now seems logical to ask: *could the president have been motored on over to the Capitol Building to see the alien artifacts for himself?* Or at least to Fort Meyer, at the Arlington Cemetery complex, where they might also have been stored in those immediate days? Or perhaps Fort Belvoir, the Army stronghold in D.C.? The latter two locales were also a fairly short jaunt away and well known to General Marshall. Either would have been a natural for many reasons, for holding the extraterrestrial recovery under heavy guard. But the Capitol Building's lower floors that seems the most likely destination, thanks to the revealing Hull-Holt eyewitness story we recall, from the Ohio pastor's daughters' otherworldly revelations in the 1990s.

.Perhaps it seems a tad outlandish at first, but when you think about it, well if *you* were FDR, wouldn't *you* excitedly go see the evidence for yourself? Everyone informed over the past twenty-four hours was likely *very* eager to see the riveting MO41 goods for themselves. Maybe they too went along, or even motored over to them the day before, or just *hours* before. And why not, since this was the most exciting find in human history, really. Who could resist? It was just a short jaunt down the street, literally, likely under heavy guard downstairs.

.If the MO41 haul was truly held that April week down inside the Capitol Building, April 16th was the perfect time to scoot over and see them firsthand. Congress was out of session and the revered building was sure to be nearly vacant. Minus a small handful of janitors, security, maintenance, tourists, and perhaps a few leftover congressional staffers, the place was nearly a ghost town on the holiday weekend.

.Franklin and his trusted brass were doubtlessly all very curious and avid to see the actual properties pulled from just outside Cape Girardeau. The MO41 hardware items were probably kept in wooden Army crates, and the soft aliens in containers of some kind, perhaps already within the Capitol Building's underground store room and its "three glass jars" that Turner Holt vividly recalled sometime later to his two daughters. For this quick cross-town trip, FDR was probably guarded by perhaps two or three Secret Service agents, seeing as how famous structure had its own security force, patrolling inside and out. The towering government facility was a perfectly legitimate place for a president to visit now and then anyways. In such a speculated scenario, it is likely that Franklin's trusted aide Harry Hopkins, perhaps Vice Admiral Dr. McIntyre, and General Marshall went along as well to inspect matters, almost like little kids on Christmas morning. Perhaps Cordell Hull and a few others were informed in advance, that they might be there waiting for the president, such as brainiac Van Bush and possibly some of his already trusted members of the Office of Scientific Research and Development. There might have been the prevailing sentiment of "there's safety in numbers."

.If the MO41 crash happened on Saturday night, there was plenty of time to fly the objects undercover into D.C. on an Army airplane, likely a C-47 cargo vehicle. They'd be taken under guard to a nearby military airfield, possibly on Easter Sunday. In the later decades after WWII, it was finally revealed in media reports that the United States Army maintained a secret airbase just outside Washington D.C. back in the 1940s. In fact, the federal government had a private plan ready to take the president and high level cabinet members to safety in case of an enemy attack on the Capitol. All deemed worthy would have been secretly whisked away for a quick emergency air evacuation when it was felt absolutely necessary. The Army Air Corps utilized this small, guarded, obscure airfield for occasional important missions, most of them likely considered top secret. It is here we can reasonably speculate that a roomy transport plane like a C-47 was flown in with the MO41 materials secured inside, guided and guarded at all stages by armed military personnel.

.From this point on Easter Sunday that a large green military cargo truck with a canvass-covered back bed - like that used in the famous Indiana Jones movie "*Raiders of the Lost Ark*" - was probably utilized to load and lug the Missouri ET items across the Beltway to the Capitol Building, possibly in the dead of night with no one around but a few security guards. Even if this process took place during the day, some sturdy young men in army fatigues lugging around a few boxes and objects wrapped in sheets or blankets, probably unknown to them into the side door or rear entrance of the nearly-vacated Capitol with no press or nosy visitors hopefully around this would actually have been quite possible, as mentioned earlier. Most likely the entire Sunday April 13th operation – wherever it went - was under the direction of George Marshall, and could not be officially noted in his records or military diary, understandably, nor anyone else's. If an intrusive reporter or photographer from any radio station, newspaper office, or magazine headquarters had been around, the military men involved would have effectively shooed him away and squelched the story.

.Now on this Wednesday the 16th, it seems logical it to theorize it was FDR's time to take a peek at the exciting cosmic treasures. To him, this probably was nearly the whole point of ordering the celestial goods shipped to D.C. in the first place, to be able to view them in person. If so, he was likely driven right up to a guarded site, possibly even the secret army airfield itself, although that was a longer drive that might not fit within the time-frame for a presidential visit logged in White House records that afternoon.

.There's another possible factor for the president to have decided to wait until this moment to see the MO41 finds for himself. And for his valued top aides and advisors to go with him that Wednesday afternoon. In his mind, and in the minds of many of his Christian cabinet members, a little more than three full days had now passed since the Saturday deaths of the three alien creatures. This was Easter weekend, when Christians were celebrating the Resurrection of Jesus Christ, who according to lore spent three days and nights in an underground tomb, after his public execution in Jerusalem nearly two thousand years earlier. Christ emerged as a miracle of God, alive and well, the story went. Now comparatively the three grey aliens had recently died in Missouri and were whisked away to D.C. to be placed in, well, an underground tomb, of sorts. They were supposedly "buried," or at least sealed up, in the sub-basement store room deep in the bowels of the famous Capitol Building, supposedly. Saturday evening to Tuesday evening, from the 12th to the 15th, that was the three-day wait. Reports may have come in Wednesday morning that all was well at the Capitol; there had been no miraculous "resurrection" of the extraterrestrials following this three-day wait in their "entombment." And there had been no report of any attempt by the grey ET race to somehow rescue or abduct the three cadavers, let alone their captured flying ship. Thus by the afternoon of the 16th, the president knew it was now seemingly quite safe to visit the recoveries, to inspect them carefully with his own eyes.

.Again we must bear in mind that devoutly-Christian Cordell Hull's final resting place was a crypt under the "Chapel of Joseph of Arimathea" within the National Cathedral. The Biblical tale of Jesus being crucified and then swiftly entombed within Joseph of Arimathea's tomb might also have played a role on this Easter weekend decision to stash the dead alien bodies, since both FDR and Hull were Episcopalians, the religious faith of that specific D.C. chapel, holding to the notion that underground stone tombs – not graves – were a proper way of dealing with remains of the deceased. The devoutly Christian Cordell Hull may thus have had a great influence on the disposition of the MO41 materials, we can speculate.

.If the destination was the Capitol Building, then the presidential party probably arrived at a side service doorway, helped from the limo and into his wheelchair by the Secret Service, surrounded by aides to block off anyone else's possible view. Mr. Roosevelt had just visited the Capitol Building a few months earlier, first to give his third inaugural address, and then a bit later a second visit to give the assembled U.S. congress and a national radio audience his annual State of the Union speech. Now if MO41 was really there, in all likelihood FDR was back, but certainly not saying anything to anyone in any speech. But he sure needed a cover story, or excuse, if asked about the trip. He may have used the excellent excuse of visiting the vice president at his office, maintained near the senate chamber, and perhaps even stopped in there briefly that afternoon to see Henry Wallace.

.When Franklin Delano Roosevelt assumed the presidency in early 1933, the Secret Service quietly built special wooden ramps leading up to the doorways of key buildings around Washington D.C. This certainly came in handy whenever FDR visited the Capitol Building, for he would need such a ramp at the least every four years for inaugural ceremonies, if not other visits. .In this April 16th afternoon scenario the president was wheeled into the same south entrance by a trusted aide, perhaps Admiral McIntyre, who frequently accompanied his patient and friend on trips away from the White House, such as a recent public visit to

D.C.'s ballpark for baseball's Opening Day. McIntyre likely needed to be present, it can by theorized, to monitor the president's mental and physical health and reactions to the shocking scenes to come. And he also needed to see the otherworldly specimens for himself, if he were to truly be in charge of an autopsy of the creatures. Everyone in the know would want to view the "little space people" before they were cut up and scientifically examined.

.The vacant Capitol marble halls would have echoed with footsteps of FDR advisors and friends; a Secret Service agent or two; and the creak of the president's wheelchair as he was pushed and escorted to the right elevator, the right floor, the right room, the right door. If it was locked, someone had to have produced the right key. Finally, in the group went, likely with an Army or State Department representative and/or scientist waiting for them, as "hosts," with lights on and space cleared for the president's party. It would have been an inspection tour like no other, that is for certain.

.There in the Capitol sub-basement storage room, under glowing light bulbs and perhaps dusty concrete floors, FDR would have been wheeled in closer, eyeing with growing shock and excitement the stupefying MO41 cache, his Secret Service protectors also transfixed nearby. The seemingly undamaged alien bodies were likely laid out on tables, or possibly were already in those very large "glass jars," swimming in formaldehyde, grey and crinkled, appearing like dead, big-headed children. These were riveting humanoids, "creatures from outer space," and Mr. Roosevelt doubtlessly stared in amazement like anyone else. He likely pondered all kinds of questions, but if there was a shred of doubt left that mankind was alone in the universe, this eerie experience ended that fast. .The weird-looking, deceased "non-terrestrials" or "little people" and their disengaged "aerodyne" were spooky in every way.

They probably made Roosevelt's skin crawl, his spine tingle, and his goose-bumps grow goose-bumps. Every human being present likely felt the same way, deep down inside. This might have been in the president's mind the ultimate Masonic prize, part of God's plan, or just plain *fate* that it all happened on *his* "watch." It was unlike anything he'd ever seen, dreamed, or hoped for. Various thoughts and emotions likely whirled around like a dust storm as he gazed around.

.Perhaps if this really *was* a Masonic room, or near one downstairs, as a devout Freemason this was now FDR's most precious possession and perhaps temporary "gift" to his favorite fraternal order. In that case, it might have been for viewing by "members only," with only the highest-ranking and most devoted Freemason society leaders allowed in that April day, or later, like the deeply dedicated Missouri Grand Master Mason Harry Truman. The MO41 materials came from his home state, in fact a town he once lived in (for one summer), and he had a "need to know" in how to handle his constituents should they start to ask questions. .

.Once the April 16th visit was over - wherever it was held - and everyone was "back to their posts," so to speak, all concerned were probably wondering to themselves: "*Now what?*" It was all very nice to have possession of this historic evidence, but *what exactly to do with it?* No doubt FDR had Van Bush ready to work on its vehicular secrets, and Ross McIntyre on its occupants' biophysical makeup. But for now well, there wasn't much else to do, frankly. They all had to wait until the secret pathology studies and engineering reports were in someday, to more fully brief insiders on the unusual situation. And for all to keep alert to any report of further non-terrestrial incursions or excursions. Therefore, all were dismissed and Mr. Roosevelt went back to the White House, where according to the existing records, he returned to the Oval Office to review some unknown matters of importance in private, with no visitors, until 5:15. Cocktails usually flowed at this hour. From our new perspective on that afternoon, we can reasonably guess that Mr. Roosevelt poured himself quite a stiff drink, absorbing all of the day's heady information. The memories of what was viewed would then have to be placed on the mental back burner as a long-planned "tea" with the Prime Minister of Canada, Mackenzie King, was waiting in the White House study. President Roosevelt huddled with King for almost an hour, according to the presidential logs.

.Is it a mere coincidence that Prime Minister King, age 65, was now in Washington? Or was he specifically called in just for this White House meeting, just because of MO41 taking place days before? It's mere conjecture, but if aliens *had* crashed in mid-America, it is plausible that FDR could have contacted Mr. King the previous Saturday night and asked him: "Have you fielded reports of any spaceship sightings or crashes in Canada?" When informed *why* his pal Roosevelt would inquire of such a thing, King's curiosity would have been greatly aroused. He might well have taken the first flight or train south from Toronto (Canada's seat of government) to Washington to see the Cape Girardeau recoveries for himself. *It's even possible he was at any Wednesday afternoon projected showing of the otherworldly materials*, or was taken to the recoveries at another time during his D.C. visit.

Such speculation would make perfect sense since William Lyon Mackenzie King (1874-1950) was no ordinary world leader. First, he was a longtime trusted friend and ally to Franklin Roosevelt and patterned his social programs in Canadian government on FDR's New Deal. Second, Mackenzie was also a devoted Freemason, bonding him further with Roosevelt and his administration. Mr. King spent some of his time in Quebec, an eastern province just north of Roosevelt's home state, New York, and it is Quebec where Mackenzie lived and died in 1950. *After his death, Mackenzie King was revealed to be a great fan of the supernatural* (in private). Talk of outer space crafts and pilots – or seeing such recovered evidence - would have excited him to no end. That is the third and most unique factor that greatly helped create a special and close relationship with Franklin Roosevelt, a great curiosity and love of the paranormal.

Prime Minister King's native Quebec has a long history of UFO sightings, including a rather odd story from a rural farmer there named Arthur Matthews, who published a book in early 1971, the 30th anniversary of what he felt was a major extraterrestrial event. Not MO41, but a sizable UFO landing on his farm, in April of 1941! Matthews claimed many other sightings of round, metallic, silver spacecrafts from other worlds, settling on or near his Quebec estate, and in later years his surviving daughter grudgingly admitted that *men from the Canadian government* used to show up at the family home for secretive meetings with her father. Whether Mackenzie King knew about all of this is unknown; it would seem that he would have been quite fascinated, however. Did the prime minister get involved in the celestial matter, opening his mind up to the unusual subject? If so, did he discuss it with President Roosevelt *before* April 1941?

In reality, Mackenzie King may well have been *very* open to the discussion of life beyond earth and visitors from the stars. He owned a crystal ball, and books on the occult. He felt his dreams at night gave him omens and portents to heed. He sought to communicate with the dead. This was all according to King's own personal diary, found after his demise; the startling facts about the unorthodox prime minister's personal life came to light only several years later. Mr. King admitted he utilized mediums and held séances, and even used a Ouija board to make contact with otherworldly spirits. In fact, Mackenzie King even claimed in his diary that he had communicated with the spirit of the late Franklin Roosevelt, in the years after FDR's sudden demise!

.Was visiting Mr. King allowed in on the great secret culled from Cape Girardeau, Missouri? We'll keep in mind that Quebec was a French-Canadian territory while Cape Girardeau was originally begun as just that. It was trading outpost established by French-Canadian explorer Jean de Girardot in 1737, since the local geographical makeup of the Midwestern land was that of a natural outcropping of solid land and cliffs, an inland "cape" that jutted out into the rough and rampaging Mississippi River. The site was a unique gathering place where explorers, trappers, traders, and Native Americans stopped when flitting up and down the deep waters, looking for food, barter, and adventure. Decades after adventurous de Girardot left his crude but substantial buildings along the river, a small town began to slowly grow, named after him. Another French-Canadian, Louis Lorimer, helped to organize and expand the "conquered territory" in the late 1700s, at least until the land was included in the great "Louisiana Purchase" by President Jefferson in the early 1800s. Cape Girardeau became a fairly important part of the new-look central United States of America in those wilderness frontier days and even hosted the historic Lewis and Clark expedition in 1803.

.Quebec as a "UFO hot-spot" may seem a bit strange at first, but in 2016, a national survey revealed in the Canadian media that this particular province easily had *the most reported UFO sightings in the nation.* There had seemingly always been plenty of these unusual encounters. What was the attraction for alien visitation there? {Or for that matter French-Canadian-born Cape Girardeau, hundreds of miles to the southwest?} Whatever the case, the possible connections became even stronger and stranger when President Roosevelt and Mackenzie King arranged two important conferences with Masonic British Prime Minister Winston Churchill in, of all places, *Quebec*, in the years after MO41.

{The bond between Roosevelt and King seemed to deepen in the years to come, and it was arranged in March of 1945 for the Canadian prime minister to again travel all the way to D.C. to meet with the frail American president. Unhealthy FDR knew he was off to Warm Springs soon, to execute his secret plan to take his own life (see Bonus Chapter). Yet it was important for Mackenzie King to meet alone and speak with Franklin at the White House that early spring, with mistress Lucy Mercer present. Weeks later, when FDR was ensconced in Georgia, the chief diplomat to Canada was one of the ill president's final dinner guests, at the Little White House. Was there some sort of special final message Roosevelt wanted this man to impart to King that mid-April of '45?}

.Cooperative surgeon and naval admiral Ross McIntyre was no Canadian, but hailed from Oregon. Dr. McIntyre was an "eyes, ears, nose, and throat" specialist, which came in handy as President Roosevelt had great sinus problems, on top of his polio and various other aches and pains. With the paranormal prime minister gone that April 16th evening, the two intimate friends since 1937, whether it was the president's health or the qualities of the deceased MO41 aliens they may possibly have just seen and/or discussed earlier. The duo likely swapped a few drinks and thoughts, then split up for the night, at 7:00. Roosevelt returned to his study for dinner, and strangely no great guests were recorded to have visited him there, or for the rest of the night. Perhaps the president was so rattled he needed time to think more clearly, study the reports, and place some phone calls, *alone*. He obviously now had a lot on his mind.

.By 10:15 that night, the logs show FDR retired to his upstairs master bedroom, the fifty-nine-year-old weary from the day's many guests, information, and activity. {Eleanor had left at 6:20 p.m. to hop a flight to California, to attend son James' wedding, obviously with FDR having concluded that air travel was safe.} Possibly the president pondered giving an historic speech about it to congress, maybe at that same Capitol Building, a radio broadcast to let everyone in the nation and around the world know the truth at last. Tell them precisely what was down in that basement room, and weighing on his mind. No that would might touch off a panic, perhaps even on Wall Street, and damage the fragile Depression-era economy even further. The matter definitely required more private study in every way, the first seeds of the "statecraft of spacecrafts" being sewn. The president needed to "sleep on it" in more ways than one.

.Much uncertainty likely pressed heavily on FDR and sleep that night might well have been difficult. Maybe it should have been. The rest of 1941 and beyond would prove quite troublesome indeed. The president would undergo more serious, energy-sapping health woes in the coming weeks and months, including a near-death crisis due to severe gastrointestinal bleeding. His favorite secretary would suffer severe health problems and would be lost to him for good in just a few weeks. The chief executive's cherished mother would pass away in September, as would his brother-in-law. Many of the difficult national problems stemming from The Great Depression continued unabated. The carefully observed, vicious warfare going on around the world would go poorly for U.S.-friendly democratic nations, with thousands of soldiers and civilians dying gruesomely every month. His new controversial "Lend-

Lease Act" would rile still more angry American opposition to global war involvement and stoke in others isolationism. And then the entire tenuous year would explode in December with two now infamous words: *Pearl Harbor*.

.Yes, Franklin Delano Roosevelt had a lot on his mind for the rest of that fateful year, for sure. It was such a roller-coaster twelve months for the president, the towering world figure was named *Time* magazine's "Man of the Year." But did any of what he experienced for the rest of his life ever tantalize, frighten, and excite him more than what fell to earth in April? Perhaps he could only share some of the MO41 facts with his most cherished and trusted allies, in private. He had trusted them in the past, these high-powered but low-key brothers who treated him and all other club members like equals in the eyes of their secretive fraternal order's laws

CHAPTER THREE

HST's Secret Society

..

"There's more to this story than you might think."

.For a fact, there existed in 1941 and to this day a very real secret society with somewhat mystical beliefs and a fairly strong code of silence, right at the heart of America, and in the heart of the MO41 crash affair, resonating outwards. A cabal of powerful American men gathered regularly, and they almost always formed an unbreakable chain in their consistent resilience and silence, in their vested interest in keeping esoteric knowledge to themselves but a mysterious facade to the general public. This specific, effective conspiracy in question flares up at every level of the MO41 investigation. The group in question likely will continue to exist, with different members now, of course, but their numbers are said to be dwindling. They subsist in most communities around the country, perhaps *every* country, actually, yet they almost never speak publicly about what goes on behind closed doors. One of their mottos is "Always conceal, never reveal." This secluded, shrouded group is known as The Fraternal Order of Freemasons..

.To be clear, it must be stated up front that Masons across America and other nations get together in private mostly to enjoy the company of their fellow good-hearted citizens who nobly donate time, energy, and money to charities and plan ways to improve the lives of citizens of their communities. They are *not* involved in evil conspiracies to rule the world, that is the nonsensical talk of sadly deluded people looking to stir up controversy and attention for various reasons. Freemasons *do*, however, conspire in private, that's a fact. They scheme, in a sense, to closely hold many secrets and rituals, kept between exclusively male members behind closed doors. No women or children are allowed. These rational adult men create and utilize secret passwords, secret handshakes, secret meetings, secret ceremonies, and secret activities that even their wives and families quite possibly never learn about, at the time of membership or perhaps *ever*. Freemasons often clam up whenever they are quizzed about what they are up to, even if it was something other members engaged in many decades ago such as the lowdown on what took place in April of 1941.

.The city of Cape Girardeau has hosted a Fraternal Order of Freemasonry since 1892. Back in 1941, the town's Masonic temple was located downtown in a brick building at 121 Broadway, on the corner of Spanish Street, where a Masonic brass plaque still remains on an exterior wall to commemorate their get-togethers. {The building is now utilized by a local business.} The town's Masonic meeting lodge in 1941 was situated on Sprigg Street, a mile or so away, shared at other times with the local chapter of the American Legion and the mysterious "Knights of Pythias" organization. This flat, brick building has been closed and shuttered for years, next door to a now-closed Ford car dealership in the downtown area. It was this site where one of the most ardent members of the society *in its history*, Harry S Truman, used to visit. A key fact to always keep in mind: from the point of the MO41 UFO crash forward, HST vaulted up the ladder of success to becoming the most famous and powerful man on the face of the earth. Mr. Truman's presence within the Masonic and governmental organizations in the MO41 saga flares up repeatedly as we shall see...

.Many leading area male Cape Girardeau citizens of the day were fraternal members, sworn to secrecy over their rituals and conduct in private. Cape Girardeau fire and police department officials were undoubtedly involved, as were doctors, lawyers, politicos, newspapermen, factory and office workers, and generally mature, thoughtful gentlemen from all walks of life. Cape Freemasons met and chatted and dined and followed secret rituals whenever they pleased, and often didn't breathe a word of their private actions beyond their locked lodge doors to anyone in town. They regularly met on the first and third Tuesdays or Thursdays of each month, as is their custom in the river town to this day (in a newer building in mid-town), although some temple social activities were advertised in advance in *The Southeast Missourian.*

.A key factor to bear in mind: *for some reason, the Brotherhood of Freemasons finds the United States Capitol Building in Washington D.C. to be worthy of great reverence and respect, glory and glad tidings.* For one example, the Capitol's dome graces the cover of their organizational artwork, in Masonic books and websites, and seems to be the focus of their most noble goals, such as bringing peaceful cooperation and democratic enlightenment between free people from all over the country. Perhaps all over the world – and also *beyond it?*

.As recalled earlier, Reverend Turner Holt stated without hesitation or levity that he was shown crashed alien materials down in the sub-basement of the U.S. Capitol Building, by Secretary Cordell Hull, in the early 1940s. Three dead, uninjured-looking grey aliens, and one damaged spaceship, cut into sections to fit into a special sub-basement storeroom. A dark "dungeon," of sorts, quite far below the working offices and floors of the United States congress. These were the MO41 materials almost assuredly. After all, how many other crashed alien ships with crews of three ETs without burns or wounds could there have been in this nation in 1941? One can reasonably conclude it was perhaps taken directly from Cape Girardeau and Sikeston, Missouri, in the day or two after the mind-numbing event, and stayed in this dungeon site for weeks or even months, guarded and examined by a precious few, including political elites who worked on Capitol Hill in D.C.

.Perhaps *the* leading citizen of 1940s Cape Girardeau, Missouri, was a very advanced, dedicated, and appreciated Freemason: Rush Hudson Limbaugh, Sr. (1891-1996). RHL was the grandfather of the very famous radio broadcaster known today for his strong opinions on the national airwaves in the late twentieth century and early twenty-first. Rush, Sr. was quite a respected and successful attorney, politician, and community benefactor in his day. He generously donated his time, money, and energies to his church and local charities and projects (although he never served in the military). By the spring of '41, Rush Sr. was almost fifty years old, and not interested in being a state congressman again, nor City Attorney, as he had once been decades earlier. He had a wife and three sons and a lovely home in Cape, across Henderson Street from the college. He worked in a law office at 102 N. Main Street in Cape, a block west of the wide and muddy Mississippi River, and a block south of the Masonic temple. It was in the conservative RHL's best interest not to rock the boat on most any controversial matter, through his entire life, for personal and professional reasons.

.According to the eighty-seven-year-old son of Rush Sr. - the honorable attorney and former judge Stephen N.

Limbaugh - his father was "a 32nd degree Freemason." This indicates decades of great responsibility and service within the Cape Girardeau community, but also an ability to remain quiet and trusted about one's club actions and organizational involvement. Yet we must keep in mind there were a number of "Limbaugh" relatives and residents in not just Cape Girardeau County, but in neighboring Scott County as well. Some of them, long gone now, may well have known the truth about MO41. Scott County, featuring fertile farmland outside of Cape and Chaffee, Missouri, may well have been *the* crash site. In his biography's interviews, Rush Sr. stated he often took trips down the local two-lane highway to Scott County to get involved in community affairs, such as organizing church activities, Boy Scout troops, and giving speeches for various groups along with visiting kin and contacts of all kinds, no doubt.

.Why is it important to understand how Masonic Rush H. Limbaugh Sr. lived his life in southeastern Missouri, and how possibly-Masonic Limbaughs existed in nearby Scott County? Flash forward to a national radio program hosted by his renowned grandson, Rush III, back in 2006. During the show, a listener called in, live on the air, to ask: "Rush, what's this about a crashed UFO in your hometown?" The famous broadcaster did not dismiss the unexpected caller or his startling subject matter. He did not reply with mocking sarcasm or snide ridicule. He did not dub the question as "nonsense" or even issue a simple "no comment." Rush III instead strongly indicated that the MO41 allegement was not only true, but that there was even more to it than was being discussed publicly! This infers he knew quite a bit about it. .

."There's more to this story than you think," was reportedly all that RHL III cryptically told the '06 caller, and thus his listening audience. Rush deftly moved to the next caller, leaving an air of mystery, but excitement to the saga.

Undoubtedly the unknown caller had been reading about the Cape Girardeau alien crash recovery claims on the internet and viewing it on television within the special documentary *"The Secret"* on the SyFy Channel. Quite possibly in private broadcaster Rush was too. But he probably didn't have to, because it appears very likely from his mysterious, enticing response that he knew more than the average American, perhaps from first or secondhand witnesses passing along scrumptious details along to Rush Sr., Rush Jr., or to Rush III himself directly. The top "suspect" for such information would be via the famous broadcaster's father, Rush Hudson Limbaugh, Jr. (1918-1990), twenty-three years old studying in law school at the time of the crash. And *a big aviation enthusiast who flew the skies near - if not directly over - the crash site, and loved hanging around others who did as well.* And according to a newspaper article, Rush, Jr. was in town Easter weekend, from Friday to Monday.

.Rush II fell in love with aviation, like nothing else in life, since he was a boy. In fact, he was *obsessed* with it nearly his whole life. Yet his own father never served in the military, nor flew an airplane. Apparently Rush Jr. hung around the underdeveloped rural airstrip just outside Cape Girardeau and took flying lessons. He passed his tests and soon enthusiastically solo-piloted aircrafts. "My father was a lawyer," Rush III told his listening audience one day in 2009, "but if he really would have fulfilled his dream, he would have run a major airport somewhere." The contemporary star radioman's dad left Cape Girardeau during WWII, serving his country very honorably in the Army Air Force, and later piloted his own private plane whenever possible while he led a group in Cape Girardeau to develop a fully functional and reliable, modern and attractive municipal airport. {For his efforts, today Cape Girardeau's municipal airport road is named after him.} Even media star Rush III's mother took up flying, taking lessons when her son was still a boy. During this time, Rush III claims, his aviation-obsessed father subscribed to many aeronautics magazines, eagerly devouring others' stories of flight, even if it was just from talking to local pilots and mechanics. Perhaps thanks to his parents' influence, Rush III confessed to his syndicated radio audience in 2009: "I've been fascinated with aviation all my life."

Rush II would go on to become a respected Cape Girardeau attorney, political and civic organizer, avid churchgoer and choir director, and was likely supportive of his father and his friends engaging in Freemason activities, but evidently did not himself join that fraternity. By mid-May of 1941 he was likely back once again from college and regularly hanging around area airstrips, including the Cape sod landing field that soon became the more polished "Harris Army Airfield" in 1942. Rush Jr. loved sopping up all manner of aviation, and likely spoke a great deal in the 1940s to anyone associated with airplanes, the aviation industry, and the military-run flight training center at Harris, which just after WWII became Cape Girardeau Municipal Airport. The famous radioman's father continued his flight fandom right up to his death in 1990.

When contacted by researcher Linda L. Wallace in early 2014, Rush Jr.'s two surviving brothers, Manley and Stephen (both in their 90s), said they had never heard of the region's UFO crash. But neither were all that necessary to learning the odd saga to pass it along to Rush III, who admittedly might have been briefed on the story's details from just *anyone* in the area, but most likely by his own father who picked up some MO41 scoop from those in the know.

.The world-famous radioman Rush - Rush Hudson Limbaugh III - was born in Cape Girardeau in 1951, and seemed at first a bit of a "black sheep of the family." Rush

III attended a local elementary school, Cape Central High School, and even the college in town, but only for one semester at Southeast Missouri State University, in 1969, before dropping out. He showed no interest in the law, farming, flying his own plane, nor joining the military, or even the Masons. At first Rush (or "Rusty" as he was called early on) had a hard time finding and keeping a job that suited him. His only great love was broadcasting, which eventually paid off with an extremely lucrative career once he left Cape Girardeau.

.The unusual, controversial subject of an extraterrestrial crash-landing was obviously not something conservative commentator RHL III wanted to publicly explore on the air. He was and remains to this day a devoted Republican in a family of very devoted Republicans, and the idea of discussing aliens, military cover-ups, and government conspiracies on a national radio program was (and still is) simply too much to ponder and palaver. Nor could he detail his esteemed right wing family's inside knowledge. No, MO41 had to be hinted at, but not discussed or dismissed, as it was a very real event, but just a little "over the top" for the conservative "Rush Limbaugh Show" listening audience, accustomed to hearing about only contemporary politics and government. If RHL III mentioned on the air that his someone - perhaps his own father - told him about MO41, he'd be the subject of ridicule and disbelief, and so would his respected dad's memory, in the minds of Rush-haters and those close-minded about the topic of alien visitation. No, keeping quiet would be the much wiser move, at least while Rush remains a national figure.

Probably Cape's most trusted police officer was Fred "Fritz" Schneider (1888-1970), a local Freemason who may well have been at the MO41 crash scene. Fritz was close friends with Marshall Morton, another Cape cop who eventually became the chief of police. Morton may also have been a Mason, but it is not clear. Rush Limbaugh I and his wife Bee knew both men well, and were distantly related to conservative Cape Girardeau County Sheriff Ruben Schade's lady love, Maxine, through her mother. Schade might have been a Mason, it is not clear, but his predecessor, Sheriff J. F. Hartle in Cape County certainly was. In a small town, almost everyone had a connection to everyone, by some manner of job, relatives, friends of friends, or community affairs, especially if they were of the same political ilk. For Cape Girardeau Freemasons to get involved in responding to the chaotic, originally-perceived "plane crash" and finding "an outer space ship" and three "little people" that needed orderly hushing up... well, keep in mind the three-word Latin motto of all Freemasons: "Orbo ab Chao." *Order out of chaos.*

Even the mayor of Cape Girardeau, Wiley Hinkle Statler (1909-1962), was a Mason. In fact, a special Knights Templar Freemason, and just a few weeks *before* the MO41 affair, he had traveled to D.C. to meet Missouri's Grand Master Mason in the early 1940s, Senator Harry Truman, on Capitol Hill. In early 1945, "Hink" met with Vice President Truman in Chicago, and then later with *President* Truman in October in southeast Missouri (along with Rush Limbaugh Jr.). Was it their Masonic brotherhood bonds that helped a seemingly obscure small town mayor get private conferences with such a very powerful American? Or their mutual knowledge of MO41? Or both?

.If the head of Missouri's state government ever visited Cape Girardeau in 1941, he was warmly welcomed at Rush H. Limbaugh Sr.'s home on Henderson Street, and at the city's Freemason meeting lodge and its "worshipful temple" as well. Why? Because Governor Forrest C. Donnell was Rush I's friend, a devout and devoted Mason, and the most powerful man in the state. And quite often when an average citizen becomes a Mason, it is because he had at least one or more Fraternal Freemasons in his family. When a political figure becomes a Mason, he also has close, trusted Masonic friends in almost every quarter of his governing territory, backing his bid for public office. Fellow Republicans Donnell and Limbaugh were quite familiar with each other, since they were top conservative political figures in the state of Missouri. On Saturday morning, April 12th, 1941 - the best guess date as to when the alien crash occurred - Rush Sr. was in a Cape Girardeau County courthouse (according to a newspaper account), earning the right to represent Governor Donnell in a critical area recount of the state's gubernatorial race from that past early November. This recount was to take place April 22nd, and Rush I was eager to prove that his friend Forrest was the true and clear winner. The county courthouse was located in the heart of Jackson, Missouri, about a dozen miles northwest of downtown Cape Girardeau, right near Sheriff Schade's headquarters.

.As mentioned, U.S. Senator Harry S. Truman was known to many Cape Girardeans. HST worked mostly in the Capitol Building and the nearby U.S. Senate Office building in mid-April of '41. He and his wife Bess lived in an apartment on Constitution Avenue in Washington D.C. According to online research, whenever Democrat Harry was back in his hometown of Independence, Missouri - just outside of Kansas City - he was the man in charge (at least nominally) of the area's finest and most influential Masonic operation center (actually located in Belmont, Missouri). *Truman once said he considered being Grand Master of the state the highest honor he had ever received.* That's how hardcore and devoted he was to this private group. He was awarded the exalted position of Grand Master Mason of Missouri in 1940 at the Ararat Lodge in Kansas City, and went on to earn still other fraternal honors. Harry completed his "worshipful master" statewide term on

October 1, 1941, and focused more on moving up in the society's national leadership as the years rolled by.

Shortly after he assumed the duties of the presidency in April of '45, *Harry S Truman met in the White House with none other than guest Vannevar Bush,* also a devoted Mason. This was arranged supposedly in order for the brainy visitor to relay in private details of the mysteriously powerful new weapon, the atomic bomb, which may well have had technology found near Cape Girardeau and also created there, in a special factory (see Chapter Five). In 1959, some years out of power, Harry achieved a special fiftieth year in Masonic service award, the only U.S. president to ever be so honored. HST remained an active member until his death in late 1972.

.As we climb the ladder of power in 1941 America, we must ponder Vice President next. Henry Agard Wallace was a *very* devoted, 33rd degree Freemason. He admitted to being something of a mystic, and had even joined the controversial "Theosophical Society," having been a member for ten years. He wrote letters to his personal "guru." Some years before MO41, Henry helped inject Masonic symbols into America's currency. The remains of otherworldly creatures likely excited him more than anyone in the country as Wallace spent most of his days presiding over the senate and working in his Capitol Building office, roaming the floors and halls of power to glad-hand and twist arms over governmental issues, both public and private.

And then there's President Franklin Delano Roosevelt. He too was said to be a 33rd degree Freemason, the highest elite status, and rather fittingly died after three terms and three months in office as president. Mr. Roosevelt made sure that at least three of his four sons were Masons, and his wife Eleanor became a member of the Order of the Eastern Star, the Masonic organization for women. Nearly every member of his cabinet and his military leaders were Freemasons. In a private ceremony, FDR was named the first "Honorary Grand Master of the Order of DeMolay" - on April 13th, 1934, for which the placing of dead aliens and their craft in the Capitol Building sub-basement – if done so "the day after" - would have been the exact 7th anniversary! For the president, keeping the secrets of the fraternal order was undoubtedly of utmost importance.

As we can see, the Masonic connections within every level of 1941 city, state, and federal government in the MO41 affair are amazing and almost mind-numbing to ponder today. Further, there's an incredible, seeming *labyrinth* of Masonic ties that bind the Missouri UFO crash recovery, these governmental and military figures, and their beloved United States Capitol Building, as we shall soon understand...

.A resident of Cape Girardeau in the summer of 1906, young Harry Truman got to know the city and its surrounding countryside. Years later, often while campaigning for office, more mature Harry came back to Cape and also traveled to other Freemason lodges and orders in the state, making friends with influential local citizens who were highly-placed, dedicated club members. Harry had joined the secret society in 1909 and was so gung-ho he eventually worked his way up to becoming Grand Master, as mentioned. As senator and later president, Truman was in fact so enthusiastic about his fraternity status he posed for a formal painted portrait in his Masonic apron and jewelry, his fez nearby. HST also wrote the Foreword to a book on Freemasonry, and evidently attended regular fraternal meetings in Washington as well, possibly at the very old but well-kept "Lodge Number One" in D.C., perhaps the oldest existing secret society headquarters in America. He was named honorary member of the Supreme Council while president. Keeping secrets from the public was second-hand nature for a political and Masonic pro like Truman, but he was also adept at public relations and communications. Just weeks before the extraterrestrial air accident in Cape Girardeau, in February of '41, Harry delivered a public radio address discussing his favorite figure in history being a passionate Freemason. The big broadcast went out over one hundred radio stations in the country. It was all about the Masonic Father of Our Country, George Washington. Within just four years, of course, HST became an American president just like his hero George. In fact, a total of fourteen of America's presidents have been Freemasons, and perhaps *hundreds* of congressmen over the centuries; the idea that a Masonic lodge or meeting room has been maintained - perhaps from the very beginning - in the sub-basement of the Capitol Building is a very real possibility, according to Masonic researchers online. *If* President Roosevelt in the spring of '41 had gone ahead with the idea of a secret congressional investigation into the Cape Girardeau cosmic crash, he likely would have tabbed Senator Truman to be a part of it, at least had HST not been chairing his military funding oversight committee.

.It's hard to believe, but true: *as president*, Harry S Truman actually talked on camera about the reality of alien spaceships! A film crew was recording President Truman on the afternoon of July 20th, 1952 - during a famous Washington D.C. "UFO flap" - when a reporter somewhat innocently asked: "Do the Joint Chiefs of Staff talk to you, or concern you about the unknown unidentified flying objects?" Harry, in a light-colored suit and necktie, smiling behind his thick eyeglasses, replied on camera to his interrogator with substantial candor. "Oh yes," he confirmed right away, *with no hesitation*. "We discussed it at every conference we had with the military." Here was - and still is - an astonishing presidential statement, considering that the official stance of the U.S. government and military had always been that there was nothing at all to "UFOs" and supposed "spaceships" piloted by aliens from other planets. That was normally the stuff of foolishness, always considered unworthy of anyone's time and beneath the dignity of those in charge of our nation to explore, either behind the scenes or with the public, *especially* on camera.

.Obviously President Truman knew he only had six months left in his presidency, but he actually let slip how very seriously this subject was taken in private by those in power, for the startled TV crew to eagerly record. Alien visitation was indeed being examined, he revealed, at *every* private military conference he and/or his staff attended. *Wow!* If there was really nothing at all to the topic, why bring it up with the very busy military leadership, immersed in fighting the Cold War, and also for a few years the Korean War? If it was genuinely disseminated at "*every*" high level conference Truman held as president, then surely MO41 was at least *some* of the subject matter from the time HST took office in April of '45 to at least July of '47, when the Roswell affair and the first really big public wave of "flying saucer reports" took precedence in the national media.

.In further explaining the UFO subject regarding his Joint Chiefs, President Truman described on camera their actions - or the lack thereof: "They never had been never were able to make me a concrete report on " At this point the interviewer interrupted, making Harry's voice trail off unintelligibly. So by this interesting revelation, we can see Mr. Truman must have asked for some sort of "concrete report" by his top generals on what *they* knew or suspected, but was evidently disappointed they didn't deliver, since he blurted out this fact in the '52 interview, over a full decade after the MO41 incident was largely swept under the rug largely by the U.S. Army during his predecessor's reign.

And Harry wasn't being totally honest, either; the General Nathan Twining September 1947 "White Hot Intelligence Estimate" on the Roswell crash – mentioning MO41 at least twice – *was* brought to the president, and HST initialed this "concrete report" on its cover page.

.But Truman's startling on-camera admission was not quite yet complete. The questioner bore in, asking the president if he had any public opinion on the subject (of UFOs). "No, I haven't " Truman stopped himself deftly, then added, "...haven't had anything on the subject." In other words, Harry had no official statement for the press or the people of the world, but then stunningly blurted out: "There's always things like that going on. Ah, flying saucers and we've had other things, you know, if I'm not mistaken." "*Flying Saucers*"?? Wow! On camera, the chief executive just stated with precision that "we've" been experiencing "flying saucers" and also "*other things*," related to alien evidence. In other words, non-terrestrial ships, bodies, and artifacts? Some even from his own home state? This was the early '50s, where Harry S. Truman was admitting that "we" - the American nation as a whole and/or its government - were "always" experiencing "things like that going on." Starting in April of 1941, the dawn of the atomic age? At any rate, the startling video is popular today on YouTube and is seen in other UFO-related projects, able to be pondered by anyone at any time.

.A number of circular airships flew in formation over Washington, more than once, sighted by many citizens and even reporters in late July of 1952. One alert witness even filmed the squadron of UFOs as they buzzed *the Capitol Building*, of all places. Radar returns were reported, photos were snapped, and eyewitness accounts were making the press. Were aliens trying to send Truman - and others - a message? National newspapers were full of the subject at the time, and it helped make belief in "UFOs" and "spacemen" more widespread and worthy of serious discussion. Perhaps until the U.S. Air Force gave a press conference to undercut and dismiss the D.C. UFO business. Was it Harry's decision to order the UFO flap covered up and lied about to the press and the public? Or was it simply ongoing Army/Air Force policy? We may never know for certain, but we do know that in his memoirs HST made sure to point out in the preface: "For reasons of national security I have omitted certain material," some of which might not be released "for many generations." What was going on that was so incredible that entire *generations* must wait to read it? Certainly the shocking censored truth about MO41 fits that bill; we're still waiting for the full story, many decades (at least *two* generations already) later.

.Like his presidential predecessor Roosevelt, Harry Truman obviously loved his Masonic rank and fellowship; he even bent over and kissed one of two Bibles he used during his official Oath of Office swearing-in ceremony, held on the steps of the Capitol Building in January of 1949. One was evidently a Bible with Masonic history to it, of course. A solemn oath, two Bibles, one kiss, precisely as his beloved George Washington accepted *his* presidential oath, back in 1789, albeit in New York City. Historical art records that President Washington was rendered in a formal fraternal portrait pose, wearing his Masonic apron and symbols, such as the time when he ceremoniously laid the cornerstone of the United States Capitol Building. Right from the beginning, Masons were drawn to the Capitol like moths to a flame; the entire building and concept of democratic government might well have been their idea all along.

.In September of 1793, the weedy, even *swampy* D.C. grounds were readied at last for an official ceremony to commence the very solid, thorough construction of this physically enormous and politically critical governmental structure. Journalists at the time reported that President

Washington and his fellow Masonic lodge members marched to the site on a hill, joined by yet other area Masonic temple members, forming quite an impressive crowd. Dignitaries and citizens from all corners stood watching with the well-organized Freemasons, many of whom were decked out in their special Masonic aprons, meticulously hand-sewn in those days. President Washington clutched a special silver trowel, cement at the ready, as he conducted the Capitol cornerstone ceremony *down in a trench*, interestingly enough. It was a fairly simple observance, the first block being ceremoniously laid *well below ground level* for the building that quite possibly one day held the greatest prize in human history, locked in a room down below its official basement. The foundation for the immense construction was to be of prime importance, structurally and spiritually, for the Masons. There were actually a whopping *seven* floors down below ground level, dug out and readied in that period in our nation's brief history. It may be that George Washington was personally participating in the construction process because he knew of the proposal to turn the basement below the planned rotunda into a Masonic crypt. For some reason, Freemasons always lay cornerstones in the northeast corner of a building, as FDR did during a 1930s ceremony at the new Jefferson Memorial site in D.C. So that northeastern entrance might also have been an entryway site for the MO41 materials, where today it is called "the Supreme Court entrance," for that judicial body's arrival at a State of the Union speech.

.Not long after the grand ceremonial experience one day in 1793, a huge, heavy, cornerstone was actually laid in place with an expert stone Mason's precision and yet apparently got "lost" to history and no one is quite sure where it is to this day. How could such a gigantic stone get "misplaced"? Why was it so important to Freemasons to help build the enormous, highly-needed structure in the first place? These are just some of the mysteries that Freemasons would prefer not to talk about to this day. However, a sizeable fresco depicting George Washington's unusual ceremony still graces the Capitol structure, and a special Masonic plaque as well adorns the building; so how can we just overlook or forget these unusual connections and questions? And just why is it the Freemasons hold it in such high esteem? After all, the chief architectural designer of the Capitol Building was not known to be a Mason, although two of his immediate planner/designers were. They reported back to Washington for instructions on exactly how the building should be laid out and constructed. Was there any great enigmatic Masonic detail to the grand structure's design that was kept secret to the general public? If so, the Masons would likely have kept the answers to themselves. It seems quite likely that many Freemasons were on the construction teams that labored for years on the project. And it should also be pointed out again that not everyone who is/was a Freemason reveals his status; sometimes membership remain a secret for many years after a man's deaths, or is possibly never revealed, only suspected. Therefore, there might have been much more to the overall U.S. Capitol project in the 1780s than the non-Masonic public will ever know.

For Depression-era Freemasons like influential Senator Truman and powerful President Roosevelt, *the MO41 materials would have been the ultimate Masonic prize, the most priceless, exciting discovery ever made, worth displaying ceremoniously in a Masonic temple or lodge, at least for a while. It would have proven their beliefs in higher, observing powers from the starry skies,* one way or another. The shocking Cape Girardeau artifacts would have been placed before the ruling elite - under the greatly revered Capitol Building - and been a great, guarded treasure the devoted "worshipful brother" F. D. Roosevelt would have very excitedly shown off to his most trusted

Masonic colleagues. It was a tremendous find that even George Washington would likely have been tremendously thrilled and yet troubled by.

.Other notable Founding Fathers, like Benjamin Franklin and Paul Revere, are known to have been enthusiastic members of secret societies, including the kindly Masons. {Franklin even wrote a book about the still-developing organization, a positive force for good he was sure.} Washington used his influence to not just attend secret fraternal lodge meetings - having joined a Mount Vernon, Virginia, area Freemason center in 1752 - but to also lay out his thoughts on the design of the new American capitol city, which some say was created in the distinct symbols of Freemasonry. And as we have seen, George's presidential successor, John Adams, initially wished to bury President Washington with great honors in the basement or sub-basement of the building, since he felt it an appropriately safe and respected structure, worthy of the great man's legacy and cadaver.

.Freemason passion for the construction of the great Capitol Building did not stop in 1793. One hundred years to the day, members of congress, various political and governmental dignitaries, and the current U.S. president, Grover Cleveland, (re)enacted a small ceremony at the Capitol to set in place a plaque honoring the Washington Masonic cornerstone ritual. One hundred years after *that*, U.S. Senator Strom Thurmond of South Carolina also conducted an elaborate Masonic ceremony just outside the Capitol Building. For the press and the public, on September 18th, 1993, Thurmond and fellow Freemasons honored the two hundredth anniversary of their influential original ceremony by pulling out all the Masonic aprons and symbology they could find.

.To bring things full circle, UFO author and alien technology expert Colonel Phil Corso stated in his rambling

1997 book "*The Day After Roswell*" that he worked "in early 1963" out of an "office in the basement of the Capitol Building" - for none other than his new boss, Senator and sometime-presidential candidate Strom Thurmond! This was just after Colonel Corso spent time briefing President Kennedy and Robert Kennedy on sensitive defense matters, working out of the Pentagon, keeping his high-tech Roswell crash discoveries from most in Washington. {Thurmond was not a U.S. congressman in '41, but was a judge in South Carolina at the time.}

.It should also be emphasized that the official curator for the Capitol Building once granted an interview on the subject of extraterrestrial items secretly being stored in the sub-basement. This person replied that no one had heard of this notion before, but that *in the 1930s, under FDR's reign, the sub-basement floor well below the structure was carefully divided into newly-constructed storerooms. Meaning that congressmen and Roosevelt people involved – Masons or not - had an existing desire to place valued, perhaps secret, materials there, before the MO41 incident.* {Supposedly, in the aftermath of the 9-11 attacks, renovations to the lowest floors of the building have changed the nature of these special rooms and halls, starting in 2002.}

.It is also worth noting that back in 1932, just before ambitious New York Governor Franklin Roosevelt and his "New Deal" administration commenced, Freemasons who would soon come to work for FDR gathered to hold a special Masonic ceremony at - where else? - the Capitol Building! This procedure was to honor the two hundredth birthday of their Masonic hero, George Washington. A special plaque was installed once again, recalling the Freemasons' interest in the influential American governmental headquarters. Yes, the United States Capitol Building held a special sway for the disabled president; a

December 1941 news story mentioned how FDR had signed a bill on an issue within the famous structure after he had "been in consultation with the Capitol Building architect." So we can see that in the Great Depression the president could learn more about, give orders regarding, and even sign legislation concerning the mighty building that Freemasons hold so dear. We can also see why selecting the Capitol's subterranean storeroom would be a complete natural for Roosevelt's hiding of the MO41 materials. A perfectly understandable idea also for so many he was surrounded by. *Where else* would FDR have ordered it stashed so securely and yet have easy access to it when he wanted, or have other elites fathom its numbing scope?

It cannot really be proven but it is certainly reasonable therefore to speculate that these same governmental Masons met in a special Freemasons' *lodge* or *temple* down inside the Capitol structure. Famed author Dan Brown believes this is very possible, and promotes this theory in one of his books. There has been such Masonic emphasis on this particular famous building, in fact, that as mentioned the structure is openly featured to this day on the cover of Masonic literature and online material, *alongside images of Presidents F.D. Roosevelt, Truman, and Washington.*

There is yet another factor to keep in consideration: Freemasons grew out of the collection of special stone Masons who helped design and build the Temple of Solomon in ancient Palestine. The Jewish people of olden days had many ties to their neighbors, the Egyptians (including servitude). Masonic founder Hiram Abiff had ties to both the Egyptians and the Jewish cultures. Mysticism abounded in both of their societies. For instance, special mystic rituals were created for Egyptian initiates long ago, specifically for young men who wanted to join the exalted priesthood. Historical authors like Manley P. Hall say this consisted of placing the earnest candidates in the darkest bowels of their tombs and pyramids, in crypts *near dead bodies*, locked away in order to test the mettle and dedication of the men involved. If one did not go mad or give up and try to escape during this timeframe, one was accepted as a priest, having been "purified" spiritually by the black and bleak, lonely, even frightening experience. Freemasons have adopted – most often symbolically – Egyptian rituals and mysticism, including this dark tomb process, even if it involves merely placing a blindfold over the eyes of a initiate or joiner, and placing him within a locked, pitch-black room just outside their main lodge meeting hall. *So could it be that Freemasons in 1941 utilized the dead bodies of the Cape Girardeau aliens under the great Capitol – kept in glass jars to remain quite visible – as part of a Masonic ritual of testing the courage and devotion of new – or even veteran – members?* To lock certain Masons away in this special storage "dungeon" or crypt well below the surface, *with* the dead ET bodies, also in order to "spiritually cleanse" and ritually test their devoted membership, as in olden times? Admittedly this is mere conjecture, and it sounds rather wild, but who knows what the ritualistic secretive society – so heavily influenced by the Middle East - was up to? The pieces of this puzzle all add up, and it also helps explain why George Washington climbed down into the deeply dug basement trench of the initial construction for the Capitol Building in his day, instead of performing his Masonic ceremony at ground level. The lowest level of a Masonic building was of great importance to the group.

Author Robert Stanley repeatedly interviewed a man who was familiar with UFOs and ETs, a person he dubbed "J.W." This source stated that when he was a boy he was taken by his father to a Denver Masonic lodge and led to the lowest, darkest part of the building. From there he was placed in an odd ritual by Masons, who apparently revere this special procedure as a test for their new members, in lodges around the world. Wildly, "J.W." stated that as an adult who had UFO encounters he was approached by two current and one former United States congressmen to become a full-fledged member of the Fraternal Order of Freemasons! Coincidence?

Mr. Stanley went on to assure of something else rather shocking, but something a few other sources have also claimed about the true nature of Masonry: that there is an outer, more public-friendly, more visible layer to Freemasons... and then there is a smaller, inner circle of elites who know plenty, are deeply into mysticism, and are *open to covert communication with extraterrestrials.* "I was told by a friend who claims to be part of this inner circle," Stanley informed this author, "and he said they are in contact with ET entities." This is of course an incredible, mind-numbing notion, and perhaps mere unprovable fantasy... *or* an actual amazing esoteric fact about the most selective and secretive side of the secret society.

{It seems outlandish to speculate, but after MO41 could FDR have been seeking a Masonic connection or audience with ETs? *He was after all the most powerful, famous, and influential man on the planet, and could command access to any inner chamber of elitist mysticism he chose.* And he certainly was on the lookout for any possible tool to apply in his struggle to emerge victorious in World War II.}

A possible tie-in here comes from information gathered on noted psychic astrologer Jeane Dixon (1904-1997). She once famously and accurately predicted in print a few years in advance the approaching assassination of a light-haired, blue-eyed U.S. president (JFK) among other publicly forecasted hits and misses. Secretly-recorded White House tapes reveal Jeane once even met with President Richard Nixon to discuss paranormal matters in the early 1970s.

Wildly, Nixon was not the first Commander-in-Chief that mysterious Mrs. Dixon met at the White House. Back in the fall of 1944, seeress Dixon met with Franklin Roosevelt in the Oval Office, taking her crystal ball (kept hidden by her fur coat). She returned for a second office visit in mid-January of 1945. FDR's son Elliot later recalled his father discussing meeting this now-famous clairvoyant, who allegedly chatted with the worried chief executive about the future of his declining health and the country's war effort, his mind fairly open to the idea of ESP, Elliot added seriously. According to seer Dixon, Franklin supposedly also wanted to know also about whether Russia would remain an American wartime ally, and beyond. What did the future hold, for Roosevelt personally and his beloved country?

Based out of Washington D.C., Mrs. Dixon also knew - or at least socially *met* - many other early 1940s bureaucrats, including Masons J. Edgar Hoover, Harry Truman, and Sam Rayburn, among others (says one biographer). Jeane studied the alignment of the planets and stars and sometimes incorporated astrology into her psychic readings, and obviously intrigued the Masonic president, but whether she learned anything about MO41 - through society and governmental contacts or mere insightful clairvoyance - remains unknown.

Marcello Truzzi, a professor of Sociology at Eastern Michigan University, claims his research shows that both Theodore and Franklin Roosevelt were interested in the influence of the stars through astrology and that FDR would quote astrological forecasts from time to time. Author Dan Brown told NBC's "*Today*" program that "The foundations of astrology really have a deep, mystical, and spiritual underpinning that the Masons" were specifically involved with, some privately obsessing God's celestial creations. Certainly one descriptive phrase that Masons use often to recruit new members to their way of life is the tag-line: *"Pathway to the Stars!"* Thus it doesn't take much to see that President Roosevelt was likely very open to the idea of life beyond planet earth *before* MO41, and certainly after.

.Putting the star-crossed Roosevelt administration aside for a moment and concentrating on members of congress during the troubling Depression era, FDR counted heavily on a fellow New Deal Democrat on Capitol Hill who represented the state of Mississippi. Senator Byron Pattinson Harrison – nicknamed "Pat" - helped pass Roosevelt's critical "Lend-Lease" legislation in March of 1941, despite supposedly being ill with cancer. Weeks later the MO41 event took place and it is reasonable now to believe that the recoveries were temporarily hidden in the aftermath within that special room below Pat's U.S. Capitol offices. It is also reasonable to speculate that the enormous cosmic secret was shared with a few key congressmen who helped ease the covert storage process, and no one would in the great building be more knowledgeable and trusted for this than Pat Harrison. He had served in the Capitol Building for thirty long years, first as a Representative (1911-1919) and then as a Senator (1919-1941), so he knew all the nooks and crannies of the structure well. Pat was named "President Pro Tem" of the senate in January of '41 and held that post until his death on June 22nd, '41. He was a member of the "Woodmen," the Elks Club, and was of course a Freemason. Very strangely - and suspiciously? - a *second* Democrat from Mississippi, (former) congressman Robert S. Hall, also was a member of all three same organizations: Woodmen, Elks, and Freemasons, and *he* suddenly died on June 10th, 1941! Mr. Hall was from Hattiesburg, Mississippi, where General George Marshall was found (at nearby Camp Shelby) on the night of the MO41 affair. In 1941, Hall was working in Washington D.C. for FDR within the Federal Trade Commission, which had regular dealings with congress and the White House. In a wilder "coincidence" still, U.S. Representative Morris M. Edelstein of New York also died unexpectedly – right inside the Capitol Building after a speech on the House floor, responding to a congressman from *Mississippi* – on June 4th, 1941. Democrat Mr. Edelstein was evidently not a Freemason, however, but he did represent FDR's former territory, New York City. Additionally, a former congressman from southern Illinois (not too far from Cape Girardeau) who lost his 1940 election but was still in Washington also died abruptly (at just age 45), on May 23rd, '41, while in D.C.; Claude Parson was a Democrat, a U.S. Representative as of January 1941, and a Freemason!

{As an addendum on the national level, there are other intriguing deaths to mention from the spring/summer of 1941. Such as U.S. Representative Alonzo Folger of North Carolina who died at age 52 in a car accident on April 29th. U.S. Representative Stephen Bolles (of Wisconsin) perished abruptly on July 8th; South Carolina's Senator Alva Lumpkin crossed over on August 1st; U.S. Representative Albert Rutherford (of Pennsylvania) expired in Washington on August 10th; and U.S. Representative – and Knights Templar Freemason - Edward Taylor (of Colorado) passed away on September 3rd. There was seemingly an unusually large number of politicians who died in the latter half of 1941; on December 1st of that year, for example, Colorado's Senator Alva B. Adams, who was a pro-FDR Democrat and Freemason, expired in a Washington D.C. hotel at age 66.}

Whether these dead *human* bodies of congressional Masons were ever utilized for a few brief days in the storerooms down below the building we'll never know, but the opportunity to test fellow Freemasons in a dark ritual or secret ceremony in this manner certainly existed.

.Perhaps the most powerful and authoritative person within the entire Capitol Building in 1941 was the Speaker of the House, Texas Representative Samuel T. Rayburn. And naturally, "Mr. Sam" was also a Freemason. Speaker Rayburn's political whims guided the 77th U.S. congress in session during the spring of 1941. As an FDR friend, political advisor, and conduit to other Freemasons within the House of Representatives, influential Mr. Rayburn might well have been told and even shown "the great secret" downstairs, if MO41 was truly placed there as it seems.

.April 12th, 1945: on the exact four-year anniversary date of the amazing MO41 event, America's newest second-in-command, Mr. Truman, could have been anywhere, such as in his upstairs Vice President's Room, an office near the senate chambers that was utilized by Henry Wallace in 1941. Or Harry could have been elsewhere in D.C., or somewhere else in the USA, or traveling abroad to help cement foreign friendships and WWII battle strategies, for example. Instead, *Harry Truman was found in a room down inside the U.S. Capitol Building*, according to biographers. And was below-decks room also actually a Masonic meeting site? A lodge or temple, built by the many secret society members who had worked in the building since its inception?

.Supposedly Rayburn and Truman were about to enjoy a libation together in a private lounge under the Capitol when the vice president received the call telling him to rush to the White House as soon as possible. HST did so at once, according to historians, and upon arriving found to his sad dismay - but not *shock* - that President Roosevelt had died under still-murky circumstances in Warm Springs, Georgia. {Did he in fact shoot himself? See Bonus Chapter.} On the day of FDR's death and the elevation of Mr. Truman to the presidency, a writer for *The Southeast Missourian* noted to its readership that Harry Truman "has often been a visitor to Cape Girardeau. During political rallies, during American Legion conventions, and activities of the Masonic Order, he has been here. Many in this county are his personal friends." *Harry's Freemason activities in Cape?* Hmm! The author of the news piece may well have been the brand new president's friend, Garland D. Fronabarger, and yet he was not a Mason. What did Harry do in Cape Girardeau with and for Masons over the years that was known to the news writer who was *not* a society brother?

.Feisty Harry Truman was a 33rd degree "Master Mason" and our nation's 33rd president. He helmed the ship of state during at least one other evidently alien crash event (Roswell), perhaps others. When the next three presidents took office, nearly the first person to come strolling in to see them, for some reason, was ex-President Truman. HST met with President-Elect Dwight Eisenhower before and on Inauguration Day in January of '53. Harry was the first guest in John Kennedy's Oval Office, to discuss something with him in private, in January of '61. Truman returned to the White House to speak behind closed doors with new President Lyndon Johnson just after JFK's funeral in November of '63. HST would have met with the next president, Richard Nixon, but personally detested the non-Masonic politico; yet photos show Harry met with Nixon when he was elected V.P. in the fall of '52 and again in March of '69, when "Tricky Dick" was two months into office. *There was something very important Harry Truman wanted to discuss privately with these powerful men, away from all others, that is clear.* Truman died in 1972, apparently taking some otherworldly secrets with him but did the ex-president impart the shocking alien visitation secret - especially MO41 - to his successors as they took office?

.Another future liberal, Masonic (somewhat) President of the United States was lurking about within the halls of the Capitol Building in the spring of '41. He was eager for higher office and loved playing the game of politics and power. He was also a good friend to Speaker Rayburn, and was one of the first to step into the "hideaway office" underneath the Capitol that "Mr. Sam" kept, just after V.P. Truman hurried out and over to the White House on April 12th, 1945. It was Rayburn who told this tall congressman the news of FDR's death, and he reacted with tears that flowed for days. This U.S. Representative later made his way from Rayburn's house to the senate side, and then later to the vice presidency. Then like fellow Democrat Harry Truman, he catapulted into the White House upon the death of the chief executive. Lyndon Baines Johnson, the young, tall, lean, politico from Texas, was a good friend and supporter of President Roosevelt, attending nearly two dozen meetings with FDR at the White House during the great man's term. Scheming Mr. Johnson collected inside information on his congressional colleagues through several sources, historians say, always using the accumulated dirt for political leverage. Did LBJ learn of the MO41 recovery and its possible storage below the basement? He certainly was a Freemason (albeit nominally, achieving just "one degree"), surrounded by brother Masons, and very close to powerful Speaker Rayburn, so it's quite possible. Through gathering gossip and subterfuge with aides, LBJ found out a lot of secrets, according to his biographers. He certainly moved up impressively in rank as the years passed, from the House to the Senate to the vice presidency to the presidency. And as JFK's veep Johnson was placed in charge of - of all things - the U.S. space program! Coincidence?

When Lyndon B. Johnson died in Texas in January of 1973, his body was flown to D.C. and taken to - you guessed it - the Capitol Building - where he lay in state in the rotunda. One of his closer old congressional colleagues, U.S. Representative Gerald Ford of Michigan, paid his respects at that time, especially since he too was a Mason. Within a year the Mr. Ford would be named the new American vice president, then suddenly became president. When he died in late 2006, Jerry Ford's body was also flown to D.C. once again in order to lay in state in the Capitol. Back in April of 1941 Ford was in his last weeks of law school in Michigan; he became a Freemason in '49, earning its highest marks, so to speak; and during his congressional days actually called for an inquiry into UFO sightings in his home state but he likely never learned a thing about MO41.

.In returning to Franklin D. Roosevelt, historians record that he joined the Freemasons at an early age, climbing the rungs of secretive fraternal power, and holding onto it even as president. He mostly attended the private group's meetings in New York City, but also likely visited on occasion "Federal Lodge One" across town from the White House. FDR is quoted as saying in a rare public Masonic ceremony: "I am proud to say that no family in the country, as a whole, is more identified with Masonry than the Roosevelt family." Cousin Teddy became a member in 1901, Franklin in 1911, both men New York-based presidents who were Masonic brothers that once in a while visited D.C. area Masonic centers, somewhat the flip side of a Masonic coin of their hero, George Washington, who was a D.C. area lodge member who once in a while visited a New York City Masonic order. Still other male Roosevelt relatives were also joiners and regular attendees. They were all interested in promoting the group, encouraging others to join, and yet keeping its fascinating secrets just that, secret.

.Perhaps Freemasonry was a key factor in why Franklin Roosevelt got along so famously with British Prime Minister Winston Churchill. FDR and fellow Masonic member "Winnie" would meet in person for the first time as leaders in the summer of '41, and at one point Churchill would become a White House guest for *weeks*, trusted with many vital secrets to help the Allies win World War II. In December of 1941, popular Mr. Churchill gave a special speech to members of congress in - where else? - the Capitol Building. That's where his pal FDR had been ceremonially inaugurated as president in early 1933, 1937, and 1941, resulting in at least three official visits, possibly more unofficially, to the famed structure prior to MO41. {An increasingly ill and frail FDR was sworn in at the White House for the start of his fourth term in early 1945, and that's where a funeral service was held for him (plus Hyde Park, the burial site), instead of at the Capitol.} Churchill was apparently not informed of MO41, and spent much of April 11th and 12th of 1941 organizing resistance and recovery from incendiary bombing raids by Germany's air force, particularly in Bristol, England. For most in Great Britain who recall those two days, it was a time of grieving, anger, and infamy.

.Who else have we seen involved in the cosmic MO41 claim turn up in the Freemasons' organization? Why, none other than General George C. Marshall, who first met with Senator Truman in private meetings on Capitol Hill in late April 1941, regarding George's testimony for expenditures for "military affairs." President Roosevelt venerated and trusted GCM more than perhaps any other member of his administration, valuing his often contradictory views. President Truman also greatly respected Marshall and utilized him whenever possible; Harry wrote that he held George in such high regard, starting from that April 1941, that he eagerly named the general his U.S. Secretary of State in 1947.

.Marshall and several other key military leaders of the day - like friends General Henry "Hap" Arnold, General George

Patton, and General Douglas MacArthur - were all Masons, according to public records today. Marshall held General Arnold in such high esteem the Arnold family proudly boasts that Hap hosted George at his home in 1945 and the two men went together to the local Masonic lodge in Sonoma, California, where a plaque still honors Arnold's accomplishments. Their mutual friend William "Wild Bill" Donovan has been rumored to have been a member of the Freemasons, although today there seems to be no definite proof. Arnold and Donovan allegedly had their own ties to 1940s UFO investigations, as noted by various books and internet sites today. Donovan was literally *named* by President Roosevelt in a later-leaked memorandum on the very limited upper echelon government discussions of the shocking "non-terrestrial" Missouri recoveries. In April of '41 "Wild Bill" was not yet in power; he was then a Wall Street lawyer who would not be named by FDR to the new Office of Coordinator of Information until that summer, based out of the former Public Health headquarters on 25th and E Street in Washington. The president's trusted Masonic son, James, would become Donovan's second in command at OCI, which soon morphed into the Office of Strategic Services, the forerunner of the modern CIA. When James left during WWII for the Marines, he was replaced by Democratic Party legal counselor and newspaperman Ernest L. Cuneo, another old New York City Masonic crony of the president's. From both a political and reporter's perspective, "FDR insider" Ernie Cuneo (1905-1988) likely knew the Capitol Building and its many Masonic inhabitants quite well, making his home in nearby Arlington, not far from George Marshall.

.Some of the president's own Secret Service protection detail may well have been Freemasons, facing the odd situation of being equals to their own boss - and other top security subjects - while behind closed doors inside a Masonic temple or lodge. The Secret Service that guarded the president would have made the hypothesized trip with him to the Capitol to view the recovered evidence in 1941, Masons or not. Would they have found even more there than a (Masonic?) special subterranean store room and extraterrestrial evidence?

.Contemporary actress Shirley MacLaine summed up these unusual matters in a 2013 book chapter, one that linked Masons, the Capitol Building, and "enlightenment from above," via "star beings," in her own words. "The Masonic Order is a relatively secret world organization that believes we are not alone in the universe," she boldly proclaimed. "The Capitol Rotunda is literally a vortex of energy," with domed buildings in general acting as "portals, gateways to the stars." The movie star researched these subjects and also concluded that Founding Father Thomas Jefferson believed "the heavens were inhabited" and that Washington D.C. - which Jefferson helped to architecturally design - needed to be regarded as not just the capitol of the country, but "the capitol of the *universe*." If this incredible statement is true, and *if such a strong Jeffersonian belief was passed down to 1940s hardcore Masons like President Roosevelt, it could lead to even stronger underlying reasons to import the MO41 materials to the capitol*, as soon as possible. Within a special "universal portal" or "inter-dimensional gateway" way down inside the great domed structure? Such notions seem outlandish, but true or not, who knows *what* the more ardent, advanced Mason leaders believed, since they were so darned secretive?

.Freemason and U.S. Army General MacArthur is famous in UFO circles for openly alluding to alien visitation in public remarks, calling extraterrestrials a potential global threat that future generations will have to prepare for, possibly in a world war, although some of his statements were taken a bit out of context. Author Bill Knell claims that his army officer father worked in 1943 under Doug

MacArthur and during that time, the general was quietly rounding up information on UFOs (or "Foo Fighters") for a 10,000-page secret military report. Supposedly this enormous document was triggered by so many field reports coming in from WWII pilots of strange lights or darting discs that zipped past or even harassed American and enemy aircraft, but evidently said nothing about MO41, one way or another. The overall conclusion of this private, classified document was that most of the sightings involved were either "unknown" but more often "non-terrestrial" in nature.

.As we have seen in other chapters, Army Chief of Staff George C. Marshall was flying around the country in 1941 for his Army camp inspection tour. But what is startling is that - shown in at least one photograph - he traveled in a personalized aircraft that featured his four-star general status on a logo, *along with the Capitol Building dome,* clearly painted on the plane's side. The existing photo was taken of Marshall's '41 arrival at an airfield in Louisiana; it reveals that the stern military man identified with the D.C. building for some reason, and as we are now aware of his Freemason status, *and* the esteemed building's tie to the crashed saucer story well, it all starts to tie in together nicely. Marshall reported directly to the president, and perhaps only to his other "superior," Henry Stimson, the aging, conservative Secretary of War. Online information about the Masons today indicates that Stimson was also a member of the Masonic fraternity as well, which should come as no surprise; FDR liked to surround himself with fellow members of his favorite group. It's who Mr. Roosevelt trusted most to help exercise authority, establish policy, and keep state secrets.

According to a Masonic book site, several other members of the FDR New Deal administration were Freemasons, including conservative Henry Morganthau, Jr., the longtime

Secretary of the Treasury, overseers of the Secret Service. Logs show Secretary Morganthau visited with the president in the Oval Office on April 15th, 1941, when most likely very classified off-the-record meetings to discuss the alien crash-landing situation took place. Henry Morganthau served FDR faithfully during World War II, and even met with ill Roosevelt the day before he died, down in Warm Springs, Georgia. The two men had a private dinner and little of what they discussed has come to light, even now. Evidently the president rather impulsively committed suicide the next afternoon, realizing his end was near anyway. Secret Service agents were not in the building at the time, but stationed outside (see Bonus Chapter). Morganthau resigned not long after Roosevelt's troubling death, and died in 1967 without commenting on secretive insider events like the president's sad end, or MO41.

Still other early New Dealers like Secretary of the Navy Claude Swanson (replaced by Frank Knox); Secretary of Commerce, Dan Roper; and Secretary of War George H. Derm (replaced by Stimson) were all said to be avid Freemasons. Even Roosevelt's Attorney General for a while, Homer Cummings, was a member of the world famous men's only club.

.Henry Wallace was such an ardent 33rd-degree Freemason he once urged President Roosevelt to change the Great Seal of America to include imagery that was of Masonic origin, and this was undertaken and accomplished in the 1930s, with redesigns of the new-look Great Seal placed on the dollar bill. Once again, the Egyptian pyramid stands front and center on the seal and on print currency as a key symbol for patriot-masons. The eye-catching artistic styles remain there to this day, although there is still some debate as to their complete Masonic authenticity. As V.P. Wallace kept his official office *in* the Capitol Building. He was there weekly, if not almost daily at times, ostensibly to help ease passage of the president's programs through the U.S. legislature; he was obviously familiar with the famous building and its Masonic members. However, since he was not amongst the names of those who attended high-level Oval Office meetings in the days after the crash, Wallace was likely out of town, perhaps even the country at the time. Henry may or may not have been told about MO41, at least at first; it remains unclear and probably always will since Wallace's recorded schedule for 1941 is unknown, if kept at all. Henry produced a (later-published) "Daily Diary" but it did not begin until 1942 and would naturally have been scrubbed before public release of any top secret information anyway.

.For various reasons, Vice President Wallace slowly fell out of favor in the months and years ahead, and his influence in 1944 Washington ebbed like a low tide. He eventually got dumped as the veep, then from the cabinet entirely, and then went home to become a Midwestern farmer. But he remained an enthusiastic member of the secretive organized brotherhood. It was nearly the case that if you wanted to qualify for FDR's inner circle, or his cabinet, you *had* to be a joiner of the Fraternal Order of Freemasons.

.He almost became a Missouri-based United States Vice President himself, but in the summer of 1960 Senator Stuart Symington also got dumped. The Democratic Party nominee for president that year, John F. Kennedy, had to toss aside his plan for naming his good friend Stu as his running mate. That's because wily Texas Senator Lyndon B. Johnson for all practical purposes leveraged (extorted) his way onto their party's ticket, by way of threatening to expose the inside dirt on JFK's racy personal life. During much of 1960 Senator Symington was ex-President Harry Truman's personal favorite for the presidential nomination, then later for the second-in-command position. Stu and Harry were old friends, both formerly officers in the U.S.

Army, and of course Freemason brothers, sometimes meeting together in D.C. or in St. Louis, Symington's home for some years (after moving from Massachusetts, his original home state). Symington also "just happened" to be a friend to St. Louis-based aviation powerbroker Oliver Parks, of the Parks Air College in nearby East St. Louis (Cahokia). Recall that the MO41 materials were quite possibly handled by Parks, even taken by his PAC men within a transport plane to the St. Louis area for refueling, before heading to Washington D.C. (speculation, but reasonably so). A 1948 St. Louis University alumni dinner photograph shows Parks and Symington seated closely side-by-side, indicating they were well acquainted. Symington began his work in St. Louis in 1938, by then very experienced with airplanes and air travel. If Parks was a Freemason, as seems possible, then he and Symington were likely more than just mere acquaintances.

Back in September of 1947, William Stuart Symington was sworn in by President Truman as the very first official Secretary of the Air Force. Before that Stu's title was the wordy "Assistant Secretary of War for Air." Symington was not tabbed for this position by HST during the Roswell, New Mexico, UFO crash saga that summer for nothing. Stu could not possibly have been named to this very important post without the full knowledge of extraterrestrial visitation, and accidents. It is conceivable that Truman promoted Stuart in '47 *because* his fellow Missourian had full knowledge of what went down in Cape Girardeau in '41. And existing knowledge of MO41 and other recovered UFO accidents may well have been a big reason why Truman pushed for Symington to be on the presidential ticket of his party in '60; Stuart would not need to be briefed on the explosive secret issue. "In real danger sometimes even a democracy can really keep a secret," Symington is quoted as telling the press. Did he, or the government in '41 or '47 consider UFO/ET visitation evidence a "real danger" to the country?

It seems fairly safe to say that if it were not for LBJ's pushing himself onto the '60 ticket, following John F. Kennedy's assassination in 1963 a "President Stuart Symington" might have been the second coming of Harry Truman, his friend and benefactor. In fact, it was hardworking Truman who got to know corporate executive Symington back in Missouri partly through mutually-beneficial political/business and Masonic/social activities in St. Louis, and helped turn Stu from big business and the military to the world of government and politics. Stu Symington headed an electric company in St. Louis in April of 1941, just a hundred or so miles north of the alien crash-landing site. He knew his unique aircraft metals well, having a few years before run a successful company founded on uses for such materials.

.In November of 1957, Senators Stuart Symington and Lyndon Johnson jockeyed for position in commanding a senate subcommittee on weapons defense systems and the immature space program, hearings held on Capitol Hill of course. Both men wanted to appear in the news media to take the lead in understanding the challenges of America's future in space as to better shine in the upcoming '60 presidential campaign, according to biographers. One of their first witnesses called to testify under oath was Dr. Vannevar Bush, who as mentioned earlier had his own ties to both examining/advising MO41 recoveries and the Manhattan Project. Bush was a Massachusetts Mason and FDR's top science advisor, having met with the president in his office just days after the crash. Symington apparently knew Bush from their years of service in the Truman administration.

As a powerful Mason in St. Louis, Symington had to have been quite familiar with Forrest C. Donnell, who also hailed from that city. {Donnell hailed from suburban Webster Groves, as did this author's maternal grandfather, a fellow conservative and Freemason.} Bear in mind that Governor Donnell was such as devout and serious Mason, he took over as Grand Master Mason of Missouri after Harry was forced to abandon that position when he was named FDR's Vice President. Later F. C. Donnell became a Missouri senator, just like Truman and Symington. In 1948, Charles B. Root - the Sikeston MIA commander during MO41 and friend of Oliver Parks - went to work at Secretary Stu Symington's Air Force headquarters. In what position? Why, as a "congressional liaison," of course, meaning Captain Root was in and out of the U.S. Capitol Building at times, although likely the MO41 crash materials were long gone from their initial sub-basement hiding place. Whether Charles Berton Root was ever a Freemason remains unknown.

.Also attending Washington D.C. Masonic meetings in the 1940s and '50s – perhaps at "Federal Lodge One" some blocks away from the Capitol Building - was the stodgy Director of the FBI, John Edgar Hoover. He might well have known many a detail about MO41, mostly via information from his Cape Girardeau field office agent, Arlin Jones. Conservative Hoover was not fond of liberals like Roosevelt, Truman, and their administrative personnel, but probably remained cordial at fraternal D.C. lodge meetings. They were all brother Masons, equal and united in good fellowship, at least in theory.

.Hoover's lifelong confidential friend and Number Two at the Federal Bureau of Investigations, Clyde Tolson, was a Missourian and possibly a Mason as well. It's difficult to conceive that Tolson was not, considering how intensely close he and Hoover became professionally and socially. Several members of the FBI likely were Freemasons, from assistants to field agents to office personnel, particularly since fastidious Hoover like to personally handpick who worked for him. Biographers say that when Hoover died suddenly in the spring of 1972, Tolson began planning a rather simple and private Freemason's funeral service, but was overruled by President Richard Nixon, who demanded a grander public event, covered by national television. Naturally, Hoover was taken to the Capitol Building, where he lay in state for public visitation, unlike the president he irritated the most: Franklin Roosevelt.

.Director Hoover famously kept bulging private files on the most famous of U.S. celebrities, from the 1930s onward. Could the most seemingly unlikely but paternal figure in all America – movie producer Walt Disney - have learned about the MO41 saga? In 1940, Disney became a secret informant to Hoover via the Los Angeles office of the FBI, according to documents released under the modern Freedom of Information Act; a whopping 570 pages regarding Disney remain redacted. Walt Disney likely expected favors in return for his cooperation.

During the war years, kindly Walt opened his Hollywood film studio doors to the U.S. military, who practically took over the place in producing short films on how to identify foreign aircraft in the skies. They also co-produced WWII propaganda (or at least super-patriotic) shorts and movies. In private, Missouri-raised Disney was at least *somewhat* enamored with two things in life: spacecrafts, and Masonry. Walt was said by some to be a hardcore 33rd degree Freemason; a member of that fraternal group in Hollywood stated that it was closer to the truth that Disney pretty much a part-time member, due to his busy schedule. Whenever the movie mogul returned to his family's home base in the Kansas City, Missouri, area, he was likely able to access the same Masonic lodge as Harry Truman, the master Mason who was of course the most powerful person on the planet from 1945 to 1953.

Evidently Walter Disney regularly consulted with American Air Force personnel on aircrafts and later became almost obsessed with the U.S. space program, reflected in his TV show and a few of his motion pictures. To that end, he struck up an unlikely friendship with former Nazi rocket and aviation scientist Werner Von Braun, who became somewhat of a technical advisor. Supposedly Von Braun was also quietly helping to guide crashed UFO technology studies for the U.S. government during this timeframe, mostly at Wright-Patterson AFB in Ohio and at a few installations in New Mexico. Also supposedly, with the covert encouragement of both the CIA and the U.S. Air Force – who promised to provide actual UFO footage – Disney began making plans to produce a UFO documentary film. It would be entertainment, yes, but informative, and evidently be a way the U.S. government could condition people to accepting the reality of otherworldly visitors. Around 1955, Walt assembled his animation team and had them imagining what extraterrestrials they could concoct for the exciting new movie project. Then... suddenly the bottom dropped out. The government abruptly backed out and the intriguing plans went into the back of the filing cabinet, according to Disney employee Ward Kimball a decade after Disney died. But the idea wasn't shelved forever. In 1995, Walt Disney Studios finally produced a one-hour documentary on UFOs and rumors of *crashes,* stored in government facilities. The television show related ET existence as matter-of-fact, and even took an attitude at times that ridiculed people who did *not* believe in alien visitation. While obviously none of this is conclusive that Mr. Disney (1901-1966) was once whispered "the secret" about MO41 he certainly had all the right connections and clues that could lead one to believe he was *possibly* fairly informed on the subject.

There are likely still *more* influential members of the Masonic fraternity that existed in the worlds of bureaucratic government; the military; the fledgling space program; journalism; the entertainment community; and the scientific research society in 1941 and beyond, but we're getting the general idea. Like it or not, Freemasons were obviously essentially running the country back then, to put it simply. But what does all of this Freemason information mean, when you boil down the MO41 allegation? Certainly it appears as though the physical evidence was taken from the Show-Me State despite the likely presence of friendly Masons at the impact site. It may well have been eventually flown to Washington D.C. by army men who were Freemasons and stored (in sections) within the revered U.S. Capitol Building, and guarded by Masons upon the orders of a Masonic president. *By accident or on purpose at some point in this chain, some Masons were apparently keeping the great secret, some in Cape Girardeau and some on up the governmental "food chain."* They already knew how to keep some matters quite confidential and did so every day. If one Freemason asked another to never breathe a word of the alien crash recovery operation, it was more than likely obeyed fairly strictly, reinforcing the stringent U.S. military/government security and silence that fell over much of the case. If the word was privately passed along, say from the president to Missouri's senators and governor to the local Cape area's politicos, to keep it all hushed up, everyone would have done so as a special bond of trust between fraternal brothers. Word could have come down possibly through a simple telephone call to a key member of the proud and popular Cape Girardeau Freemason Society chapter. Private information may well have been shared at lodge meetings by top local leaders behind closed doors, or at the more sealed and secretive Masonic meeting later that month and then kept to a minimum ever since.

.So this is where we stand with the tangled web of Masonic angles in and around the MO41 enigma today, more intrigued than ever. Secrets, specifics, and speculation what-ifs and what-not fascinating fragments, factoids, and frustrations… connections abound all around. HST popping up again and again in his political and Masonic forms. Like so much of this case, absolute proof is tough to track down, then firmly nail down, yet there is a trail of enticing circumstantial and "coincidental" evidence that leads us to at least a better understanding of how things were *really* done in this country back then and perhaps to this very day. This was, and still often is, a nation of secrets, and even secret societies going on in our midst. So there evidently really was and will continue to be - just as Rush Limbaugh III stated - *more to this story than you might think.*

CHAPTER FOUR

JFK Almost *Had* to Have Known

"I'd like to tell people about the truth behind UFOs, but for now my hands are tied."

.To be clear, there is no smoking gun link between John Fitzgerald Kennedy and the 1941 UFO crash and retrieval by the United States military near Cape Girardeau, Missouri. But one can make a circumstantial case that JFK at some point *had* to have found out about the amazing celestial incident – and that it whet his appetite to learn more about the enticing subject overall.

It should be mentioned first that some writers have already explored the notion that as president, J. F. Kennedy learned about the reality of extraterrestrial visitation to Earth, wanted more data on this, and was pondering sharing such secret information with the Soviet Union or potentially perhaps the American public someday, before he horrendously murdered in November of 1963. That this historic UFO-allocating proposal was so upsetting to the inner-governmental American powers that be they arranged for the president to be liquidated, leaving a patsy to take the blame as a "lone nut" to cover for a high-level conspiracy. Since this territory has already been covered by others it is not necessary to stray very far into it here, but within a special "Bonus Chapter" later on we'll take a look at the strong probability that there *was* a conspiracy to kill JFK and then cover it up in the same manner as the body-snatching and fakery that took place in the 1945 Franklin Roosevelt suicide case, first brought out in the pages of *"MO41, The Bombshell Before Roswell."* For now, let us dwell on Mr. Kennedy's past, raising the serious question of whether he was briefed on – or snooped into - the facts within the Cape Girardeau UFO crash, at some point in the 1940s...

.At the time of the mid-April '41 Missouri affair, twenty-three-year-old J. F. Kennedy was a post-graduate student at Stanford University in the Bay Area of California. He was thin and at times sickly, but still handsome, charming, and very bright. And as his son, the late John F. Kennedy, Jr., stated on camera in the 1990s, *curiosity* was a big personality factor regarding his world famous father. Digging into the unknown and learning the facts. In fact, it is what JFK Jr. admired most about his slain parent. His dad had a "healthy curiosity" about so many things in life.

Nicknamed "Jack," the popular and gregarious Kennedy sibling's best qualities had managed to get him through Harvard University and to successfully author a book called *"Why England Slept."* Thanks to his wealthy, scheming father buying up many a copy, the book became a bestseller. In it, JFK argued that the British Empire should have taken a much more active role in stopping Adolph Hitler's brutal aggression in 1930s' Europe. Publicly in the early 1940s, Kennedy espoused the growingly popular but controversial opinion that the United States should also get more actively involved in the global conflict. He slowly became an interventionist. To that end, his draft "number came up" in late 1940. It was the perfect opportunity to back up his words. By the spring of '41 he was preparing to take a physical for the Army so he could "suit up and get in the game," as they say today.

.In a stunning turn of events for the always-powerful-and-successful Kennedy family, Jack failed his physical exam. It turns out JFK was riddled with too many serious health problems, such as colitis and Addison's Disease, which along with a bad back wrecked his physical stamina and his chances at military glory. Deeply embarrassed, Jack grimly determined to turn the situation around and spent the next five months working out, building his muscles, stamina, and overall toughness. In the late summer he took a special physical for the Navy instead ...and flunked again. His father Joe apparently intervened and the son tried once more. This time Jack passed his exam, in what one historian called "a complete whitewash." Still not really physically fit, he was sworn into the U.S. Navy on September 25th, 1941. Instead of going to Annapolis, Maryland, for proper, time-consuming naval academy training, green Mr. Kennedy was instead given quite a plum assignment. Quickly he was commissioned as an ensign and appointed to the U.S. Office of Naval Intelligence in Washington D.C.! This was put into play by the then-Director of ONI, who used to know Joseph P. Kennedy as a Naval Attache at the American Embassy in London, a fear years before. Friends in high places. So by mid-October of 1941, Jack Kennedy had eased into the best of possible three possible worlds: rubbing shoulders daily with military brass; interacting in D.C. with the FDR administration to firm up his planned political future as a loyal New Deal Democrat; and keeping out of any rough overseas assignments via a cushy job that allowed him time for socializing with attractive women, so important to Kennedy men. Somewhat immature and certainly inexperienced militarily with no education in naval operations, it seems very strange and perhaps even outrageous that suddenly "Ensign Kennedy" would be assigned to such a sensitive and desirable post in the world of great secrets, far from danger.

.What is more intriguing is the question of what JFK found out once he was placed in his new Washington position of trust. At one point he was assigned the "Foreign Intelligence Branch" at the naval intel headquarters. {And what could have been more "foreign" than extraterrestrials?} Carefree Jack Kennedy lived in an apartment called Dorchester House, located at 2480 16th Street, where his sister already resided. This was the same long street that hosted the city's popular and powerful "33rd Degree Scottish Rites Masonic Temple," with its immense pillars, museum, and library. 16th Street is itself very old, part of the allegedly Masonic original layout of the city by the Founding Fathers and their hired architect, although Kennedy was not a Mason, evidently.

{Ironically, around this time (October 19th), a U.S. Representative who worked in the Capitol Building and hailed from just north of Boston, near where Kennedy would be a U.S. congressman one day, suddenly died in office; Irish-Catholic Democrat Lawrence J. Connery departed this world in Arlington, Virginia, eerily where Irish-Catholic Democrat JFK would be buried in 1963, both at age 46!}

The normally cheerful and sociable Ensign Kennedy spent the remainder of 1941 working with respected intelligence officers, frequently summarizing reports created from overseas bulletins. JFK prepared data (often on Japan) and briefing papers for his powerful superiors, such as the Secretary of the Navy (Henry Knox) and his Undersecretary (James Forrestal), "and other top officials," according to military records. This could also have easily included high-ranking members of the Roosevelt administration. All of this gave the dashing twenty-four-year-old access to military and governmental intelligence reports, special bulletins, phone information, big secrets, and general gossip, which as an intel operative he would likely dutifully report back to his superiors, if it was of any military or diplomatic value.

At this point let's keep in mind the great possibility that Naval Vice Admiral Ross McIntyre (1889-1959), the president's personal physician and the navy's Surgeon General, may well have secretly handled the inspection if not the actual autopsy of the MO41 otherworldly bodies, possibly at a naval facility in town - Bethesda Hospital? - that spring or summer. Data on this ongoing investigation into the makeup of the Cape Girardeau aliens was undoubtedly placed in folders and filing cabinets. The ET creatures and their crashed ship may also have been whispered about amongst high grade officers at the headquarters. Since the Army had a liaison office down inside the Capitol Building, it seems like the Navy would also have been installed there.

In short, there was seemingly plenty of dirt to be hoovered up by the highly curious John Fitzgerald Kennedy during this period in his life. He began to make contacts, both socially and professionally. People who might have learned of MO41 were all around...

A very well regarded Navy man who probably dealt on occasion with sensitive and classified matters within Washington's Office of Naval Intelligence and on Capitol Hill was a mature businessman named Sidney Souers (1892-1973). Coincidentally, Souers had spent some of the 1930s as an insurance company executive in St. Louis, with a partner – according to Stu Symington (1901-1988) – from southeast Missouri. During nearly the entire Great Depression Sidney was busy coordinating insurance data while also participating in the U.S. Naval Reserve intelligence corps. He knew so much and handled it so professionally that he was activated in 1940, and appointed by President Roosevelt as the Assistant Director of the ONI in July of 1944. {Again we must remember a secret program that was revealed publicly in the 1990s: insurance companies sometimes spied on Americans to assemble intelligence data for the U.S. military/government, such as is suspected with Walter W. Fisk in that era.} Sid Souers then moved up in rank in '45, thanks to his friendship with new President Truman, who a year later named him as the very first director of the new Central Intelligence Agency. And while some critics and cynics feel the leaked briefing papers are bogus, many in the UFO community believe the famous "Majestic 12 Documents" are genuine; they show Admiral Souers was tabbed in 1947 by Truman to a special committee to investigate and exploit alien technology and biology, in the aftermath of the Roswell incident. *Could that alleged high-powered committee appointment have been based on what Sidney already knew about MO41?* It is obvious he had the Missouri connections, the ONI military intel, the powerful position, and enough Washington political supporters to qualify as a person quite in the know. And if *Sidney* did, did JFK?

Another Naval Intelligence figure allegedly aware of the reality of otherworldly visitation was a college astronomy and astrophysics professor named Dr. Donald Menzel (1901-1976). He moved around to various universities in the depression until he settled in at Boston's famed Harvard University in 1932. He was on staff there when teenaged Jack Kennedy was a Bachelor of Arts in Government student at Harvard, from 1936 to 1940. Many decades later, UFO researchers like Stanton Friedman began to suspect that Dr. Menzel knew *much* more than first thought about the subject of unidentified flying objects – which publicly he debunked with very flimsy reasoning – and also that he was friends with Kennedy. A series of correspondences between the two men have been unearthed; one letter from August of 1962 (JFK's presidency) was regarding a special radio telescope to scan the heavens; it was addressed to "Jack" and informally signed "Donald," clearly indicating an intimate friendship. As it turns out, JFK was on a "Board of Overseers" at Harvard University, and when listing his selected "point of interest" he surprisingly replied "astronomy." *Who knew John F. Kennedy was interested in the study of the cosmos? Was it because of MO41?*

It turns out that sometime during WWII, Menzel joined the U.S. Naval Intelligence department, naturally, although he could only have met up with Kennedy at ONI in late December '41, into mid-January of '42, if the professor joined right after Pearl Harbor. Don Menzel spent the war years helping with cryptology, astrophysics, and communications, rising to the trusted rank of Commander, and more importantly for future covert government work, held the nation's highest security clearances. Dr. Friedman found a man who worked with Dr. Menzel in 1947, and this source reported that Donald rushed off to New Mexico around the time of the July Roswell UFO crash, which was a repeated habit further noted also in Menzel's personal notebook over the next two years. Could it be that Dr. Menzel was in some way already familiar with alien spaceship technology through the MO41 recoveries being studied by top scientific minds during WWII? After all, this examination of the materials was done in the Washington area since it involved Dr. Vannevar Bush's scientific allies based there. At any rate, like Admiral Souers, Dr. Menzel shows up as one of the members of the alleged "Majestic 12" study group, supposedly researching not just the Roswell crash recoveries, but other UFO data as well – providing those controversial documents are authentic, something still in dispute.

Just as JFK was settling into his life of working for ONI, so was its new director in mid-October of 1941, starting one week before the youthful ensign. Admiral Thomas S. Wilkinson (1888-1946) was now in charge of intelligence operations and ongoing programs, especially "domestic surveillance," and perhaps the most startling and strange one is revealed in an online website article entitled *"The History of the Office of Naval Intelligence, 1882-1942."* According to the author, Admiral Wilkinson did not enjoy a quiet and highly successful tenure at the office within the new ONI building (which he moved into back in April of '41, interestingly). The admiral was reassigned to the Pacific in June of 1942, where he served with distinction in WWII. However, Tom Wilkinson was "still haunted by what he perceived as his personal failure" in the disaster that was the Pearl Harbor attack on the navy's ships by the enemy in December 1941. Within seven months of the war's end, "Wilkinson drove a borrowed car off the end of the Norfolk-Portsmouth ferry and into the Elizabeth River and drowned." If that wasn't bizarre enough – accident? suicide? – then the next sentence in the same ONI website summary will suffice: "He was the last Director of Naval Intelligence to preside over the operations of Parapsychology, Paranormal, and Psychic Phenomena Division in ONI." Uh, *what now*? The Office of Naval Intelligence had, as of mid-1942, *an ongoing operation to look into paranormal or otherworldly activities in the United States?* Well that is a most curious revelation! The kind that a curious young ONI employee like Jack Kennedy most likely would have wanted to learn more about. The kind that would have held a big fat file on the exciting alien spaceship crash recovery from southeastern Missouri. In the end, all we know for sure is that Admiral Wilkson was buried in Arlington Cemetery in '46, not too far from his employee Kennedy seventeen years later.

As mentioned, in 1941 another Kennedy sibling was in Washington, and had possible access to secrets as well. Jack's sister Kathleen (or "Kick" as she was nicknamed) lived at Dorchester House and worked at the headquarters of a Washington D.C. newspaper. She also hobnobbed with the social set in the district. In fact, she was so adept at upscale mingling she became a society columnist for the *Times-Herald.* Kathleen (1920-1948) got her journalism job around the time of MO41's occurrence. Always looking for scoops, *it was her business to pry into other people's business*, to put it simply. It was in her best interests to nose out juicy D.C. secrets of any kind. Jack and Kick spent plenty of their free time *together*, gossiping, going to parties, and sightseeing, free from their often oppressive father, who it should be pointed out had a curiously close relationship with the FBI's director, J. Edgar Hoover. It was due to this friendship, in part anyways, that JFK was ironically "kicked" out of town within a few months.

.According to investigative author Ted Schwarz, Naval Ensign Jack Kennedy was also "a White House liaison" in 1941. If this startling claim is true, it means JFK took sensitive U.S. Navy reports, important briefs, and oral messages to the Oval Office area, for the president's most trusted staffers, perhaps even to Franklin Roosevelt himself. In some cases Kennedy might well have been given Oval Office responses and return information to carry back to the Naval Intelligence brass at headquarters. Top secret data that could not be transmitted by telephone, telegraph, or telegram in those days. Again, any matter pertaining to MO41 would fall into that very classified and sensitive category. If he truly *was* a trusted "Liaison Officer," JFK would quite possibly have also taken data at times to the Naval Liaison Office within the Capitol Building's lower floors!

.While not attending to business, John Kennedy socialized, apparently like nobody's business. Biographers report that JFK hopped around to various D.C. social events and mingled with the capitol's elite: generals, admirals, cabinet members, senators, representatives, diplomats, reporters, probable spies, friends of friends, etc. It was likely an exciting experience to be so young and wealthy with plenty of free time in peacetime Washington, speaking regularly to those in power who sipped a few too many cocktails, loosening lips. As an intelligence ensign, it might well have been Kennedy's *job* to sniff out secrets, get people drinking and chatting, and find out who was talking too much. Jack's good looks and personal charms could well have been utilized by Naval Intelligence for their own quiet operations; if a footloose bachelor like Kennedy bedded down a D.C. socialite, for example, he could find out further low-down through romantic pillow talk. Kennedy's attributes played right into intelligence hands; he sure wasn't hired at the office for his typing or filing skills. Additionally, it should be noted that it is often a regular chore for U.S. intelligence agencies to try to tap into what other intel outlets are up to. Thus the Navy was curious as to what the Army knew, and vice versa. Therefore JFK may have found out a lot. *Too much*, in fact. And that it was quite possibly the young Jack Kennedy himself who talked too much, about what he found out

.According to Steve Hager, author of the e-book *Secret Societies*, Ensign Kennedy was transferred by his Naval Intelligence superiors for possessing - and apparently *spilling* - too many secrets "that could be more than a bit embarrassing." What "embarrassing" hidden knowledge would have been considered so volatile in early 1942 as to get the young naval figure wiretapped, then shipped out from D.C. to South Carolina, then all the way to the South Pacific? Bachelor Jack's romantic dalliances and apparent inside scoop on something very big and important eventually drew the attention of the Federal Bureau of Investigation. Under FBI Director Hoover's personal instruction, the feds began secretly bugging Kennedy's main lover, Inga Arvad (1913-1973), and their romantic

D.C. rendezvous sites (and later his South Carolina getaways). At the time, Kennedy was sexually involved with this beautiful married-but-separated lady suspected by some of being a Nazi spy, although not one scrap of proof ever surfaced proving this startling allegation. FBI audiotapes were made of the lovebirds and years later allegedly relayed to the Kennedy brothers during the early 1960s, as special Hoover blackmail. Thus we can speculate reasonably that a subject pretty enthralling and top secret had to have been spilled from Kennedy to Arvad, likely to try to impress her. It is one thing to date a suspected Nazi sympathizer, but it is another to be so intensely recorded. Those pillow-talk conversations... Hoover was clearly suspecting and searching for something quite big. Also, we can say it was a pretty hot topic to have Naval Intelligence catch wind of it and ship him south, then Hoover utilize it as blackmail fodder two full decades later. Yes, it is sheer conjecture, but... *could JFK had been talking at times about the astounding MO41 incident?* It would certainly fit the bill all around in this covert scenario.

.We must recall at this point that it quite likely that J. Edgar Hoover (1895-1972) himself knew all about MO41 and was in on keeping it secret, through his field agents shadowing certain people and tapping their telephones. Hoover is a very strong suspect in the (alleged) following and phone-bugging of Cape Girardeau fireman Walter Reynolds, for example. Reynolds apparently told his family of this while on his deathbed, that he was at the UFO crash site that night, where FBI agents were apparently present, watching him then and perhaps in the aftermath.

According to author Schwarz, President Roosevelt was personally informed of his young Naval Liaison's illicit affair with Arvad and likely approved the transfer of dashing JFK to an active fighting unit, to get him out of D.C. *and* S.C. with his many collected – and blabbed? -

secrets. In addition, patriarch Joe Kennedy did not like Inga Arvad's background or her possible damaging effects on any future planned political campaign for his handsome son. Joe may well have consulted Hoover about the Arvad romance, neither man happy about it, that is clear. What is even clearer is that biographers have reported for years that it was at this time, in the fall/winter of '41/'42, that John F. Kennedy first spoke openly of running for political office as a stepping stone to someday achieving the presidency. All of these factors came together by mid-January to grease the skids of JFK being placed into action in the Pacific in about a year's time.

.In March of 1945, a worldlier Jack Kennedy became a private citizen again. He had been honorably discharged following his tour of duty in the Pacific, having survived the now-famous "PT-109 Incident." And yet... he turned up in the most unlikely of places: bombed-out Germany. Kennedy oddly tagged along in mid-July with Naval Secretary James Forrestal (1892-1949). That's along with various Navy and Army brass when inspecting conquered Nazi military outposts, ports, and headquarters, following the allied victory declared on May 8th. Citizen Kennedy was even introduced then to the Supreme Allied Commander of Europe, General Dwight Eisenhower, in Frankfurt. It is clear that much of the focus of this well-decorated military contingent in vanquished German territory was searching for meaningful Nazi scientific data, technology, and personnel to bring back to America, thus keeping it all out of the hands of the Russians and British, who were also present and roaming around captured properties. Some say it was for acquiring files if not hardware on recovered crashed alien technology.

President Truman ordered this critical mission done by people he trusted. Why in the world did discharged Kennedy go along? What did he know that qualified him to take part? This was likely pretty classified stuff, sensitive operations in trying to swipe valuable men and materials away from our equally-curious allied war comrades.

.The "official story" that biographers duly record is that Navy Secretary James Forrestal was eager to influence new President Harry Truman at the Potsdam Conferences going on that July. Yet if so, he utterly failed. James did not reach Potsdam until the day the conferences ended! If he took JFK with him after their devastated German tour, then Kennedy missed attending the conferences as well, and supposedly that was why young Jack was allowed in. Again, it is part of the accepted part of the future president's history that he wanted to become a journalist and record the great Potsdam confab for Hearst Newspapers. Yet he evidently failed to do so. Supposedly, Joseph P. Kennedy had called Forrestal and talked him into picking up his son in Paris, to fly him to Potsdam on the Navy Secretary's private plane, supposedly so that John could brush up on his reporting skills. So we can see that official claims don't add up with what took place.

As mentioned, many UFO writers seriously feel that this July '45 military task force was also searching for possible Nazi-retrieved UFO crash artifacts, or duplicated technology. It has long been rumored – but remains murky and unproven - that Hitler and the Nazi regime had gotten their hands on a crashed UFO back in the 1930s. If so, it would have been of great interest to the American military, currently examining the Cape Girardeau artifacts to create something useful for the war effort. Since the startling allegation about a retrieved Nazi "disc" has been covered by other sources in other venues, it won't be dug into here. But the personnel involved in the U.S. task force is the key for us trying to understand MO41.

In 1981, a Cape Girardeau college professor named Harley Rutledge published a book on local UFO sightings in southeast Missouri during the 1970s. He included an eye-catching personal story about a German man who had sent him information on a once-secret project the German military was working on – starting in 1941. It was all about "flying discs" German military officials and scientists had begun researching and attempting to construct for the Nazi war effort. The European source sent the Cape author documents and copied photographs of the two unusual circular spacecrafts, allegedly very advanced, until the mysterious informant abruptly cut off all communications and was not heard from again. If the story is valid, it raises the question of whether wartime American military officials and scientists had a pro-Nazi spy in their ranks, sending information to German contacts after April of 1941, in order to create a MO41-type spaceship of their very own. Or if the Nazis really had gotten their hands on a crashed ET ship. And also there's the possibility that the German information was forwarded to a Cape Girardeau resident because of MO41 tie-ins in the supposed Nazi-era technology. And that perhaps this subject was precisely what men like Forrestal and Kennedy were searching for in 1945.

Along on the U.S. military caravan with JFK in Germany that July of '45 was a naval officer named Henry A. Schade. He had been a captain until promoted in late 1944 to commodore and assigned intelligence duties relating to gathering up German technology in Europe and rushing it back to America to examine and turn into useable, reproduced war materials. Although he was born and raised in St. Paul, Minnesota, not southern Missouri, it is possible Henry Schade (1900-1992) was related to Ruben, Ben, and Clarence Schade of Cape Girardeau. {Sheriff Ruben who was likely at the MO41 crash site; MIA clerk Ben was on the Sikeston UFO recovery team; and Clarence was the former Army enlistee who spoke briefly of being told about the cosmic crash when interviewed in the 1990s.}

According to his own bio, in the first half of 1945, Commodore Schade was focused on finding and examining "rocket technology," whatever the Nazi war machine was developing – and why and how – *as to what could be launched into sky, if not outer space.* At the behest of President Truman, Secretary Forrestal and Commodore Schade and other uniformed U.S. military honchos took their tour of Berlin and were joined by - as two surviving photographs prove - JFK in a civilian suit and sunglasses. Was he allowed into the technology-searching crew because he was already familiar with MO41 and the fact that our planet was being visited and observed by advanced extraterrestrial races?

Henry A. Schade went on to receive military decorations and plum jobs in and outside of government, eventually living in Southern California, where he died in Pasadena in the early 1990's. {Ironically, in the early '90s Ruben Schade retired in Cape Girardeau, sold his home there, and moved to southern California (Orange County, not far from Pasadena)}. Did Forrestal, Schade, and Kennedy find any recovered or copied extraterrestrial vehicles from Nazi vaults? Whether they did or not is unknown. The whole mission-to-Germany still seems very strange and suspicious, likely classified and tucked away to this day.

.Adventuresome Kennedy in late 1941 had naturally taken a liking to the power and glamour on Capitol Hill, perhaps even the quiet goings-on within the depths of the grand building itself. As soon as the coming war was over, JFK focused his energies on working there. He ran for the U.S. House seat from Boston in 1946, and won. Soon he was a D.C.-based congressman with valuable social contacts all over town, holding a priceless military and intelligence background, and a very great interest in how the American government really ran behind the scenes. In January of 1947 Kennedy was quite experienced in how to get around in Washington power circles and this is quite evident from a fascinating section of a secret report written by an Army Counter Intelligence Corps officer, working under the Army's Chief of Staff (George Marshall's old position) in mid-July of '47. It was a classified document written *by* the CIC's special "Inter-Planetary Unit," which G. C. Marshall apparently began within a year of the '41 Missouri crash and recovery operation. *John F. Kennedy was literally named and clearly identified in the document, which explosively dealt with extraterrestrial matters.*

.In a summary of the top secret events in the Roswell area of New Mexico, the CIC/IPU intelligence agent wrote in the '47 report that only a small handful of people outside of Army officers knew about the extraterrestrial crash discoveries in the sunbaked southwestern desert. One of those was Marshall, the wise and experienced Secretary of State. The only other informed person mentioned was "Representative John F. Kennedy, son of Joseph P. Kennedy." JFK and Roswell! The banal report description of this seemingly obscure rookie congressman (out of over 300) noted that he was once "a naval officer assigned to Naval Intelligence during war." Why was it necessary to point out his intelligence background? Why and how could young Congressman Jack Kennedy learn of the shocking ET finds kept fairly tightly under wraps out in 1947 New Mexico? He was mostly stationed out of a congressional office inside the Capitol Building in Washington, and/or from his home district in Massachusetts. Just like the possibility that Kennedy was helping to locate Nazi captured UFO technology and scientists in July of '45, the answer may well link in MO41, and Freemasons too.

.First, it seems possible that the MO41 discoveries - or at least some remnants thereof - were *still* packed inside a storeroom (or Masonic site?) below the basement level of the Capitol Building in the autumn of '41, for Ensign

Kennedy to have somehow, someway have talked his way into seeing. Or, they might well have been stashed at a D.C. army base like Fort Meyer or Fort Belvoir. Or they were possibly stored with "Air Material Command" in Wright Field, Ohio, or were taken to a New Mexico site by '47. What seems most likely, however, is that by the summer of 1947 the MO41 affair was merely a leftover rumor or old intelligence report that Congressman Kennedy had once learned of, perhaps even by chance. It is still something worth keeping in mind as the plot thickens

.As we have seen, John Fitzgerald Kennedy knew a lot of powerful people even though he was still in his first months on the job as the very junior member of the House of Representatives in July of 1947. According to the IPU report, JFK found out about the startling Roswell alien affair thanks to a key contact where the two men worked. "It is believed that information was obtained," said the once-secret report, "from source in Congress who is close to Secretary for Air Force." No names for this source were given in this report, but one can take an educated guess as to who these two men were.

.The U.S. Air Force had no official "Secretary" until a few weeks after this report was originally dated. At the time there were a few assistant secretaries in control. But soon enough, in September of 1947, William Stuart Symington of Missouri was sworn in as the very first official Secretary of the Air Force. Before that his title was the wordy "Assistant Secretary of War for Air." Stuart may well have been an admired, older friend to Jack Kennedy in '47; certainly at one point they became fairly close acquaintances with plenty in common. The two liberal ex-servicemen both ran for the senate in 1952, and despite a Republican landslide that year, the pair of handsome Democrats each won handily in their home states, Missouri and Massachusetts. {In fact, Stu had been born in

Massachusetts and attended an Ivy League college.} Both men enjoyed outdoor activities and the intrigues of power and politics. Symington even brought Kennedy to Missouri for a political speech in 1957. The distinguished duo eventually grew so close ideologically and perhaps socially that historians have written at length that JFK's original pick for the position of vice president on the 1960 Democratic Party ticket was none other than Senator Symington. Well before that, hardworking Truman got to know and support corporate executive Symington back in Missouri, partly through mutually-beneficial political and Masonic social activities in St. Louis, and helped turn Stu from big business and the military to the world of government and politics.

.Stu Symington headed an electric company in St. Louis in April of 1941, just a hundred or so miles north of the alien crash-landing site. Emerson Electric headquarters was not far away from the riverside Parks Air College, near East St. Louis, that local pilot and businessman Oliver Parks operated. A PAC airfield apparently hosted - at least for a while - the recovered MO41 alien artifacts a day or two after its army recovery. Parks was well connected in St. Louis, even including a friendship with that town's most famous citizen, history-making pilot Charles Lindbergh (an enemy of FDR). Symington was evidently a friend of air training guru Parks; a 1948 St. Louis college alumni dinner photograph shows the two men seated closely side-by-side. Symington began his work in St. Louis in 1938, by then very experienced with airplanes and aircraft metals. If Parks (1899-1985) was also a Freemason then the two men were likely even chummier. Also, Symington might have been familiar with the St. Louis FBI field office which basically controlled the satellite office in Cape Girardeau in 1941.

Thus, while there is no smoking gun proof laying around, W. S. Symington almost *had* to have learned all about MO41 at some point, it would seem. His position in both his personal and professional lives would have required a briefing, and there existed just too many connections to people who were quite aware of the alien crash and its aftermath. And if he *had* been briefed, once again, did J. F. Kennedy?

.It may well have been known to the Army CIC/IPU author of the '47 secret UFO report that Under-Secretary Symington was to be sworn in soon to take the highest reins of the Air Force; Stu was that high up and respected in the organization and involved in daily matters. It's hard to believe Symington could possibly climb the Army Air Force ladder without having at least *heard* about the shocking 1941 incident that took place so close to home, relatively speaking. After all, President Truman trusted Symington to run the Air Force during a sensitive time of the Roswell incident and perhaps other alien crashes, so Symington's prior knowledge of MO41's intimate details by mid-'47 seems quite viable.

.We know that Kennedy spoke about the Roswell UFO crash rumor to *someone in congress who knew Symington well*, according to the confidential IPU report. This unnamed source in the Inter-Planetary Unit document could of course have been most *anyone* in either body of the Capitol Building, the House or the Senate. To narrow down the likelihood, it had to have been someone who knew Symington well and trusted. Hence it likely would have been a congressman from Missouri, and someone who may have known about alien visitation from a few years earlier. Say, *Senator Forrest C. Donnell*, perhaps. Donnell was a 1947 U.S. congressman who as mentioned previously in April of 1941 was the governor of Missouri *and* a very devoted Freemason. Now in the summer of '47 Forrest was the former Grand Master Mason of Missouri, once having presided over the "Tuscan Lodge #360" in St. Louis, where "Most Worshipful Brother Harry Truman" was "a most frequent visitor" and "33rd degree Mason," according to its website description.

.Locating a more concrete connection between Senator Forrest C. Donnell (1884-1980) and Representative John F. Kennedy would then be the final masterstroke key to link all of this together. So far, that seems lacking, but it all fits together within reasonable conjecture. *However, logs show that Forrest Donnell was in President Truman's Oval Office on the morning of July 3rd, 1947, the day news from Roswell, New Mexico, could well have come trickling in to the president.* This confab – with a few other senators present - took place minutes after a special "off the record" meeting Harry held with a D.C. newsman, existing logs show, discussing something obviously rather sensitive, where no notes were to be taken by anyone. About an hour later, ET-aware George C. Marshall was brought in for a meeting with the president. A few days later Stu Symington also arrived at the Oval Office to chat with Truman, this the day after Roswell UFO discovery stories hit some newspaper headlines around the country.

.One must ask at this point: *why would JFK be allowed the white hot secret of the Army's New Mexico alien recovery operations in '47 if he did not already have prior knowledge of the MO41 Army retrieval?* Again, speculative, but also logical.

.One important figure who fell into this web of intrigue - and then fell out in a dreadful, deadly way - was FDR's 1941 Under-Secretary of the Navy, James Forrestal. That is, Forrestal was tabbed by President Roosevelt to be the Number Two man at Navy headquarters in mid-1940, so most likely he grew at least somewhat acquainted in the department's D.C. intelligence offices with Ensign J. F.

Kennedy in late '41. The two men may have become friends when Forrestal (by then promoted to Secretary of the Navy) took private citizen Jack with him in July of '45 on that trip to vanquished Germany. {In May of 1944, Navy Secretary Forrestal signed a special citation for Kennedy, for his heroism in the PT-109 incident in the South Pacific and a month later Joseph P. Kennedy badgered Forrestal into giving Jack a medal for it, too.} The duo strangely drove off together to visit Adolph Hitler's war-damaged home in the mountains, and his once-secret underground Nazi lair, that mid-summer as WWII raged in the Pacific. Neither man was a Mason, apparently, but both were at least Ivy League Catholics and respected navy officers who had seen the ravages of battles first-hand. More than likely, what secrets the odd couple uncovered were quietly taken back to their old U.S. Naval Intelligence headquarters in Washington and perhaps even presented in report form to President Truman in mid-'45.

.So impressed was Harry Truman in 1947 that he promoted James Forrestal to the first "Secretary of Defense" cabinet position. The swearing-in ceremony for this new position took place just weeks after the rumored Roswell UFO crash incidents. Logically, Truman would only have promoted someone to the lofty new post who had experience in understanding ET matters, considering all that had come falling into American hands (literally). Both Forrestal and Kennedy may well have learned about ET secrets in both '41 and '47, and eerily both men died sudden, controversial, violent deaths. Both were autopsied at Bethesda Naval Hospital, in Maryland. Coincidence again? {Forrestal's possible murder, or "suicide," took place *at* this medical facility.}

.A full decade later, a more mature Senator John Fitzgerald Kennedy decided to run for president, as his father wanted and pressured him to do someday since the early 1940s.

JFK laid out his plans with only the most trusted of advisors, and interestingly utilized Franklin Roosevelt, Jr., during the primary campaign. In the fall 1960 campaign, Democratic Party nominee Kennedy met with Eleanor Roosevelt at her upstate New York home. Later he traveled to Warm Springs, Georgia, where he gave a public speech on the front steps of the famous "Little White House" where Franklin Roosevelt died. Afterwards, in a somewhat unpublicized story, he rather curiously met inside the cottage with the widow of one of his PT-109 shipmates, and her son. Not content with a conversation before the cameras in the living room of the cottage, Senator Kennedy led the young man back into "a private room." Since there were only a few rooms in the house, this likely meant Kennedy conducted a private conversation with the teenager in either the very room where Roosevelt died, the back bedroom, or the spare bedroom (where a Secret Service guard rested when guarding FDR). Kennedy "mostly asked questions" about the boy's life and schooling. Did JFK bring up the sad story of the FDR suicide? Or scuttlebutt about MO41? Unfortunately the rest of the confidential conversation on October 10th, 1960, has remained – and likely always will – a secret. But it was nineteen years earlier – nearly to the day - that a young Jack Kennedy had arrived in Washington with presidential ambitions, to work for President Roosevelt, and eventually JFK became the first and only American president to die in office after FDR did so, both men evidently with bullets in the brain.

Kennedy was to go on to become president in the early 1960s and was surrounded by many of the same Secret Service men who guarded Roosevelt and handled his deceased body on April 12th, 1945, in the cottage. In fact, when JFK was inaugurated, it was at the U.S. Capitol Building, where the PT-109 widow and her son were special guests, guarded by these Secret Service agents who possibly knew of MO41 and its temporary storage site inside the immense structure. As so often is the case in the Cape Girardeau UFO affair, synchronicity, or incredible coincidence, abounds.

. As everyone knows, JFK loved to "play the field" sexually in the 1940s, '50s, and early '60s, when he was mostly based out of Washington. "He was a fearful girler," recalled a famous journalist who knew him well. This seemed to cement his noteworthy friendship with Franklin Roosevelt, Jr., who behaved likewise, both products of the ultra-privileged political/social upper class and both affiliated with the Navy. Despite his marriage vows, J. F. Kennedy was seemingly addicted to sexual encounters with a wide variety of women. When he became president, he famously had an affair with legendary movie star Marilyn Monroe (1926-1962), and according to sources recounted in various books, as President Kennedy - and his brother, Attorney General Robert Kennedy (1925-1968) - told gabby Marilyn some state secrets during "pillow talk." *One of these classified topics was evidently that of alien crashes*, according to an explosive later-leaked CIA memorandum from the summer of 1962. Monroe evidently told friends over tapped telephone lines that JFK and RFK had talked to her about the president's quiet trip to "a secret air base for the purpose of inspecting things from outer space," according to the once-classified memo. Allegedly, the lusty chief executive admitted to seductive Monroe that he viewed in private the remains of recovered alien bodies and hardware. Monroe friend and confidante Robert Slatzer (1928-2005) also backed up this story, in a 1990s television interview a few years before he died. Slatzer said Marilyn recalled to him that President Kennedy informed her that the displayed deceased alien creatures had large heads, big black eyes, skinny bodies, and grey skin tones. In other words, it's been alleged that in '61 or so JFK supposedly saw in person recovered and preserved ET crash victims that match the MO41 discoveries (and perhaps Roswell). Was this curiosity first instilled in Kennedy from twenty years earlier, as a bachelor ensign in 1941 D.C.?

.British author Timothy Good stated in a 2007 book that he developed an inside source (or two) that told him that President Kennedy in 1961 quietly "expressed the desire to see the alien bodies" that that were the result of a tragic extraterrestrial "crash site" (year and site unnamed). It was his first year in the executive position of the highest power. According to Mr. Good, it was arranged for the young commander-in-chief to visit to a military airbase in Florida to secretly view the bodies of the creatures. Of course, anyone can make up tall tales, even JFK himself, but in this case the '62 CIA memo; the Slatzer interview; the '47 IPU report; and the Masonic info we have just digested all seem to come together quite nicely to create a certain amount of credibility to the amazing allegation.

.Early on as president, JFK invited a large group of upper tier Freemasons from around the world to the White House, for a modest tour and an intimate greeting outdoors, on the lawn, since the crowd was so large. The Eighth International Supreme Council of Freemasons - the highest of the high - mingled before the cameras with the new Commander-in-Chief on April 10th, 1961, for some unknown reason. Ironically it was nearly the twentieth anniversary *to the day* of MO41. If non-member Jack Kennedy had no interest in being a Mason, or learning their secrets, why were the most authoritative group members brought together for a social event at the highest seat of American power like this? Obviously JFK took time from his busy schedule to speak to the most influential and knowledgeable of all Masonic brothers. What they discussed remains unknown.

{Some researchers have highlighted President Kennedy's public speech at the Waldorf-Astoria Hotel in New York

City on April 27th, 1961, where he railed against "secret societies." But it is clear in listening to that entire address to newspaper editors gathered that JFK was referring to the Soviet Union as the "closed" or "secret" society in question. Communists, not the Freemasons. In September of 1962, Kennedy proved his respect and affection for Freemasonry by stepping off Air Force One in Illinois to attend an airport ceremony by local Masons for opening their new lodge. Clearly, the president was *not* anti-Masonic.}

.What we do know for certain is that as president, J. F. Kennedy initiated an aggressive space program to at the very least place a man on the moon. An astronaut in a manmade spaceship. Who ended up accomplishing this lofty goal? Freemasons! That's right, enthusiastic members of Masonic societies landed on the moon and boldly explored there, that is a startling fact the organization proudly advertises to this day. Back in July of 1969 the second man to ever step foot on the moon, U.S. astronaut Edwin "Buzz" Aldrin, fulfilled late presidents Roosevelt and Kennedy's desire to have an American "conquer" that enticing lunar body and then return safely in an advanced, controllable spacecraft to planet earth. A special U.S. flag was planted at the landing site, of course, making it somehow "American domain." After the manmade spacecraft's return, this flag was returned to the well-known and respected "Masonic 33rd Degree Scottish Rites Temple" - the one on 16th Street not too far from where Jack Kennedy lived back in late 1941 to early '42. While on the moon's bleak, dusty surface, Buzz Aldrin carried with him a special Masonic "deputation" and "declaration," stating that the moon was from then on to be considered part of "the Masonic jurisdiction."

.{Although apparently astronaut Neil Armstrong - the first human on the moon's surface - was not a Freemason, many other well-known and more obscure astronauts *were* Masonic members, including Gordon Cooper and Edgar Mitchell, both of whom publicly espoused their belief that earth is being visited by intelligent alien species.}

.And finally, it has been learned over the years that the site where John Fitzgerald Kennedy was shot – and essentially died – was once a Freemason's gathering place. That's right, of all the locales in Dallas, JFK's November '63 motorcade route was carefully directed by White House planners and Secret Service advance men to take an awkward, slow turn into Dealey Plaza, which used to be the location of a Masonic lodge, in fact the very first one in Dallas, according to research at kentroversy.com, a website dedicated to the many weird mystical/coincidental factors involved in the president's murder. FDR would have been pleased when he was taken through this very same burgeoning public park of Masonic origin when *he* was paraded through town in '36.

Want another weird Masonic JFK assassination tie-in? Kennedy was shot in the same exact three bodily places that famed Freemason founder Hiram Abiff so long ago was stabbed in: the back, the throat, and the rear of the head. And when it came time to pick governmental figures to investigate the Kennedy assassination, President Johnson selected Earl Warren to head a commission; *Warren was former Grand Master Mason of California in the 1930s, and was aided by information provided to him by J. Edgar Hoover, the very Freemason who had been keeping tabs on Kennedy and the Cape Girardeau crash since 1941.* Weird!

Still more on mindboggling information on JFK's shocking murder is included in the special "Bonus Chapter" herein. Hopefully more data and documents will be released in the future pointing to some clear and definite answers on both Kennedy's murder and his possible knowledge of MO41.

But one alleged John F. Kennedy quote still haunts many UFO researchers...

Five months before he died, in June of 1963, President Kennedy supposedly told a curious Air Force One employee – a flight steward/loadmaster - named Bill Holden, "I'd *like* to tell people about the truth behind UFOs, but for now my hands are tied." If true, this indicates John Fitzgerald Kennedy had indeed learned plenty, but was handcuffed by someone powerful and influential in government – a special UFO committee? the CIA? Hoover? - who didn't want the truth to come out, even as of 1963. It is at least possible American intelligence personnel made sure JFK never spoke of it, or anything else, ever again. Is it *still* that way today?

..... **SECTION II**

... *Local Surprises* – Southeast Missouri

Personal Diary Research

CHAPTER FIVE

Author's Field Trip: 2013 Cape Girardeau

"The military came in and took it all back to an Army base."

.The first thing people ask about MO41 is, *"Where's the crash site?"* They want to go there and snoop around, dig in the dirt, and become the great hero who produces the first ever historic piece of indisputable alien spaceship metal from the downed wreckage of the 1941 affair. And I don't blame them. I admit I have desired to do the same exact thing. It would help tremendously in presenting actual scientifically-tested hard proof of the great 1941 Missouri UFO crash to all the skeptics and believers, media people and politicians alike. Such a contemporary event would be truly historic and exciting. One for the history books. But this noble goal requires an intense but cautious and low-key ground search based upon clues to the accident site. It would also take some skillful public relations, legal permission to dig, metal detecting, science lab connections, and pure luck. I was determined to be the great hero who found his pot of gold, his great white whale. Unfortunately it all proved to be much tougher than I first expected, especially when I got sidetracked by fascinating and sometimes very surprising new facets of the story being unearthed, some by my elementary detective skills, others by strangers, and some simply by chance…

Since this author had a day job and limited time off, a small budget and other responsibilities in life, I couldn't just zip five hours across the state to my old hometown of Cape Girardeau any time I wished. Even though I was born in Cape; grown up and been educated there; and spent my first 34 years there, I was now living elsewhere in Missouri. Field trips possibilities for more intense scouting around were today very limited. But in May 2013 I did get a chance to commence my "quest for hard proof" by traveling to Cape and then talking to some area residents about the crash. Unfortunately, most folks were not familiar with the saga, despite some TV specials and online articles that have mentioned it.

Keeping in mind my accumulated general clues, but lacking a very specific farm site for a "dirt search," I did dig up a few new possibly-connected stories surrounding MO41. Or stumbled into some. Commencing with a rather surprising story via a somber, trustworthy woman who was a longtime friend of my mother. "Ramona," as I'll call her, gave me assurances that her son "Dack" (another pseudonym) learned of the 1941 crash before it "went viral." When asked how, from the internet or TV, she replied, "Neither. Dack overheard two old men discussing it while he sat in the lobby of the Ford Groves dealership." That establishment was for many decades a downtown Cape Girardeau Ford automobile sales and service lot, on Sprigg Street. The property was based around a two-story building that featured garage bays for repairs below, and lots of office space above, on the second floor. "This happened about fifteen or more years ago," Ramona added, meaning the encounter likely took place sometime in the mid-1990s. At that time, Dack told Ramona, he was surprised to overhear the aging twosome knowledgeably discuss "the alien ship and the dead bodies," and how the military arrived "and took it all back to an army base."

Unfortunately, Dack said he did not know the exact date of this encounter at Ford Groves, nor the names or backgrounds of the men involved. Or any specific location they might have mentioned for the crash. At first I wondered seriously if Dack was merely relating "the tale of two gents" as the duo would have reacted to the July 1998 *Southeast Missourian* front page news article on MO41. But that cannot be possible. Ford Groves was closed to the public by July '98 so Dack and the two old men simply could not have been there at that time. Therefore it seems obvious the elderly area duo had to have been discussing inside information - perhaps *from firsthand knowledge?* - or at least scuttlebutt from hearing about MO41 from others who were there, at the local farm crash site, a little over fifty years earlier.

.A friend of mine who also hailed from Cape surprised me around this time a similar story, that he had heard of the MO41 tale around fifteen or so years ago. This fellow happened to have worked in the Ford Groves building, but only after it was sold by the Ford dealership and became a taxi cab service garage, where my friend repaired their yellow vehicles. Was my buddy recalling the story has heard from a source who knew of MO41 firsthand? Unfortunately, his recollection was also fuzzy on the exact time and the source, but as I researched around town, the Ford Groves site mysteriously came popping up again and again. I was further surprised during my 2013 trip to find out how historic and important this city block truly was in old downtown Cape Girardeau...

It turns out the upstairs of this same downtown Ford dealership was once quietly used in World War II as a factory to create small devices that changed the world! For certain, the top secret government-guided project greatly aided the nationwide push to win the tenuous war. The "manufacturing plant," as it was referred to then, employed Cape Girardeau citizens to make small wire-wound "resistors" for application in weapons, bombs, and communication devices, utilized also in American ships, submarines, trains, and aircraft to aid the fighting effort overseas.

"Resistors," I discovered through research, were considered essential for use within the electrical components of countless items. While resistors had actually been around for several decades, apparently few if any U.S. citizens or inventors had previously created specially-coated, wire-wound editions. The oldest and most common kind were of a filmy carbon variety, according to some online research. Precisely who came up with the wire-wound form of resistors is not clear. But the idea was mysteriously seized upon by the owner of the Ford Groves auto dealership - Frederick A. Groves - and parlayed into an impressive secret effort to upgrade mechanical devices of all kinds, all around the world.

.Now here's a further odd twist in the resistors story: the smallish items were utilized in radar units, to detect various approaching aircraft (or spacecrafts) and *even in the atomic bomb*, according to an article in *The Southeast Missourian* in the days following the unofficial end of the war, mid-August of 1945. Considered a "control device used to balance and regulate electric circuits," the tiny wire resistors played a major role in advanced technology that won the war and advanced American communications for decades. It was almost hard to believe: *leaving MO41 aside, my seemingly sleepy hometown made a huge difference and impact on twentieth century civilization, thanks to this diminutive device alone.* It was an inescapable fact that made me a little more proud to be a native Cape Girardean.

.The wire-wound resistors were even applied in early editions of computers in the 1950s and '60s. Communications and technology blossomed out in the years to come, thanks in part to the product first made upstairs at Ford Groves and shipped around the nation. Cape resistors helped change the world in so many ways. And a seemingly obscure Cape Girardeau auto dealer named Fred Groves helped lead the way. But who was this long-deceased car seller, and where did *he* come up with the idea, the technology that he somehow knew would work and aid everyday items and military-use gear? Even with a search engine on my personal computer, I found answers hard to come by. All I know is that the production of said new-look resistors *seems* to oddly fit in with the MO41 saga, in roundabout ways. And once again, this may all be mere coincidence, it's hard to tell.

."A special type order found themselves rushed to the Oak Ridge, Tenn., atomic bomb plant," and not long thereafter the results were felt "in the awful destruction at Hiroshima," reported Cape Girardeau's daily newspaper, just two days after the first atomic bomb drop in Japan, 1945. The resistors concocted upstairs in the Ford Groves building were a very substantial and successful secret at the time, worked on day and night by over one hundred employees. They allegedly created "three-quarters of a million resistors of many types."

Surprises kept coming, some on a personal level. For instance, I was startled to learn that the secret factory operation was managed by Mr. Walter W. Heath, my own stepmother's father! Walter was also the manager of the dealership, working directly for owner Fred Groves. I had never heard this family history before. My stepmom sat down with me and calmly explained her father's past, and that also her dad often went hunting and fishing with none other than MO41's likely newsman, Garland D.

Fronabarger! The two men were pals. What is more, *Walter's daughter told me she too heard the story of a crashed ship and dead aliens just outside of Cape, around the time when she was a teenager in the 1960s.* Once again, I am quite surprised. She cannot recall precisely *who* told her the amazing tale, or any specific facts involved, but obviously the wild crash claim was rumored in town by some long before it broke big forty years later. Could ol' Frony have been the source of the rumors? My stepmother replied, "No, I don't think so. He never told anything like that to *me*, anyway." Could it have come from her father, an important cog at Ford Groves? The answer is unfortunately uncertain, thanks to the fog of time. She's just not clear on *who* precisely informed her, but the story was still in the air in the 1960s, tellingly, three decades before Charlette Huffman Mann came forward with the story that made MO41 famous.

.My mind wandered back to a nagging, persistent question: *"Of all the places in the nation to make a part for the atom bomb, why did the Ford Groves building in Cape Girardeau qualify?"* According to the *Missourian* article, owner Mr. Groves had "contacts back east" who linked him in the spring of 1942 to the critical enterprise, which went into full operation that autumn. No specific names minus a helpful sales rep in New York City were revealed as any sort of Groves special connection in the news story, but it makes one wonder: just who suddenly came up with this carefully-coated wire-wound resistor approach, rather than the old carbon resistors? Was it Fred himself, or one of the automobile service operators under his command? And precisely who in the U.S. military and/or government approved it for Frederick A. Groves and Cape Girardeau to mass produce, and why?

.Furthermore, where exactly did the parts for a coated, wire-wound resistor and its Cape Girardeau factory production come from? "Much of the equipment was built right in the plant," the 1945 article claimed, "and employees improvised" with what was laying around Ford Groves and the Cape Girardeau area to create the items. Just where did they get some of this cutting edge material? I have no answers, and I don't want to speculate outlandishly that it came from MO41, but who knows?

.In researching the Manhattan Project - the 1940's creation of the atomic bomb in pre-war and mid-war America - I found out the delicate process was eventually coordinated for practical application in wartime by a gruff Army overseer appointed by FDR, a man who grew up in New York City: General Leslie Groves (1896-1970). That's certainly "back east." Was he related to Fred A. Groves? It might simply be a coincidence, but it is of further intriguing interest to know that General Groves worked with the likes of Robert Oppenheimer *and Vannevar Bush*, who as we know now was heavily involved in researching not just secretly-recovered MO41 technology but correctly applied nuclear sciences for perfecting nuclear bombs. Documents suggest that Van Bush may have pumped new life into that critical defense project by studying the "atomic secrets" of the recovered alien "wonders" recovered from the farm outside Cape Girardeau, perhaps including a "neutronic propulsion device" taken from the MO41 wreckage.

A Bush-L. Groves connection and a possible L. Groves-F. Groves connection. Is this why Cape was specifically selected to help make an atom bomb part? As a kind of reward for some of its citizens keeping quiet about the top secret, historic ET crash and its army recovery? This seems too pat, too speculative, and too unbelievable. This was likely all a mere incredible happenstance. Um, right?

.Around this time I learned to my further surprise that in the mid-1930s Fred A. Groves the downtown car dealer owned farmland in – of all places - the Chaffee area, southwest of

Cape Girardeau! Some of this land was listed in the newspaper then as rural property between the tiny hamlets of Randles and Arbor, not far from Chaffee; it was likely to be sold soon in order to help create a new five-mile road that would connect these tiny country hamlets. While Fred and his wife (and daughter Marjorie) lived near SEMO University in Cape, serving on their Board of Regents, and enthusiastically promoting local business growth through the Chamber of Commerce, farm-owning Mr. Groves was also on an "airport committee" trying to find land outside of town that would be a proper site for a new, modern airfield. Likely this meant some of the property that Fred just happened to own between Chaffee and Cape. Yes, the very same general area of the 1941 alien crash, albeit perhaps not the precise property.

.It is certainly unproven but the possibility struck me: what if Fred Groves had been called on the night of Saturday, April 12th, 1941, and rushed to the UFO accident scene with a mechanic or two? It was at first expected to be a gnarled "airplane crash" with twisted, flame-damaged metal and people's lives were at stake, or so all originally believed. Fred's service garage featured professional metalworkers, mechanics who had great experience in handling burned, mangled automobile and truck metals, like steel and aluminum. They likely had acetylene torches, powerful repair tools, and cutting devices that possibly even the fire department did not own, or have any experience with. A sharp-minded Cape policeman or fireman might well have telephoned Mr. Groves and pleaded for help when the call for assistance first came in. *Did Fred A. Groves rush to the UFO crash scene also because he felt it might have been on his own land?* Or a friendly neighbor's? The Cape car dealer may have found out plenty, either that night or soon thereafter, and parlayed his information into a lucrative deal not long after, during the war. It's pure speculation, but at a plausible, possible scenario, certainly.

.What is even more thought-provoking is that the August 1945 *Southeast Missourian* news article on the critical resistors manufactured in Cape has no specific byline. The name of the informed writer was not provided. Could it have been written by Garland D. Fronabarger? He often wrote without credit for the newspaper. He also personally knew Harry Truman. Frony's son worked in the factory itself, and the manager of the production was his old friend. Whoever created the article knew a great deal about the big local secret project, which could only have been revealed with official government permission so soon - August 11th, 1945 - after the general cessation of the war in the Pacific. President Harry Truman - who had once trained for the United States Army *in* quiet Cape Girardeau - had not even officially declared America's triumph, with "V-J Day" (which was announced in early September '45). How could acceptance be given so very soon for the publication of an article revealing a crucial and secretive part of our "super-weapon of war" (as FDR once put it)?

.During my Cape Girardeau trip, I was graciously allowed to enter and view the former home of Reverend William Huffman and his fine family, on North Main Street, overlooking the Mississippi River. I was happy to find that it remains a well-kept and charming older house. The kindly current owner pulled out the property's manifest for me. Together we viewed the legal documents that William and Floy Huffman signed long ago to first acquire the place in early 1943, then sell the property in 1945. This certainly confirmed that Reverend Huffman was indeed in town in the right era and neighborhood, but evidently he only *rented* the site of his interrupted evening at home in mid-April of '41. William was to work full-time at Red Star Tabernacle later that year, so he was evidently allowed to move into the church-owned abode early with his family. It's where anyone should start when retracing his footsteps from his journey to the farmland alien accident scene. It's also where William was approached by a local man with an ET photo he snapped, about two weeks after the bizarre rural crash event.

.During my time in May 2013 in town, I took photos of the Huffman home; the current Red Star Baptist Church; the old downtown Masonic lodge; the former police/fire department headquarters; the old Ford Groves building; and G. D. Fronabarger's old house. I visited Cape's newspaper headquarters; the town's public library; City Hall; the current police headquarters; and several other places of interest. I drove through rural farm properties and imagined what might have taken place on their land in April of 1941. But no obvious crash site seemed readily apparent.

.Around this time, I received a somewhat surprising phone call, long distance from Arizona. It was from Mr. John W. Fronabarger, the now-elderly son of "One Shot Frony," the popular reporter/photographer from Cape's conservative newspaper. The 85-year-old said he's been living in retirement near sunny Phoenix, Arizona, recovering from a recent operation. He was clearly intrigued by the recent allegations involving his father Garland, and the entire UFO crash claim, but just could not recall if his dad once even hinted to him or any of his relatives about an alien spacecraft accident from 1941. John did relate a few other helpful tidbits of information, however, such as his work with the coated wire-wound resistors during World War II in the Ford Groves second floor manufacturing plant! To my surprise, John said he helped to create the unique items in the secret enterprise. "I still have a box of rejects here" in his Arizona home, John chuckled. "I was only seventeen when I worked at the plant, for Walter Heath, and I knew Fred Groves too. One time while I ran a chemistry experiment there, I was closely observed by two men, looking over my shoulder. Later I was told that one was a general, and the other was an admiral." This begs the critical question: *what were such very high-ranking military men doing in an obscure small town's manufacturing plant, during a very busy war effort? Weren't there far more important matters to attend to?*

.Certainly the impression could be given herein that there was more going on within the Ford dealership and in the Cape area than met the eye during the war years. Maybe there was, maybe there wasn't. For instance, John chuckled as he recalled how his news-hungry father would catch hell for openly photographing with his 4x5 "Speed Graphic" such high-grade officers when they came to town, arriving during WWII by plane at Harris Field outside of town, just north of Scott County farmland. The brass quickly let Ol' Frony know in no uncertain terms that they didn't want the American public - nor the Axis powers - to know where they were and what they were up to. They didn't want *any* images snapped at all, for reasons of security, and photo-snapping at the airport was banned. It seems obvious such men didn't relish having their purposeful wartime cover blown. *But what were these important men doing, exactly? And how did Frony find out about their presence and snap their picture as they arrived covertly?*

.At least on *one* specific occasion, the August '45 newspaper article stated, a shipment of the special resistors was "rushed to Oak Ridge," to aid in the top secret atomic bomb-making program at their headquarters in eastern Tennessee, a few hundred miles away. Could some of the Cape-visiting military brass have escorted the load? Evidently so, at least at times. According to the *Missourian* article from August of 1945, "Military and chartered planes often came after them," and that "special messengers from the plant were flown all over the nation with equipment."

Presumably therefore they didn't *always* have or need military brass as escorts. In fact, their presence would have made their missions more high profile and obvious, thus more dangerous as far as attracting potential spies, saboteurs, and thieves were concerned. It made more sense to send undercover, obscure couriers to Cape to escort the critical defense system parts. Thus, something *more* seemed to be going on in Cape. Were the top military men in town partly to see people and places - and objects? - once associated with MO41? I could come up with no clear-cut answers, only lingering suspicions and questions.

.What was produced in Fred Groves' downtown building did not stop at applications within radar, vehicles, communications devices, and atom bombs. No, the little wire "resistors being made were needed for television and communications of various types," according to *The Southeast Missourian* article trumpeting its enormous impact in mid-summer of '45. While television was still in its infancy, incredibly, the little upstairs manufacturing plant and its unimpressive-looking product obviously impacted the whole world for decades to come via TV set production and still other ways to send and receive data, such as mentioned earlier, through computer technology that was emerging after the war, as crude as it was compared to today's advanced models. Mr. Frederick A. Groves in hindsight and historical retrospect seems now like a bit of an unsung national hero with huge, far-reaching – worldwide? - implications for his impromptu Cape company's tiny product and small factory's toil.

.Whether the newfangled invention had anything to do with recovered alien technology or not, the question still nags: how did Mr. Groves come up with this "wire-round resistor" idea, for mass production? Fred was a relative nobody on the national scene, a small town car dealer, and only started his war-based "Groves Corporation" enterprise for the resistors at some point in '42. Did he alone come up with the idea, or possible have a mechanic at the garage who hit upon the clever product? Was it produced by someone else in the Ford Motor Company engineering division, and somehow passed on to Fred? The special resistors proposal was studied and discussed by those in power - in the Ford enterprise presumably and in the U.S. government specifically - for over a year, according to the news article, then low-key Cape Girardeau production was approved and began in the fall of '43. An inside connection or two to the MO41 crash... or knowledge of the alien affair, used as leverage with General Groves to gain the defense contract... either *might* explain also why Fred got his factory and why the aforementioned old-timers from that vehicular sales and repair establishment knew about the crash fifty years after the war era manufacturing was a distant memory? Admittedly, this is pure speculation, without a basis in solid evidence. But it's compelling to ponder.

.A little further research revealed that Fred A. Groves continued his resistors factory in the upstairs of his Cape dealership into December of 1945. Likely realizing he was a car dealer and service manager at heart, Fred made himself a little extra bundle by selling the special technology plant to a Walter Davis, who moved the enterprise to a larger location situated near my old high school in Cape Girardeau. {Mr. Davis also lured away my step-grandfather from Mr. Groves, to manage the new enterprise.} The new factory was actually a building that I had walked past on my way home from school many times so long ago. "Davis Electric" kept the resistors production going for several years, until time and advancements in technology left the one-story factory in the heart of Cape nearly obsolete. Eventually the production plant was taken over by Walter Davis' son, and it managed to compete and grow with the changing times, at least into the early 1990s, when it finally wound down and was shuttered.

.I was further surprised to discover that *right next door* to the old downtown Ford Groves dealership sat the city's community building that acted as the regular meeting room for three major civic organizations: the well-known American Legion, with its military ties the obscure "Knights of Pythias" *and the Cape Girardeau lodge of the Organized Brotherhood of Freemasonry*. That's right, some of the most influential area citizens of the day were in and out of the flat, nondescript brick structure (now shuttered) a few feet away from some of the Ford vehicles parked on the Fred Groves lot. In my time in town, the Masonic lodge was always on Broadway. I found out that building was opened in the late '60s. In the 1940s, the elongated building at 17 Sprigg Street was a busy and active place; it is where - with or without signing in the guest book - Harry S Truman attended meetings when he came to town, for instance, along with his Masonic Grand Master replacement, Governor Forrest C. Donnell. Missouri's popular governor was a future senator like Mr. Truman, and good friends with noteworthy fellow conservatives in the area, such as Rush Limbaugh I, Sheriff Schade, and quite possibly Fred Groves himself. It would not be surprising if Justice of the Peace Milton Cobb - Reverend Huffman's neighbor - was also a Republican and Freemason, after his many years of service in the Cape area, along with the local newspaper owner/publishers, the Naeter brothers. Radio station owner Oscar Hirsch was a member, so was the mayor, along with cops and firemen. It's difficult to believe that civic leader Fred Groves was not a Freemason, since he was such a kindly community forerunner and the meeting hall was so close by he could nearly *crawl* down the sidewalk to attend meetings, if he so choose.

.{Trivia: Fred's wife was a member of "The Daughters of the American Revolution" and I suspect Mr. Groves joined the "Sons" version also but can't prove it. She attended group meetings in Washington D.C., where Leslie Groves was often based. Records show General Groves joined "The Sons of the American Revolution." Coincidences again?}

.I began to wonder around this time if Navy Commodore Henry A. Schade (mentioned in Chapter Four) was amongst those visiting Cape and the downtown WWII resistors plant, to check on this vital material... and visit with his relatives? As mentioned he could conceivably have been related to Ruben, Ben, and Clarence Schade. Henry's mission in capturing European rocket and scientific technology (a Nazi-captured UFO?) was apparently considered a success; I discovered he went on to receive decorations and plum jobs in and outside of government, eventually retiring in Southern California (where he died in Pasadena, in 1992). Ironically, in the late 1980s, Ruben Schade retired from the Cape Girardeau newspaper, sold his home in town, and moved to... southern California (Orange County, not far from Pasadena).

.In returning to my phone conversation with G. D. Fronabarger's offspring John, he went on to recall several people I knew from Cape's old days, including my father and grandfather. It reminded me what a small town Cape was, and how almost everyone seemed to know everyone, in a direct or roundabout way. John remembered how his outgoing dad was familiar with nearly everyone in town and would not hesitate to rush out of the house on news stories at all hours of the day and night, searching for the latest scoop. "My dad was a member of the First Baptist Church but I'm pretty sure he was not a Freemason *but he was secretive about some things*, and talkative about other things." This was an intriguing response, but it didn't clear up at all whether Garland genuinely saw the alien situation and sat on the story, or perhaps heard about it later from others. It surely makes some inside knowledge very *possible*, since as John and I agreed: *when the U.S. Army and the American government told you to do something in the 1940s, you shut your mouth and quickly did as you were told.* And this included the area's police and fire department representatives. There was precious little dissent or rebelliousness in those days. But attitudes in this nation towards authority and government secrets have changed as the decades passed. Yet to his son at least, Garland didn't discuss any sort of top secret alien situation before his death in the early 1990s.

.To bring things full circle, John Fronabarger told me he was even familiar with the Limbaugh family, and went to school with Rush Sr.'s son Stephen, "from grade school to college." The famous broadcaster's father, Rush Jr., once represented John in a legal case involving Garland's second wife selling off her husband's possessions late in life, including many photographs. Today Frony's offspring feels that some in the Limbaugh brood know the real story of just what happened in 1941 but can't talk about it for fear of ridicule, considering the well-known family's very conservative political standing. "The government knows the story too, and they don't want to release secret files. I used to have high clearances in my job and that's how they work. They have secrets, they keep 'em. They don't want to rattle somebody" who is still alive and might be affected by the release of information, within or outside the government. Additionally, John felt that in 1941 any news of aliens visiting the planet would genuinely have started a "panic," at least in some, and might even do so to this day. Keeping quiet would have been of utmost importance for many years afterwards, possibly for the good of mankind, even.

.I also learned at this time that John's father, the intrepid newsman, had an obsession with the local airport. He'd hang out there, take photos of the visiting dignitaries – despite being warned not to – and go up in airplanes for recording the countryside with his Speed Graphic. I wondered seriously if he did so at times to photograph the MO41 site from the air, but I had no proof. I did find several aerial digitized snapshots of Cape Girardeau and Chaffee, however.

.I did some more searching of this near-the-airport location - southern Cape County and northern Scott County - during my next trip to my old hometown, in late September, 2013. I felt sure that I alone could find the crash-landing site. It was buried treasure that only I could unearth. But I still came up goose eggs. There were *plenty* of area farms to search, I realized, but only one held the key. It was such an enticing mystery!

I also spoke at this time to members of the Red Star Baptist Church, received more lowdown on Reverend Huffman and his family, and toured downtown Cape sites. All this despite being rerouted at times by Cape Girardeau traffic cops and security guards, aiding the filming of a major motion picture - "*Gone Girl*," starring Ben Affleck and other notable actors - in and around town. {I was even further surprised to find that Affleck was visiting crew members of the movie production team right across the hall from my hotel room.}

During this early autumn trip, I also toured the eastern half of Scott County, slowly poring over rolling hills, wooded areas, and farm fields not too far from the mighty Mississippi River. I realized after a fairly detailed search that this was not quite the proper crash locale, and that in my next venture to the area, I would endeavor to concentrate solely on the flat crop-land outside northwestern Chaffee and near a unique "rock island" landmark, but not too close to the busy interstate highway. The proximity of the historic crash site seemed to come into clearer focus on my next go-round

.

CHAPTER SIX

2014 Trips to Chaffee

"People said it was an 'outer space ship' that had crashed"

.In 2014 I again took a springtime journey across Missouri to Cape Girardeau, continuing my "quest for proof." It was a long drive and costs mounted. But once settled in town, I drove up to the William Huffman home on Main Street. I set my trip odometer and proceeded down that aging avenue to Broadway. From there I followed its westerly path leading to Highway 61, and headed south. These routes were the most obvious main avenues available in 1941 and happily are still around (mostly). I traveled down what was left of "Old 61" - as the highway is now called locally - to Chaffee via the first of two different routes available to access farmland outside of town, using Highway 74 to tiny Dutchtown and then down Highway 77, and also later utilizing Highway M, past that strangely large rock outcropping, into the heart of older parts of Chaffee. But in reality, going all the way into the city was not really the point. No one has said the UFO accident happened *in* that town, or in *any* town, but just *outside* Chaffee in the agricultural countryside. I wanted *north* of the city, and nearby Rockview, but research *within* Chaffee turned out to be helpful as well…

.Utilizing either of these very likely paths from the Huffman home to the existing farm sites "south of Cape, north of Chaffee" - the most likely crash locale - I discovered both were a perfect "10 to 15 miles" from the Huffman property, the description the Christian pastor/fund-raiser told his family in April of 1941. {In one interview it was described as "12 to 13 miles," still good.} I searched around as best I could with oncoming and tailing traffic bearing down. No great crash site was readily obvious as I drove around and around, in a kind of maze of flat farmland and thick clumps of trees here and there, followed by the developed outskirts of both Cape and Chaffee, commercial and residential areas which may not have been built by 1941.

.During some downtime on this trip to town I re-read a 1981 book by SEMO University physics professor Dr. Harley Rutledge, a man I met a couple of times in my Cape Girardeau days a decade after his publication was released. "*Project Identification*" had no mention at all of the MO41 incident, and according to one researcher, Harley had no knowledge of the affair, yet late in life he was suffering from Alzheimer's disease, which sadly took the college teacher's life in 2006. Thus it is not certain that he wasn't made aware at some point, and it simply passed from memory as he grew older. Remarkably, Harley described in his book leading in April 1973 his fellow astronomy buffs – including his son (whom I went to school with) and some students – to open fields outside of Cape Girardeau, for better nighttime viewing, away from reflective city lights. One particular favorite site turned out to be the very area of the 1941 UFO accident! Rutledge mentioned repeatedly setting up telescopes and other equipment in the grass of land alongside a state road not too far from the region's airport, which was technically not considered either "private property" or "trespassing," but public property.

In his book, Harley covered a considerable list of UFO sightings in the Chaffee and Cape Girardeau, and in other southern Missouri areas over the decades, including Cape newspaper accounts of a spate of unusual reports coming January of 1967. By '73 and '74, Harley was hooked, regularly readying for more UFOs via one or more teams set up near the few roads that lead to Chaffee, south of Cape. And at times, he was seeing and photographing some pretty strange and unexplainable lights, or glowing objects, some hovering and some streaking along at incredible speeds. Taking into account that at least some of these eye-catching lights were simply airplanes headed towards or from the airport, the majority of the reports Harley and his stargazing friends witnessed and described fit with the other stories of UFOs in Cape and Scott Counties I had heard or read of previously. But they did not fit in with the manmade aerial technology of the day. And the teams of astronomy lovers who found the streaking lights fascinating had ties to both Cape and Chaffee, Sikeston too. It was all so incredibly ironic they were scanning the skies for possible extraterrestrial activity in the very locale of the 1941 crash incident without ever knowing the saga, right where I was now driving and searching myself.

Just before, and for quite some time after this Chaffee trip, I had been discussing MO41 with a woman I met online. She lived in Chaffee – where she grew up – and worked in downtown Cape Girardeau. "Juanita" was a friendly, helpful soul who told me that when she was a little girl, her mother and grandmother used to mention the spaceship crash outside of town in a matter-of-fact manner, she recalled. The references tailed off a bit as Juanita became a teenager, interested in the usual adolescent issues. "I wish I had paid closer attention, and that they were here today to give us more information," sixtyish Juanita ruefully confessed to me. "But here's something else I've told almost no one. My husband and I were sitting on our porch at home one night and saw this amazing bright light, hanging in the sky, north of town. South of Cape Girardeau. West of the airport." A familiar location! Whatever this weird, shining object was, it apparently hovered in place right over – or very nearby - the site of the 1941 crash. "Then this *thing*, this *light*, flew east, not real fast, past the airport, towards Scott City. My husband and I were mesmerized. We stared, frozen in place. Unable to move for like twenty minutes, or more. I've never seen or experienced anything like it before." When did startling event this take place? "About a decade ago. Maybe 2003 or '04." I had no words in response. I didn't know what to say, or even what it meant, but there was the tantalizing possibility that what she described was a modern, truly extraterrestrial event that had something to do with checking up on the April 1941 incident location. Mother Nature just doesn't produce a slow-moving blaze of light that moves across farm country like this. Whatever it was, the object or lit creation wasn't subtle or keeping hidden, it had to have been quite visible to anyone nearby, including the staff, pilots, passengers, and visitors to the Cape Regional Airport that night.

.While touring slow-paced Chaffee, I spoke with a few residents; absorbed the sights and sounds of the rather sleepy business district; toured the even quieter suburban neighborhoods; and visited the local library for regional research. I found out some interesting tidbits, including the 1942 Chaffee high school yearbook, which included a final message for graduating seniors: "*Happy landings!*" Perhaps a mere coincidence, but a most fitting slogan after what took place near town the previous April. {The 1941 Chaffee school yearbook was not in the library's collection.}

.Another fascinating fact at the Chaffee public library drew my attention: a report on the spring 1940 tornado that tore through Chaffee. "Within the hour, auxiliary police forces from Cape Girardeau and Sikeston arrived to help" beleaguered citizens deal with the damage from the sudden and shocking storm, one story described. It certainly shows that in times of emergencies police-trained men from Cape knew how to get themselves assembled with needed equipment and arrive down south to help affected Chaffee *in less than an hour*. Much like the unforeseen but upcoming April '41 perceived "airplane crash" emergency, it would seem; perhaps the '40 tornado response became a template for the MO41 reaction. The information on the Chaffee twister also revealed that supplemental personnel from Sikeston could speedily pull themselves together and zip north to the hamlet within an hour as well, although these were police "auxiliary forces" and not the uniformed cadets from the Missouri Institute of Aeronautics situated at the Sikeston airport. "Auxiliary police" were part civil defense-trained citizens with some amount of military background, and part police-trained Cape area residents who wanted to help out in times of need, almost like a volunteer firefighting force. By the early 1950s, the number of auxiliary policemen in the Cape Girardeau area rose to over sixty, according to some additional online information provided, mentioned long ago by a familiar former top cop: Fred "Fritz" Schneider, a strong candidate for having shown up at the MO41 crash scene. {A check of Missouri Highway Patrol officers at the scene proved fruitless; records at Troop D Headquarters in Poplar Bluff, Missouri (the nearest station) do not go back to 1941 - as usual, but it also seems unlikely they'd have rushed to a farm's "airplane crash," just highway incidences.}

.While researching in the small town, I also wanted to know more at least about the Chaffee fire department, having seen a photo of a 1926 fire truck in the city's possession in the pages of another library book on local history. For certain the village maintained a small but working firefighting department; my library research showed that Chaffee had trained and utilized when needed a volunteer group also, one that had access to the town's fire truck. To try to learn more I zipped over to the current firehouse. Oddly - for the middle of a work week - the station featured a "CLOSED" sign on its window, with no one about. I vowed to look them up online instead, later and did, but in contacting them I received the same predictable results: "Sorry, we have no records left from the 1940s."

.As I looked around Chaffee, I could not help but notice not one but two different advertised locations for area Freemasons to gather. The first was a small, rundown house with a green road sign prominently featuring a Masonic symbol. This appeared to be the current fraternity "lodge," for likely a contemporary whittled-down Masonic membership, with local interest obviously fading badly since the 1940s. An older, two-story brick building downtown featured two very sizeable and eye-catching Masonic signs that once lit up a main avenue in the business district, beckoning a larger contingent of fraternal members back in the day. The structure now stood nearly empty and for sale. In theory, it might well have been a place that held some juicy, otherworldly secrets, but evidently was not officially in use until 1955. Where precisely the '41 meeting place was situated, I did not discover, but it certainly appears there were a substantial number of Chaffee secret society members back in the day, as was more in vogue everywhere in the country at the time.

.Next I intended to visit Chaffee's hospital, to see if they had any records of admittances or emergencies in April of 1941. Unfortunately I found out the town's small medical facility only opened in 1969, far too late for such helpful logs. I then vowed to try Cape's Southeast Missouri Hospital, where I was born. Perhaps *they* had some yellowing files on admittances in April of 1941. Before going to this expanding medical center in my old hometown, however, I visited with a relative who once worked there. "You should probably forget that," she informed me. "Hospitals are clamping down on releasing *any* sort of information on admittances and care, for fear of lawsuits. They will barely even tell you anything on patients when you phone them *today*, let alone release old records that might get them sued for Privacy Violation." I found through another hospital source - who once knew and worked with Garland Fronabarger, ironically - that 1940s paper records at the medical center were once again long since ditched and/or destroyed. Thus, another dead end.

.Through a friendly Chaffee librarian I learned of a local woman named Mary, whose late brother was once a Missouri state senator. Mary wasn't around for my visit, but arrived at the library just after I departed town. It turns out she was not familiar with MO41, but knew of a second crash involving the Sikeston MIA. This early '40s accident featured one of their training airplanes making a sudden crash-landing after problems arose on a routine flight. It came down on young Mary's family farm, apparently in the 1940s. When Mary came home from school that day, she recalled, she noticed many vehicles parked on the lane leading to her house. MIA personnel were present on the property, checking on the downed plane and its pilot who had been forced to make an abrupt landing on the soil near Morley, south of Chaffee, but was evidently unhurt. {Sometimes the MIA pilots utilized flat area farmland like this for practicing landings and then resumptions outside of their more controlled airport scenario, I learned from Linda L. Wallace; these "emergency touchdowns and takeoffs" prepared them for eventual difficult wartime conditions overseas, among other aviation lessons learned.}

.Mary's recollections didn't reveal a MO41 tale, but they did show that Sikeston MIA people were accustomed to flying over northern parts of Scott County and then driving to rural landing sites that made them perhaps far more familiar with the countryside and its roadways than I had originally figured. Thus they might well have been much more skilled at navigating their way from the Sikeston airport in the dark of night on unlit roads - initially Highway 61 - to the MO41 crash scene than I had first imagined. It was a small clue, and yet it fit well with the Huffman story, that not long after William made it to the MO41 scene and viewed the physical evidence and issued his prayers, the alerted military suddenly showed up to take over. Uniformed soldiers seemingly hustled fast to the site to accomplish this task and now such a described scenario seemed more plausible than ever.

.Through the helpful Chaffee librarian, I also learned of a local couple who lived just south of town. They were friendly old-timers who knew some local history and many fellow area citizens. I took down the couple's contact information and also talked to the librarian about the supposed major clue in the area that there is a remaining memorial of sorts to the MO41 crash victims. As I spoke, I turned and peered out a window. My eyes rested on a distant but noticeable sight. It was a large white cross, planted atop the hill that juts up over the city, rife with trees and undergrowth all around this noticeable monument. This obviously Christian *memorial* seemed to loom over the whole city. I was most surprised. Later I discovered the tall cross was erected by the woodsy property's owner, perhaps to express his religious faith. Or was it something much greater and more important to the community? The cross was deeded to the city to keep up after the owner's death.

But it sure seems to fit the bill in a general sense, seeing as how it was put up in the 1970s, a full "generation after" MO41, in accordance with the *Topix* "JustWondering" internet clue that described some sort of physical construct honoring the men who gathered to help that alien April night. Yet it is definitely not *at the site* of the crash, "wherever something tragic occurs," as the *Topix* forum writer put it initially, for the alleged memorial's location.

.A thought occurred to me as I scanned the local Chaffee area scenery: Charlette Mann also said she saw *grass* in the foreground of the alien photograph, along with the two trees. This would have meant that the ET was propped up (presumably close to its crashed ship) in some farmer's *yard*, not really out in their mostly-brown-dirt, recently-planted fields. So unless the alien was dragged across a field a long way from the crash site (unlikely), the right location had to have been pretty darn close to a local, now-aging farmhouse. Reinforcing this logic, I also recalled the cyberspace allegation by "AllSouls" from *Topix* that just after World War II a rain-collecting cistern was plugged into the debris-sprinkled ground near the impact location. Such metal rainwater tanks are installed down into an owner*'s lawn* near an existing structure, not dug into a crop or some distant uncultivated field. A cistern is also best utilized by catching *gutter and down-spout rainwater from a barn or house*. Thus once again the crash-landing was more likely to have taken place in a farm *yard*, than in a farm *field*. MO41 "ground zero" must have been quite near a wooden house whose owners and employees would have acted *very* quickly to get the resulting fire put out, lest they lose their abode and all their possessions. Perhaps their nearby barn, henhouse, and tool-shed too, depending upon the speed of the burn within the debris field. Should I thus be looking for a barn... or where a barn *used* to be?

.I recalled that "AllSouls" stated that the farmer's old barn that had stored metal crash debris had been torn down not too long ago, which probably led to a very barren patch in the rear of a compound where grass was possibly still unable to grow. As I drove I noticed that almost all the older homes still standing were made of wood, appearing small and faded, weather-beaten and outdated by today's architectural standards. Newer homes (and barns) were certainly present, clearly made of brick, stone, metals, and vinyl siding, obviously much finer and more modern, sturdy construction. This factor helped narrow my focus as well, but ultimately what I thought would be discovered so easily seemed to be beyond my grasp, at least for the present.

.That afternoon it was time to take a scheduled private tour of Cape Girardeau's downtown "River Heritage Museum," which was located in the city's former police and fire department headquarters. I discovered my paternal grandfather in a photograph in the building. The structure was where my grandfather - during his ten-year total tenure as City Attorney - occasionally visited with authorities on legal matters that shuttled and shuffled across his desk at City Hall offices. Grandpa undoubtedly rubbed shoulders at times with men who have been mentioned herein, first responders at the MO41 scene, whether he was told later about the incident or not. At the time of UFO accident, however, grandfather was in private practice at this 503 Broadway office in Cape, although apparently he was also at some point in 1941 a "U.S. Commissioner," a position akin to a judgeship in town. He was therefore unlikely to have been called to the scene at any time. He died in 1983 without, evidently, speaking of the crash to any family members.

.Although the museum was normally closed to the public on a Tuesday, the kindly guide gave me a brief tour of the building, indicating that most exhibits were pretty self-explanatory. I could see with my own eyes how small the structure was for containing both cops and firemen in 1941; there was almost no way for someone to have called in a report to one department and *not* have it overheard or learned of by the other department, the two forces of public servants were likely intermingling constantly as they passed the empty time between assigned duties. The upstairs was for the fire personnel – like Walter Reynolds - to utilize as living quarters, sometimes sliding down the stereotypical metal fire pole that was still firmly in place, or more mundanely taking the stairs. It also likely held communal meals and card games between the two departments.

.On display in the initial main room was a new "presidential exhibit." This was a display of articles and photos from press coverage of the handful of U.S. presidents who had once visited Cape Girardeau over the past one hundred and fifty years, albeit most either before or after they were in office. One example of this, to my surprise, was none other than Franklin Delano Roosevelt. And Eleanor too. They came to Cape on a train to campaign as FDR was a potential vice presidential candidate in 1920. The duo were escorted through downtown, then Franklin spoke (as Eleanor and aides watched) before a crowd on the hilltop Courthouse Park, overlooking the Mississippi River. This shows that FDR was at least somewhat familiar with the river city when he was sitting in the White House twenty years later, pondering MO41 and handling its discovery aftermath, whether by phone or Oval Office meetings with his military brass and governmental bureaucrats. As I viewed the display, I wondered if any of the Cape Girardeau contingent that showed up at the '41 UFO accident scene had also been around to actually meet and greet FDR when he had arrived in town two decades earlier. Somewhat possible, but unless you were a longtime veteran of the city police or fire departments, or involved in politics and government, then not too likely.

.Another exhibit claimed that in October of 1949 President Harry Truman campaigned in Cape Girardeau. I was quite surprised as I had never heard or seen that data before. Perhaps because it wasn't true. I contacted the museum later and they apologized, saying that the dating for the news article on Truman in the exhibit was incorrectly written down on the back of it as "1949, when it should be 1940." Ah-ha! That made Harry "just" a senator up for re-election back then, out stumping for Cape votes when he gave a campaign speech at the same university I would attend decades later. But indisputably accurate is a printed date on a mounted, yellowing old telegram at the museum. 1949. That's when *President* Truman made sure to contact Cape's mayor in this swift manner, to officially notify him of immediate funds being sent to help repair the city following the devastating tornado that damaged or destroyed many buildings, including the old wooden Red Star Tabernacle that Pastor Huffman worked in some years before.

.It came as a further museum surprise to me that *two* U.S. First Ladies visited Cape Girardeau in 1957. On April 11th - *very* close to the sixteenth anniversary of MO41 - President Eisenhower's wife Mamie visited the city. In October of that year, the late Franklin Roosevelt's widow, Eleanor, also stopped in town for a spell, to address the university's students and faculty. It would seem improbable that Mrs. Roosevelt learned about MO41 at the time, but one never knows, it is so shrouded in mystery and secrecy. This was of course her second trip (that I knew of) to and around the city, following the October, 1920, campaign visit. The two beloved and famous First Ladies' appearance in the same year in the seemingly obscure town seems to be a mere odd coincidence, as it was not even an election year. Still, I had no idea after so many years of living in Cape that such luminaries ever graced my hometown. I recalled that Eleanor Roosevelt had actually hosted an NBC television show in her widowhood. On one program she interviewed a military man who said he saw a strange metal flying disc, around 1950. Eleanor replied she had not much faith in most "UFO sightings" but found her guest's story fascinating. Her reply made me wonder if Mrs. Roosevelt was ever told about MO41 in the aftermath of that TV show. And had she ever been to Cape Girardeau besides 1920 and 1957, perhaps flying in under the radar (literally)? Local newshounds like Garland Fronabarger weren't *always* made aware of every dignitary gracing our community, and even if so such celebrities may have requested, or insisted, that their unannounced visits *not* be splashed across the pages of *The Southeast Missourian.*.

Around this time I was contacted by my aunt, who was living in Texas with her family. She never went by her actual first name, but my father's sister was named "Eleanor" after the First Lady in the 1930s. My paternal grandparents being New Deal Democrats revered the Roosevelt family during the Great Depression. Now my aunt had a special memory that surprised me. It seems when growing up in Cape Girardeau, *Missourian* photographer Fronabarger came by the Smith house on Bessie Street to visit my grandparents and his visiting first cousin, my grandfather's brother-in-law, Carl Fronabarger. Garland and Carl were like brothers, and when my aunt – then a small child – mentioned at one point in 1955 her interest in photography in front of the two mature men, Garland helpfully suggested she buy herself and use a handy small pocket-like camera, a Kodak "Brownie." The photos produced by this Kodak were scalloped-edge types, my aunt stated, just like the one that Reverend Huffman's granddaughter recalled. This all brings to mind very quickly the story of the unnamed local newsman – rumored to be "Frony" - who used a large flash camera at the MO41 crash site in April of 1941, then whipped out a smaller camera, which Charlette Huffman Mann specifically recalled in interviews as perhaps "a *Kodak Brownie.*" So it would seem that fourteen years after MO41, Garland was talking to my aunt from his own personal experiences with the little Brownie, it was clear. Hence G. D. Fronabarger remains to this day – now more than ever - the Number One Suspect for having been the camera bug who utilized a little Kodak like this for snapping the unusual-edged photograph of the dead alien, propped up by two men at the alien accident scene.

.I knew that my trip's scrutiny of the Chaffee area was woefully incomplete. I drove back there again the next day, but once more limited time and the seemingly unlimited number of farm candidates for the MO41 crash site made the journey nettlesome. I did not have the time to check on an area that was perhaps one third the size of the overall farmland encircling the small town, this stretch of property to its east, not far from the "old 61" and the current Highway 55. The unexplored section lay beyond that unusual tree-filled, cross-topped Chaffee hill; it was an agricultural area "west of Grammar" bordered by the interstate and Scott City to the northwest. I realized that on my next jaunt to the Chaffee area, I needed to gain access to this notable locale and be patient, for it was full of winding two-lane roads, aging farms, occasional forests, and huge swaths of crops, shown on *Google Earth* satellite maps online.

.During this particular spring trip to areas outside of Chaffee, I had ventured close to a particular farm property south of the town. It featured a nice wooden farm compound very near some railroad tracks. The front yard featured many religious icons, flowers, and a unique rock formation. It all reminded me that I had noticed this same property many times as a boy, being driven past, on the way south to a nearby small town where my mother worked as a school teacher for a quarter of a century. Was this eye-catching lawn memorial near the train tracks honoring MO41 victims? I decided not to rudely drop in unannounced and knock on their door but instead took down the address, snapped some photos, and vowed to write the owners when I got home. I did so, included a SASE, and waited. I heard nothing for months and simply forgot about it.

.By late spring of 2014, I received some unexpected visitors to my western Missouri home. It was the elderly couple of the house with the unusual rock outcropping and track-side memorial garden! This was a total surprise to me, but a fortuitous one. It turns out this was also the same longtime pair of locals who were recommended to me earlier by the helpful Chaffee librarian! A remarkable coincidence. They were now in *my* town and decided to swing by and respond to my letter in person. It turns out the wife - I'll call "Wendy" - actually knew my mother. Wendy was quite keen on telling me something: *she remembered hearing about the strange accident back in 1941,* and "it was not an airplane crash." What precisely landed abruptly in or near Scott County? "We didn't call it back then a "UFO." Or a "flying saucer." What people said was that it was "an outer space ship," that had "little people" on board, you know," Wendy assured me. That certainly got my attention, although her longtime husband mentioned he had not heard of story before my letter arrived. "I was ten years old in 1941, and I remember some folks talking about it," Wendy assured me. "I was told it crashed on a farm not too far away, between Chaffee and Cape Girardeau." This was precisely what an anonymous poster or two on *Topix* boldly described as the proper locale, too. But here was a rarity: an actual member of the community who vividly recalled the incident, its proper terminology at the time, and its general location that fit with other descriptions. Priceless!

.The spaceship crash was definitely an exciting topic back in '41 as it was very clear the dead beings were not from this world, but another, Wendy emphasized. The aging couple stated that they had been asking around in the past few months, talking to friends and relatives about the tale, but had not gotten a positive response - yet. They'd keep trying, since it obviously a subject that personally piqued Wendy's interest and memory banks. There were no further MO41 tidbits or details from this kindly couple, but this was certainly a pleasant surprise visit worth my time, and hopefully the sweet-natured married pair's too. It reinforced my desire to return to Chaffee sometime later in 2014. And that is what I did in mid-October, trying to narrow the search... which Mother Nature did for me, with a surprising amount of rain.

.In recalling the description by AllSouls on *Topix,* the phrase "my grandparents owned and farmed the land where the crash occurred" stuck in my mind as I explored in wet weather. *"Farmed the land"* was the key phrase, indicating the MO41 property was geared towards raising *crops,* not odoriferous animals for eventual slaughter. So now I was searching for a *pleasant-smelling* property that featured a torn-down barn, an aging cistern near a house, maybe only a few trees in the yard, and cropland beyond, with no herds of noticeably smelly animals about. More of a "mom and pop operation," not a big, smelly, industrial-sized agri-business, which were around, here and there, in the area.

.While in Scott County, I roamed through the public cemeteries in some tiny towns, in search of any "memorial" to MO41 participants or clue to the ET event. Nothing really caught my attention. I stopped again at the Chaffee Public Library and did a little more historical research, then went on my way, still soaked by the continual obnoxious light rain and unusually cold breeze for mid-October. Conditions were becoming an increasing problem for the ground search.

.When back in Cape I took the time to tour various "*Gone Girl*" film locations, including the downtown courthouse park where my kin - and FDR - also once roamed. This was where a key set of scenes in the Ben Affleck movie were shot a year ago or more. Inspired, I went to the see the motion picture for the first time, aired at the local theater where it had its Cape Girardeau premiere just ten days earlier. Decorations from that gala were still in place in the lobby. I remembered this was the Wehrenberg Theater that had replaced the one where I used to work when I was a local college student, so long ago. It was strange to see some familiar Cape scenery in the movie, which didn't always highlight the finest parts of the city, unfortunately. Overall it seemed to be a well-made R-rated movie for adults, despite a rather slow first half-hour and a somewhat unsatisfying, ragged ending, which I hoped would leave things open for a sequel someday. Naturally one that would return the cast and crew to my old hometown for more filming, thus producing more revenue for the city and fame as well. But I had other ideas for fame for my town. If only I could dig up some actual proof of MO41, on the "target farm." I could then inject another side of world attention and public tourism for Cape Girardeau and perhaps the Chaffee countryside – which folks there may or may *not* desire. Not everyone, or every public enterprise, wants attention, especially from curious UFO hunters, I realized.

.I pondered the special technology that was created in the secret Cape Girardeau WWII factory downtown, so I took the time to take a gander at that locale during this trip. Surely that hush-hush work had nothing to do with the local alien accident, um, right? Some of the amazing alien technology from the MO41 crash *was* explored within the completed television program that aired in 2014, *"Hangar 1: The UFO Files"* episode "EO3: Alien Technology." While they did not really give new details, MUFON made the bold and surprising claim that successful behind-the-scenes reverse engineering of the MO41 alien artifacts led to "the greatest leap forward in technology" in man's history, mostly through advances in the field of "transistors," not "resistors." How was this achieved? Supposedly by funneling some of the ET technology recovered in Missouri to - of all people - "a Purdue University grad student."

.Based out of western Indiana, north of Indianapolis, Purdue has always been a very respected college with some highly skilled graduates, but why in the world would the secretive United States government give one or two 1940s college graduate students there the most critical and sensitive materials ever found? According to the *"Hangar 1"* program, a government official – perhaps a Purdue grad? - simply gave it to the prime Purdue source by telling him "It was from an unnamed foreign government" with a "see what you can make of this" attitude. No documents, proof, background, or interviews with anyone involved in this Purdue contention were aired. Still, the History2 Channel program clung to its daring statement that "the 1941 Cape Girardeau crash was Ground Zero" for America's "technological boom" of the last seven decades.

.Thanks to the pouring rain outside, substantially marring my trip, I had time to ponder. What could have been another, more believable, more logical site for scientifically examining the technology culled from the wreckage? Certainly it was scrutinized in Washington D.C. by Dr. Vannevar Bush and his "Non-Terrestrial Science and Technology Committee," but *where*, precisely? Around this time I reviewed my copy of the 1997 book *"The Day After Roswell,"* co-authored by Colonel Phillip Corso. While I kept in mind there were said to be many factual errors in the text (and the story veered off into some pedantic areas at times), the book presented some very interesting nuggets of information for MO41 fans.

.Colonel Corso's tome mentioned a few times the ongoing rumors that the U.S. Army and Air Force were fiercely and secretly holding onto *other* crashed ET discs in some well-guarded military bases around the country, besides New Mexico laboratories and Wright-Patterson AFB in Ohio (in the 1940s, "Wright Field"). An Army facility in the Beltway was of particular great interest: Fort Belvoir, in the D.C. area. It *may* remain to this day a great key to unlocking the government's shuttering of the alien visitation truth.

.Fort Belvoir was "the Army's most important base in the entire Washington Military District," Corso explained, adding "it was where some of the army's most top-notch research into UFO technology" was undertaken. Belvoir naturally housed the Army Engineering School and some testing labs and outdoor sites for new weapons. It also featured a training school for National Security Council officers, plus "an elite Air Force unit." One that was well-trained in quickly and quietly responding to reports of crash-landed non-terrestrial vehicles and entities. Was this unit created because of MO41? Was this General Marshall's "Interplanetary Phenomenon Unit"?

.Beyond even all this, Phil Corso tantalized, Fort Belvoir was a top secret facility for the storage and examination of highly classified records and files of many (perhaps all) recovered alien hardware and bodies, "including photos and even motion pictures." These cosmic goodies were "closely guarded secrets while the facility remained shrouded in mystery," author Corso claimed, having admitted to actually visiting the base several times over the course of the mid-twentieth century. According to Colonel Corso, *an*

office for the "Office of Scientific Research &
Development" (Van Bush's team) was created within the
confines of Fort Belvoir (and now we know why). Bazinga!
Therefore Fort Belvoir would have been *the* next logical
place – after the "dungeon" under the Capitol Building - to
stash these stunning goods for secure classified filming and
photograph purposes; lab-controlled scrutiny and
experiments; visiting military and governmental
observation; and still other reasons, all during the 1941/'42
time-frame. Fort Belvoir would have been a fairly covert,
convenient locale for Roosevelt, Marshall, Bush, and other
chosen leaders and academia too, to slip in and look
otherworldly things over with no fanfare, either the
physical evidence itself or the files thereof. But that does
not mean it held *all* of the technology, of course…

I knew that some investigative U.S. authors had written
about the rumors and allegations of captured UFOs being
examined and back-engineered over the decades at Wright-
Patterson AFB. As home of the "Air Material Command,"
it saw a great, sudden explosion of growth on their property
from the time of MO41 going forward. The airfield went
from thirty buildings to *three hundred*, and *fast*, with all
new offices, laboratories, hangars, and test facilities,
according to Linda Wallace's research. The great question
then arises: why did the United States government and
military take the time and money to design and construct
these secret high-tech facilities where captured alien
materials were apparently brought *in the years just after
1941, but before Roswell in '47?* Obviously some serious
funding requests; general plans; architectural designs; high-
tech machinery; trusted base guards, employees, and
construction workers; and general operations had to have
been put together for quite some time leading up to the
mid-'45 opening of the airfield's grand new off-limits
facility. And certainly any strange, unfathomable alien
hardware and technology from Missouri needed a proper,

well-guarded, more permanent home in the late 1940s, possibly one with an airfield to test reverse engineering resulting from it. MO41 technology turned into secret manmade aerial and weapons projects required a more deliberate and encompassing understanding by trained, highly-educated experts dedicated to defending America with whatever means necessary. These needs would require the American Air Corps' AMC to create a special "Foreign Technology Division" *and* a secret UFO study facility. Supposedly some former Nazi scientists also ended up in New Mexico, the other major site of so many other recovered UFO examinations and reverse-engineering rumors. Now to be fair, certainly the ex-Nazis ended up also working on mere U.S. rocket and airplane technology, not just helping to reconfigure highly classified, advanced alien hardware in great secrecy.

.The Wright-Patterson "Foreign Technology Division," that was allegedly the source of leaked extraterrestrial images used in a controversial 1988 television special called "*UFO Cover-up - Live.*" I remembered watching that show. It was hosted by M*A*S*H* co-star Mike Farrell. The unusual syndicated production claimed to have inside government intelligence on recovered aliens and their crafts. Criticism and debate followed the show, but no one could argue that its most remarkable feature was the FTD visual graphics, leaked, of an allegedly recovered deceased alien creature. This "Grey" was supposedly pulled from a crashed ET disc, apparently in the 1940s. Some of the twenty grey alien designs utilized on the program were early computer graphics (concocted in the late 1970s), and others were merely artist illustrations, and most featured serial numbers supposedly from the actual filing system of the secret Wright-Patterson facilities mentioned herein. Still featured nowadays on some UFO web sites, the W-P FTD images and background info seems to fit perfectly with the MO41 ET descriptions we've learned.

.A large, hairless gray skull with a big brain and jumbo black eyes yet no ears. Long thin arms, torso, and legs. Three long fingers on each hand and a long thumb. A simple set of inner organs with no great digestive excretion area or gender identity the 1988 TV show aired the eye-catching display in a more three-dimensional format than what a book or website photo can show. Allegedly, the dead extraterrestrial cadavers were said to have been kept at the Ohio airbase until the early 1980s, autopsied and inspected at great length. This process allegedly revealed that a sample alien's lungs and heart functioned *as one organ*, as well as its kidney and bladder as a single organ too. It also supposedly gave off a distinct "burnt rubber smell" that might indicate it excreted its waste matter through its skin. *Thus the little alien pilots would have been perfect for space flights, with no need to make trips to the bathroom!* Apparently the W-P secret studies found that one "grey" was identical to the next, just as Reverend William Huffman said he saw close up. As if they came out of a mold, or a cookie-cutter. Thanks to the investigative staff behind that 1988 special, we may well have discovered fascinating, very relevant information about the very foreign beings who landed in a heap on a quiet farm outside Cape Girardeau, formerly kept secret by the American government.

As the rain continued the next day, limiting my Cape Girardeau/Chaffee research tour, I learned more by simply reviewing Ryan Wood's marvelous book "*Majik: Eyes Only.*" Information within on American intel operative Tom Cantwheel helped; the ex-CIA and Army CIC man reasonably claimed before he died near 2000 that the Missouri (and Louisiana) spacecraft recoveries were controlled by the U.S. Army and studied intensely behind the scenes in the 1940s by American and imported German scientists, at Kirtland AFB and Alamagordo AFB, plus Wright Field. The special designs and technologies taken from MO41 were applied into a new "S" craft, Cantwheel explained, a manmade disc mockup, a flawed round spacecraft with human pilots, one that could achieve noteworthy speeds and heights in altitude. This "reconstruction commenced in 1945," elderly Cantwheel explained; likely this was done with fading President Roosevelt's approval and excited interest. Sadly, in the next two years the highly classified secret program struggled due to lack of funding (which had to be artfully explained to congress during wartime). Plus whenever the finished result was flown in great privacy, pilots proved prone to illness and even death from decompression and radiation while inside the cobbled craft. Mr. Cantwheel's claim dovetails neatly with the 1947 "White Hot Report" mention of just such a hybrid project which was eventually scrapped altogether.

This all raises the question of what curious aliens – very similar to the MO41 recoveries – were doing in the New Mexico skies, when they came crashing to earth again, in early July of '47. This was during the period of the "S" craft testing, the new manmade-alien technology of the day. *Were extraterrestrials eager to check on the S-craft's ongoing test flights in the remote, restricted desert?* It had their own hardware, "ripped off." One hot summer night, a violent thunderstorm hit the area and not long after, in the light of the calm next day or two, at least two UFO crash sites were discovered on the hot desert floor, many miles apart. They were soon seized upon by the Army, who sent in their teams that seemed to know just what to do. Trained by the template in Cape Girardeau six years earlier? Did they realize that one ET crash somewhat led to another? As fate would have it, '41 got hushed effectively while '47 got the publicity and worldwide fame that sticks to this day, fairly or not.

UFO investigators have since traced data that showed that some material collected from the '47 crash was flown to Dayton's Wright Field, plus Los Alamos labs, while some flights *to* Roswell's AFB imported special Army units from Albuquerque's Kirtland AFB. Back in the '40s, there seemed to be both a commercial and military air route between Dayton and Albuquerque, the two entities combining for maximum wartime effectiveness (see Chapter Nine).

.After the Roosevelt/Truman years, it seems obvious newly-minted U.S. intelligence operatives expanded their operations and dug into what the military was doing with the recovered wreckage and technology. There have been all kinds of claims made over the past decades about what the Central Intelligence Agency - created by Truman in '47 - found out about the subject. One example of what might well be the truth - at least as of the 1960s and early '70s - comes from Victor Marchetti, who once worked as an assistant for CIA Director Richard Helms. According to Marchetti, summing up his CIA tenure's in-house otherworldly whispers: "There were rumors {sic} of little grey men whose ships had crashed." That extraterrestrials are quite real and quietly observing first-hand our troubled planet. And that "the U.S. government, in collusion with other national powers of the Earth, is determined to keep this information from the public." Once more, this sounds like a very accurate but general description of the overall MO41 affair, and some other UFO crash cases. It made me wonder if there was one single scrap of alien metal left in the soil I was determined to pinpoint and dig up; had the military and intelligence agencies already been back to the Missouri crash site farm long ago to extract all leftover pieces of proof?

.Not being the most high-tech person in the world, I returned my focus to the ground search outside of Chaffee, the surprising amount of rain having at last moved on but time was running out. It was unfortunately now a "mud search." What a mess. I had a job to go back to soon, across the state. Just looking around now while driving, with vehicles roaring past or up from behind on puddle-filled rural roads... and impatient drivers glaring or even honking as crops and farms tended to blur together... well, it wasn't the fun, sun-drenched, and glamorous "history in the making" I had envisioned for this trip. After all my in-person 2014 investigations, of all the roads I took in all kinds of weather, I only drove down a dead end in a figurative sense, a little sadder, poorer, but wiser. "Maybe next year," was my motto. If only I had paid more attention to that unusual rural "tree-topped outcrop." The virtual "rock island" strangely popping up in the middle of flat area farmland, just north of tiny Rockview and Chaffee. I had passed it repeatedly, last year and this year. It stuck out like a sore thumb, topped with lush trees and thick brush, towering over the landscape, southwest of Cape and its airport. The maps call this isle of rock "Lost Hill." This remarkable anomaly turned out to be a significant clue later on...

CHAPTER SEVEN

2015: Carl's Recollections

"The nurses went white with fright because they had never seen anything like it before."

. In the spring of 2015, I determined to drive back to my old hometown of Cape Girardeau once more for a little "searchin' and researchin'," and also again to nearby Chaffee, a town and surrounding countryside I was not satisfied that I was familiar enough with. I prepared for another road trip across the state. Just before my departure, a surprising e-mailed nugget of supportive new information came rolling in.

. What arrived was from a man named Carl Armstrong, a longtime Cape Girardeau citizen with substantial interest in UFOs and the MO41 tale in particular, understandably. Carl had recently written to *The Southeast Missourian* and urged them to create a rundown of the long-ago MO41 affair for their sister publication, one that specialized in age-oriented information for senior citizens. After all, he had a small but wild-sounding clue to add to the 1941 episode, and was curious if anyone from any era would respond to such a proposed article with further information. Unfortunately the publication's editor turned Mr. Armstrong down.

. According to Carl, he had recently watched the History Channel program *"Hangar 1: Alien Technology"* with its early-on mentions of Cape Girardeau and MO41. This brought to Carl's mind something his own sister Olive had told him many years ago. It turns out married Olive lived in a Cape Girardeau house that boarded a respected area school teacher, to help bring in extra income. That bachelor educator's name was Herb Schaper, and he worked at the small Cape Girardeau building on Bloomfield Road called Campster School. This site will take on greater meaning later in our story.

. It seems Herbert Alvin Schaper (1908-1997) was friends with some nurses at one of the two Cape Girardeau city hospitals in 1941 (not sure which). Herb may have become familiar with these women due his polio condition, which affected an arm and a leg. These healthcare professionals had supposedly once told Herb an alarming tale of being on their shift at the medical facility "where some of the entities were brought in" from some sort of crash just outside of town. Whether the "strange-looking bodies" were dead or not, Carl did not say. However, by referring to them as "bodies," instead of "patients" or "survivors," we can safely infer the unusual unearthly creatures were dead. They had been imported from the crash site and evidently required scrutiny - or even possible revival efforts? - by trained medical personnel.

. What made this even more memorable for Olive, and later for Carl, Herb supposedly told her how remarkably surprised and even *staggered* some of the female hospital staffers had been that night. "The nurses went white with fright," Herb recollected to Olive - or so Carl recollected to me via e-mail - "because they had never seen anything like it before." A very human reaction, a very believable little story. Yet it seems somewhat inaccurate and puzzling in some aspects of MO41 with what we now know. Or what we *think* we know at this point

. If Carl Armstrong's claim of Mr. Schaper's story is to be believed at face value, then we must ask if the deceased MO41 alien victims had really been scooped up - by *whom*? - and carted across the community to a Cape Girardeau hospital. And if so, *why*? They were clearly dead at the scene, perhaps upon impact, at least in the now-legendary William Huffman account, and seemingly implied in Armstrong's claim. This created another problem within the overall storyline. *Why bother to rush dead bodies to a medical facility?* Especially if the Army had arrived at the accident scene by then, taking over with a warning of silence for all. An alleged trip to any area hospital would have led to all sorts of eyewitnesses, admittance documentation, and flying local gossip, anyone in charge of the rural crash scene surely would have realized. If the United States Army was truly in command and wanted to make sure no one knew about the bizarre accident, they would likely not have allowed the nonhuman creatures to be rushed by responding Cape medics to a hospital, nor anywhere else.

. Furthermore, Reverend Huffman apparently did not specifically recall - nor did Floy Huffman or Charlette Mann - any medical contingent on the MO41 scene, although William did say there was a small crowd of various citizens there, staring at the crash and its blaze. In his granddaughter's retelling, Pastor Huffman said that just after he finished his prayers over the dead bodies, the uniformed soldiers arrived and hemmed in the mixture of slack-jawed onlookers and well-intentioned responders. They warned all to keep quiet and swore the preacher to silence. So Huffman left, the dead aliens still on the ground, flat on their backs in the grass.

. A follow-up e-mail by a relative of Carl Armstrong stated that Olive recalled hearing that the general directive "*what you see here stays here*" was firmly declared by authorities regarding the stunning finds. This reinforces the notion that the bodies stayed right there at the farm until the army members swept them away and back to their base. However, this could well mean that when the nurses returned "empty-handed" to their hospital that night, they were still shaken and pale, with at least one or more excitedly telling Herb Schaper there what just occurred, quite naturally dumbfounded by what they just experienced outside of town. It was *history*, something no American had *ever* laid eyes on before, or even daydreamed of, quite likely. Now the emotional nurses were part of it, maybe even quite proud of their role as eyewitnesses. No one was going to keep them *all* completely quiet.

. We know that the fiery crash produced an emergency response by the Cape Girardeau police and fire departments. They felt sure (originally) that an airplane had gone down and its passengers were likely in bad shape. It would have made perfect sense therefore to have notified one or both of the city's two hospitals. The most likely medical facility notified would have been the newer and perhaps better equipped Southeast Missouri Hospital. It was smaller in those days but closer to the main highway (61) than Cape's other hospital, and perhaps better known to cops in terms of medical personnel. The other Cape Girardeau health facility was the older, Catholic-based hospital, St. Francis, near downtown. If a Southern Baptist preacher like Huffman was imported by a police associate to the crash scene, then it makes sense for the local authorities to have chosen the non-Catholic hospital for an urgent care team, especially if they were going to send a vehicle over to pick victims up. If a Catholic first-responder was involved – perhaps even the town's Catholic mayor, W. H. Statler – then possibly a priest was also called upon to go and deliver the last rites, whether Pastor Huffman knew of this or not. And if so, then maybe St. Francis Hospital was notified after all. The Catholic hospital *could* have sent a medical team and a priest with nuns at some point, full of mercy and compassion, SEMO Hospital notwithstanding. Certainly in those days doctors *did* make "house calls," and this would have been a doozy.

. This new story would make much more sense if educator Herb Schaper had stated that he had actually *seen* the noticeably blanched, rattled Cape nurses simply reacting in such a manner back *at* the hospital *afterwards*, the women actually having returned *from* the crash scene with only memories. In this speculated, slight revision of Carl's e-mail message, *the bodies were not brought to the nurses, in reality, but the nurses were brought to the bodies.* Such a scenario would mean that in the many retellings of the '41 tale, over and over and over as the decades passed, a small fact in the chain of events got mixed up, quite understandably. The *hospital* didn't review the bodies, only the hospital *nurses* at the site did, and they reacted later with such tremendous emotions that Mr. Schaper either saw this, or perhaps heard about the strong reactions afterwards at the medical facility. It's possible a little was "lost in translation" or re-telling the tale.

. No one has produced any record at all of any aliens being lugged into either Southeast Missouri Hospital, or St. Francis Hospital, both still in operation in Cape Girardeau today. And there is no other corroborating other account of MO41 where the ETs were whisked away by the army or police/fire departments to the hospital, or by other crash site witnesses before the army arrived on the crash scene. Unfortunately, there's still another problem with Carl's claim. He recalled Olive Keller mentioning Herbert Schaper's description of the nurses' excited talk about the location of the crash site, pinpointing it as "out near County

Park." That's a few miles *north* of Cape Girardeau, not south, where so many other indicators are pointing. Could it be that this tidbit of information also got slightly altered over the years? A bit of a UFO buff by nature, helpful Carl stated to me that he knows some of the farmers in this Cape County Park area, and yet has never spoken to them about the crash, nor heard from them that there ever was such a major, unforgettable UFO incident on their land. And evidently Mr. Armstrong never discovered the exact crash-landing site there, either. What's even more frustrating, Carl related to me that his sister Olive is still alive as a possible source of further details, but now unfortunately suffers from Alzheimer's Disease, her mind often unable to recall much of anything with reliable clarity. But he assured me she related the hearsay information to him *decades* ago, as a young woman. And Olive's son confirmed this, relating in an e-mail that she told the same tale to her two kids many years ago as well.

. Yes, the "white-with-fright nurse tale" is pure gossip, handed down and filtered through generations, a little troubled, seemingly. But *sometimes gossip turns out to be true*. Or at least partly true. The surprising Olive Keller saga is certainly compelling and another slice of possibly true-life events in Cape Girardeau in 1941.

. In recalling the tale recently in an e-mail to me, Olive's son added that she used to speak to her family about *Missourian* reporter/photographer Garland Fronabarger being *at the MO41 scene that night*. Frony again! "He took pictures of the bodies and was sworn to secrecy afterwards," Terry said he and his sister remembered Olive mentioning long ago of MO41 details. I asked how they could be sure G. D. Fronabarger was involved in the crash first response. The male offspring simply replied: "I don't know how Olive found out about the Fronabarger side of the story." This small clue, however, can lead us to believe that either Olive Keller had heard about the crash from more than one source, possibly ol' Frony himself, or that one or more of the nurses really *were* imported *to* the crash location where they personally eyeballed Garland Fronabarger, working his Speed Graphic camera craft. After all, how would some pale, genuinely scared nurses in a hospital, repulsed by the strange, lifeless aliens, know that Frony was at the tragic site, taking pictures? Somehow a nurse who had been in the know on this important detail was able to tell Herb who told Olive, evidently, sounding very much like a nurse who was called to the scene, watching G. D. Fronabarger work the site, notepad and cameras in hand. Also, from the description of "bodies" at the scene we can again assume the extraterrestrial visitors were all *dead.*

. "The general location was thought to be the county farm area," outside of Cape Girardeau, Mr. Armstrong reiterated. Now I was mildly confused. Earlier Carl had said "County Park." Now he was saying it took place near the "County Farm." However, a little more research showed that during the Depression era Cape County Park was formed out of the County Farm, which was also known as "the Poor Farm." There weren't anywhere close to where I had been looking, to where all of the previous clues to the crash site were pointing to.

. In looking over Carl's north-of-Cape area on a modern Google aerial computer map, I noticed there are very few contemporary farms in this vicinity. Some property was developed as County Park land, and others for suburban sprawl. Still other parcels remained undeveloped, covered as they were then and now in thick woods, with a lake and an Elk's Club (private property). Nothing much stands out as a strong possibility for an "alternate site" for MO41.

. While I briefly toured the general locale that Carl had mentioned, I also kept driving around in the south-of-Cape area, searching, map-checking, and ultimately finding nothing that deserved closer scrutiny, frankly. My ground search was going nowhere but in circles. {"Crop circles," in a sense!}

. Many months after all of this new crash data was exchanged and pondered, Carl surprised me even further with another startling claim. "Did you hear about the UFO that came down to land not far from the Campster School? A safe landing, this time. This was probably years after the '41 crash," Mr. Armstrong wrote in an e-mail in March of 2016.

. WOW. *What's this?*

. "It landed and was seen by people in the Campster School area. Aliens stepped out of the craft. They walked around in a field for a while, then got back in and took off." The alleged incident was so substantial, my source alleged, that the Cape Girardeau police were involved, holding back a growing crowd of curious onlookers at or near the Campster School, before the strange visitors took flight. All accounts of this were cautiously squelched, Armstrong assured me, so that the local radio station and newspaper could not record or air it publicly. Presumably the staggering incident was quashed by the police, the army, or worried local officials. Or all three.

. This fresh, enigmatic tale had actually been told to him by a Cape Girardeau friend, Carl said, but Mr. Armstrong had just related quite an astonishing tale, something that seemed pretty outlandish on the surface. Campster School was just a small, two-room schoolhouse. It was originally built a few years before the Civil War, then torn down and rebuilt beautifully with stone in 1940, with just a couple dozen students at most. Carl assured me that his source told him that eventually the amazed crowd numbered in the *hundreds*, observing with fascination the aliens doing something out in the lush pasture. How could such a big crowd view such a shocking otherworldly event and later every single one of them remained quiet? Or took no photos or home movies of the incident? Even in later decades, in a more open-minded American culture, media, and society... *no one* wrote this down and mailed it in anonymously to *any* mass media source since the occurrence?

. This was a whole new drama to me, a real surprise. It was frankly difficult to swallow and believe, and there was apparently not a shred of proof to back it up. Bloomfield Road runs north and south where it cuts through the distinctive, recently-developed Houck Woods neighborhoods in southwestern Cape Girardeau. Today, the simple, aging Campster School building is a private home at the northern stretch of this road, and perhaps two miles further south along this locally-famous road there were sites that would take on added significance in MO41's astonishing drama (see next chapter). Could this second landing saga – if true – have been "car trouble"? That is, more technical or mechanical difficulties for alien visitors to the Cape Girardeau area? Or have involved a vehicular *crash* of some sort, like MO41? Or an assault upon the ET craft, either by a manmade jet fighter, or another extraterrestrial presence?

In working the internet during this time, I found worldwide lists of UFO crashes from the past century, so many of them seemingly obscure and based on rather sketchy rumors and fragile eyewitness accounts, or perhaps even downright fabrications. But one in particular caught my eye and seems worth mentioning here. It is the intriguing "Zelyony Island" UFO crash, in western Russia. In this saga, alleged eyewitness accounts claimed that a kind of "aerial dogfight" was going on in the sky, where one silvery, gravity-defying alien spaceship "zapped" or "shot down" a second. And that one of the cyberspace accounts for this claimed crash-landing stated that it took place in mid-April 1941, in fact just *days* after the MO41 affair!

.According to further but unproven online claims, Zelyony Island was the site where the "losing" UFO came crashing down in an undeveloped area rife with trees, brush, and rich riverbed sentiment (sounding much like the Cape Girardeau/Mississippi River area). Zelyony is in fact a brushy island in the middle of the "Rostov-on-Don" river area, not too far from the Ukrainian border. Today it is more developed, the surrounding city boasting more than a million citizens, yet some Zelyony areas are still left alone as they allegedly contain strange radiation, "rare and abnormal chemicals," and a weird "vibe" for the lack of a better term. Supposedly, *some* people who enter this possible UFO crash area suffer a kind of "spatial disorientation." Also, some stories claim plant growth has clearly accelerated here also.

.If around April 20th, 1941, or so, an alien "showdown" really did occur and one race's wingless and saucer-shaped airship was left to burn and its crew die on planet Earth in Russia, *could something like this have also taken place in the Cape Girardeau river area?* Did such a possible sunset "cosmic clash" leave one or *two* ET ships crippled and crashed both north and south of Cape? And was the Russian incident even a kind of "revenge grudge match" for MO41? Was it all coincidence that these two wild UFO affairs took place near large rivers in nations not yet involved in World War II fighting? {Russia would be very soon, when Nazi Germany attacked in June and even took over the Rostov-on-Don area for a week later in 1941 and then again for seven months in '42/'43.} And did this Russian UFO crash incident spark the communication by Greys, in secret talks with Soviet intelligence operatives?

This is where a possible Soviet Union connection to MO41 gets even wilder…

Perhaps being a latecomer, it wasn't until around this time in April of 2015 that I stumbled upon someone named "Skinny Bob" on *YouTube*. Four years previously this month, well, that was the seventieth anniversary of MO41 and also when the big-headed "Greys" suddenly appeared – some alive, some dead – within amazing old images now on the internet. Again I was most surprised, not having even *heard* of this video before. "Skinny Bob" was the nickname someone gave a rather friendly extraterrestrial "person" in the astounding video, and it stuck. The fascinating footage was uploaded to *YouTube* by an anonymous and mysterious source, quickly creating many tens of thousands of hits. The Skinny Bob "viral video" event occurred just a few days after the latest batch of the world famous, controversial *"Wiki-Leaks"* materials appeared. Those were the once-classified information packages unleashed by anti-secrecy campaigner Julian Assange, the controversial Australian activist/writer turned computer hacker/leaker. Assange had warned in interviews as of late 2010 that some startling classified government files from select countries *containing UFO information* were going to be leaked in the near future, and on April 13th, 2011, the world may well have seen the results. And it was quite a revelation, all right. I was just now stumbling upon it. The timing was excellent from various standpoints.

"Skinny Bob" to me and many others seemed pretty darn real, not "CGI" fakery. An apparent living, breathing, somehow-communicating alien, allegedly one of a few non-terrestrial visitors in covert sustained interaction with Russia's Soviet government. This delicate behind-the-scenes process allegedly began in or near 1942, just a year or so after the stupefying Cape Girardeau incident (and about the same time as the creation of the U.S. Army's special "Interplanetary Phenomenon Unit"). Therefore *it is very possible that just after the MO41 and Zelyony events in 1941, historic "first contact" was somehow arranged, but wasn't secretly filmed by the devious KGB until the following year.* Limited secret meetings and private communications supposedly took place on occasion from '42 to '69, between some representatives of the visiting grey-skinned ET species and a select few high-ranking Soviet intelligence officers. The filmed results available on *YouTube* remain for all to witness to this day, rather mindboggling and exciting to behold, yet frustratingly brief. It *may* at last be *real proof* of this race of inquisitive visitors who crashed in Missouri and New Mexico and likely other sites in America, plus various locales around the world (like Russia) over the past decades, maybe longer.

.What was posted online in 2011, more precisely, was grainy film footage featuring an old KGB logo; some relevant information on the circumstances involved; a ticking digital clock of film recording time; and shockingly bold but brief images of an extraterrestrial in a kind of flight suit, seated in a chair, moving his arms and head around, *fitting our MO41 ET profile nearly perfectly.* Just like Reverend Huffman and Charlette Mann said: "Bob" had long thin arms and legs; three fingers and a thumb on each hand; a big bulbous head with large black eyes; and grey hairless skin. The video clips certainly *look* authentic, even the most hardened skeptic would admit. But is it? Computer-Generated Imagery, made by talented Hollywood-based film experts, could conceivably produce such a series of clips, but only at great cost. Why would anyone bother to burn through a ton of money to concoct such tantalizing but fake images? For what profit? No one has ever come forward to admit they were the guilty party who created such a fantasy for cyberspace public viewing. No one has duplicated the amazing imagery, either. And no one has seemingly earned a penny from the very public uploading of the file.

.The calm *YouTube* non-terrestrial was, as mentioned, allegedly *secretly* filmed at first, according to the online originator Ivan0135's notations, then in a later session he (or another similar identical ET creature) *knowingly* poses for the camera. "Skinny Bob" was allegedly involved in sporadic private contact under a mutually signed treaty, according to the video's background information provided. He appears to be seated in a chair and then inspecting something off-camera that requires leaning forward and moving his arms and head to examine. His eyes blink, and at one point his forehead pulses a bit. The human-like entity later almost seems to calmly and patiently *smile* for us.

.*If* the surprising film footage is genuine and the Russians actually sustained communicative contact from 1942 forward, it leads to some troubling questions. Were any of these supposed secret ET-USSR exchanges in any way a reaction to USA's MO41 affair and its hushed aftermath ordered by FDR? If so, why? Why were these bold extraterrestrials making congenial contact with an oppressive communist nation led by despotic dictator Joseph Stalin? Were other nations, friendly and unfriendly alike, also quietly contacted in the early '40s, or beyond? And just what happened to these daring, communicative aliens? And of their Russian intel handlers? Where is the highly compartmentalized old KGB file nowadays, to help prove this amazing allegement? And where's the rest of the footage promised by "Ivan0135"? And how was it swiped or copied in the first place? Of course we'll likely never know the answers to these important questions   unless someone comes through again with even more shocking, leaked government files and footage in the future.

.In returning to the Zelyony incident, there are further spooky parallels to the MO41 saga. Allegedly the Russian army rolled into the crash scene to hush surprised first responders and crash witnesses that night. The determined soldiers scooped up all the debris and hauled the load away to first nearby Rostov, and then to their nations' capitol (Moscow). {Although some say it eventually ended up in "Kapustin Yar," the "Area 51" of the Soviet Union.} The crash recoveries were then scrutinized by top Soviet scientists under great secrecy. Sound familiar? Also, people were supposedly ordered *not* to enter the crash area for quite some time, and local legends sprang up, about strange noises and behavior going on within the forbidden accident site. To this day, some people call the crash scene "an evil place," but contemporary UFO tours still take brave folks into the mysterious zone nowadays, becoming a bit of a tourist industry, which makes one suspect certain aspects of the lore. Is its reputation being inflated in order to bring in tour groups and exploitive revenue? Certainly Cape Girardeau has never featured anything of the sort regarding MO41, nor have there been any dire tales of dangerous side effects from its alleged crash sites. At least, I sure couldn't locate any.

Again, my trip to town was becoming problematic. Costs mounted. My big plans for still more research and the ol' "quest for proof" in Cape and Chaffee and points in between were soon waylaid for a few reasons, unfortunately. All I had in 2015 was this new and baffling claim to chew on while I put the finishing touches on *"MO41, The Bombshell Before Roswell: The Case for a Missouri 1941 UFO Crash."*

.I did note that according to seasoned paranormal investigator Linda Moulton Howe's gathered accounts of other UFO incidents, there are several races of extraterrestrials visiting our planet and *some of them don't always get along.* Incidents of violent encounters *between ships and species* may have occurred at times in *our* global airspace, or at least reports saying so have been gathered. Just like Zelyony... and perhaps Cape Girardeau? Apparently not all otherworldly observers of Earth are of a noble and high-minded purpose when they come here, or perhaps anywhere. I had never even thought of such a prospect, previously.

I didn't want to get carried away with baseless speculation regarding MO41, but after considering all of this surprising data and more, there seems to be at least a *possibility* that there was more to the original Cape Girardeau UFO crash story than I first perceived, involving a possible ET collision or dogfight's spread-out landed wreckage. Or at least *more than one crash site* that Saturday night in April '41. This creeping and *creepy* notion would be reinforced in the coming year...

CHAPTER EIGHT

2016: Kyle's Recommendations

"There's better than even odds there were two crash sites."

.In early 2016, I received another surprise, this time an online message from a new source, whom I'll call "Kyle" (pseudonym). Kyle turned out to be an ardent Freemason in Cape with a recognizable last name to me. He was a friendly soul fond of conversation about people and places from the old days in my hometown. Kyle contacted me with some titillating data and recommendations that soon had me seriously considering once again the previous year's fleeting notion that there was not just one landing wreckage scene to the MO41 affair, but *two*.

"In my opinion, there's better than even odds that there were two crash sites," Kyle told me in a series of internet chats and then over the phone in a follow-up interview. It was his unproven theory, yes, but it was something he seemed pretty confident in. "This is from people who lived in the area, their accounts," Kyle explained. The "primary crash site" – PCS – took place on the described flat farmland situated just north of Rockview/Chaffee, southwest of Cape, and west of the airport, again matching other descriptions. Near "Lost Hill," the outcropping I had dubbed "Rock Island." Kyle recommended I narrow my search there. That was the "main event," likely featuring the dead alien bodies seen and described by Reverend Huffman. However… *more* extraterrestrial debris came down about a mile or so away, Kyle asserted. *This was the same southern Cape Girardeau area that featured Bloomfield Road cutting through Houck Woods, as pinpointed by Carl Armstrong's friend* (see Chapter Seven). Aliens had supposedly landed there peacefully sometime in 1946, to walk around in a field, Mr. Armstrong claimed; now I was finding out there might well have been extra crash material located here back in 1941! Coincidence? *Or was this the very reason that ETs supposedly set down and poked about in a field search for something, five years or so after MO41 took place?*

According to Kyle, this "secondary crash site" – SCS - was supposedly located on the *eastern* side of Bloomfield Road, in a semi-developed area of grassy lots, thick trees, and even some nearby cropland that was once owned by the esteemed Houck family and a second revered local brood, the "Gregors" (pseudonym). Kyle related that the SCS metallic objects supposedly fell onto the lawn of a fine house that was built by patriarch Giboney Houck way back in 1907 and was later purchased and owned by the Gregor family. By 1941 the Houck family mostly lived in a brick castle-like home across Bloomfield Road a bit to the west. According to the 1942 Cape City Directory, some of the Houcks worked in Cape on the same street with members of the Gregor family. There was even intermarriage between the two close households. Was there really a second UFO crash site in the vicinity of such a pair of well-regarded local families? "The Houck family kept that area closed off," back in the day, Kyle asserted. Was the alien affair the reason why? And was it now accessible, and search-able? Kyle certainly recommended it.

I sought out more background data, and found some, thanks to the internet's airing of old newspaper articles. It seems that during the Great Depression, Giboney Houck (1878-1960) was a well-known Cape Girardeau businessman, landowner, and former Missouri state congressman. Giboney once ran for U.S. congress, but lost. As mentioned, he lived in a large, distinguished brick home in Houck Woods, its design based on Dalhousie Castle in Scotland. Today, this unusual-looking house with the long winding driveway – longer than many streets - is still there, not far from the nearby new Dalhousie Country Club, golf course, and upscale residential complex.

"My grandfather Jake used to know the pastor at Red Star Baptist Church in those days, although grampa was a member of Southside Baptist Church," Kyle informed me. "Jake worked for Giboney Houck back in the late '30s, but when the UFO crash occurred he had moved on," yet Kyle's family knew the land and its history well. "My father and my uncle were born and raised in a small house by the driveway gates of the Houck estate. I think that little house is gone now, but the secondary crash site is not far from that. As I understand it, it landed near the Gregor house and the Red Clay Pits." {Presumably this meant that Kyle's kin were not living in the "two-room house by the gates" when the MO41 event took place and thus the family did not have first-hand eyewitness experience with the celestial incident. And whether Kyle meant his grandfather knew Reverend Huffman or his 1941 Red Star Tabernacle boss, Reverend Harrison C. Croslin, at the time of MO41 was unclear. Jake's son (Maury's dad) was about eight years old at the time of the crash, and ironically is now a deacon at, of all places, the Red Star Baptist Church in Cape!}

A "red clay" mining operation seemed like such a strong clue, easily investigated today. Naturally, like all other aspects of this frustrating case, these clay pits on Bloomfield Road are now gone, built upon and vanished, as satellite photography reveals. {Kyle recommended I use that tool also, but frankly I already was.} However, a second, older satellite map image once provided to me by Carl Armstrong showed some captions to various Houck Woods sites, and the "Silica Mine" was clearly listed. Right near the Gregor House, with some undeveloped woodsy lots and cleared farmland not far away… it all added up like Kyle told me. This SCS was also not too far from the Campster School and its nearby "Schwab's Farm," like Carl (and his source) related to me. The whole ball of yarn, spun in dramatic bits and pieces, was adding up, slowly but surely. Thus the notion that there was once a second crash scene in this area was increasingly enticing, especially when I recalled two different assertions from *Topix* forums some years earlier. One claim stated the UFO crash happened "near the interstate and Houck Woods." A second said he had asked a friend about the MO41 affair's site when visiting Cape Girardeau so his host surprisingly drove him "to a gravel mining pit" and said it took place nearby. Both comments may now be seen as accurate, despite not jibing with the original "primary crash site" (PCS) farmland story, which was why I had initially ignored them.

."Look at satellite and topographical elevation maps carefully," Kyle instructed me, "and you'll see the flight path of the spacecraft. It came from the south, or southwest, headed north. Or *northeast*. Much of it hit the farmland just north of the Rockview outcropping, that large hunk of old rock that sticks up strangely, with trees on top, surrounded by crops as you get closer {from Cape Girardeau, headed south} to Rockview and Chaffee." As mentioned, I had previously noticed this eye-catching landmark when repeatedly driving past in the last few years. Kyle's info matched Barry's (through Bill and Chief Lewis).

.As per usual, I drove the five hours across Missouri to Cape Girardeau, then steeled myself to more intently finding the proper farm for the MO41 "main event." Now I was in for another surprise: a farm where the primary crash is most likely to have occurred was once the setting for a motion picture! I was informed by a Cape source – who was on the production staff – that a small independent movie called *"Fire Lilly"* was filmed on this farm near the alleged crash site, back in 2008. While the finished film caught no one's fancy and died a quick death upon its public release, the main point of recording some of it on a farm south of Cape Girardeau and outside Chaffee was the fact that the actors and crew could fire guns legally, beyond Cape and Chaffee city limits and safety codes. The plot of the picture had nothing to do with aliens, just feuding rural young adults mixed up in love triangles, its movie trailer aided by a Sheryl Crow ballad, especially poignant since the famous singer/songwriter was born and raised in southeast Missouri. {Sheryl's father went to college with my parents, where I too attended decades later, at Southeast Missouri State University in Cape Girardeau, where Crow has performed in concert a few times.}

When I pondered this intriguing update I reckoned that every day the indie movie performers and the crew worked with "Rock Island" looming in the background and the UFO crash spot was very close by, maybe within view. Were any of these motion picture people ever told by a knowledgeable local farmer what might have gone down over six decades earlier?

Kyle reiterated to me his candid theory on the aerial accident. "I think the alien ship either hit the treetops on the rock outcropping, or just slammed down to the ground just beyond it, for some other reason. Most of it landed on a farm within a half-mile of air miles at most, but not all of it. The rest hit the Gregor's lawn. See how on the map?"

Again Kyle recommended a topographical map that visually displayed terrain features.

.An immediate and obedient search of a terrain map indeed showed me that if the alien ship was truly approaching Cape Girardeau from the southwest, it traveled in an almost-forgotten "former Mississippi River corridor." That is, the low-level fertile swath of soil where the great river *used* to run, having changed course for some reason, perhaps through a natural disaster thousands of years ago. The powerful flowing waters eroded bedrock along the way, but left rich sediment behind, along with "Lost Hill," my strange-looking "Rock Island." If one followed the satellite map's "lower corridor" further southwest from this area, you'd notice Lake Wappapello, about sixty or more miles from my hometown. And guess what was under construction for great expansion from 1938 to mid-1941? That's right, this manmade dam and lake/reservoir project was just being completed around the time of the UFO crash. The U.S. Army Corps of Engineers had just reshaped and altered the land – mostly with water - for many miles around with this large new lake, all by bottling up and controlling the St. Francis River. Once this substantial project was finished, perhaps some of these same Army engineers were moved to the new Pentagon construction in Washington D.C.; that major undertaking was begun in mid-1941 with guidance from a familiar name in the post-MO41 Cape Girardeau saga

It seems that just weeks after MO41 took place, President Roosevelt had agreed with the Secretary Stimson that his War Department headquarters in Washington - the old D.C. "Munitions Building" - was too small, old, and unfortified. The stunning and perhaps frightening outer space crash incident may well have helped spur and speed the proposal of a newer, stronger military headquarters in the District of Columbia. In May of '41 FDR ordered the Army Corps of

Engineers to develop a specially-fortified new headquarters. This effort was planned and funded that summer, and ground was broken for construction in October. Of all people, then-Major *Leslie Groves* pops up – possibly in *both* corps projects! Groves had been based out of Kansas City, Missouri, for a period in the mid-1930s, working as an assistant to the commander of "Missouri River Division." Groves was likely very familiar with the St. Francis River/Lake Wappapello studies and design, and perhaps another project near Cape Girardeau…

In a recorded 1965 interview available on the internet, Leslie recalled his greatest influence: Colonel Earnest Graves (1880-1953), who was in the Army Corps of Engineers long before Groves, retired when he knew him. Graves was "responsible for the so-called Mississippi River flood control plan," Leslie explained, and part of that was to siphon off river water in drainage ditches (manmade riverbeds) to nearby farms – precisely what was in place at the site of the south-of-Cape UFO crash scene in what is locally called the "Diversion Channel." Groves might have even had some input initially in the St. Francis River/Lake Wapapello project. However, in 1938 Leslie was assigned back to Washington and by the fall of '41 was placed in charge of the five-sided concrete bunker-like Pentagon's construction by his beloved Corps of Engineers, seeing it successfully through for FDR just before he took over the atom bomb project, which as we know apparently entailed some replicated Cape Girardeau UFO recovery materials *and* small Cape factory "resistors." The world-changing "Manhattan Project." It all seemed to strangely tie in to my home area, these historic subjects and decisions that affect humanity to this day.

Another possible MO41 factor I had to consider was then and is today a potential ticking time-bomb: the volatile New Madrid Fault Zone. In late 1811 and early 1812, frighteningly destructive earthquakes from this unstable area south of Cape Girardeau reached what today would be estimated as 7.4 or larger on the Richter scale. Over and over these shockwaves reverberated across the nation, even reportedly ringing church bells in cities on the East Coast. The fearsome, forceful quakes even changed the course of the Mississippi River in the region, but thanks to only small villages dotting southeast Missouri in that era there was not a great deal of civilization or population destroyed, as there would be today if similar eruptions occurred. Many, many other smaller quakes have been registering in this locale over the centuries, however, and any extraterrestrial race that was carefully monitoring planet Earth and the spread of human civilization would naturally be attracted to the Cape Girardeau/southeastern Missouri region to keep track of this dynamic geophysical situation.

.Theory: *Could otherworldly aliens "out for a Saturday drive" have been looking over the new Wappapello project and old earthquake zone, before traveling too low through the old, former river corridor towards Cape Girardeau? Is this why they smashed into abrupt, unforgiving "Rock Island" on a warm and windy April evening? Or were they attacked and shot down by another visiting species? And that before crash-landing on a farm nearby, did some of the ET ship jettison on purpose to a SCS location about a mile away?*

I had all of these mindboggling themes to mull over during my Cape Girardeau trip. Overall Kyle's two-crash location data seemed like an authoritative and substantial break in the case. But checking on it in person would be another matter, I sadly discovered once again. The five-bedroom, five-bath Gregor House was private property, and to my surprise and disappointment, still off limits. Additionally, a friend fond of archaeological expeditions told me he had once offered to run a metal detector on the site for any old manmade artifacts but was rebuffed by a rather agitated female property owner. *Was she in reality nervously protecting evidence from the old UFO secondary crash-landing site?* An online real estate page advertised the property for sale a few years ago, featuring 3.2 acres of lawn around the stately, well-kept house. Did it now have new ownership? I longed to run a metal detector on the land as soon as possible, as did my buddy, but accessing that private land – even with new owners - would seemingly be difficult, if not impossible.

A little later in the spring of 2016, I stumbled upon a surprising online quote from an actual member of the Gregor family. I'll call him "Zak." When the subject of extraterrestrials and UFO crashes came up via a mutual friend on Facebook, Zak Gregor wrote a brief but eye-catching response: "Yeah, right outside my parents' house!" *Well, well!* Confirmation? It sure seemed like it. When pressed for elaboration on this statement, Zak had no further response. But in all of the Journalism classes I had in school, I learned that the first rule of reporting the news is that you can't run a story until it has at least two separate and independent sources that confirm it. And now with the Gregor mansion SCS saga, we appear to have just that. I made a quick, polite attempt to respond to Zak Gregor to learn more, then one to his brother. I also sent a lengthier explanatory letter in the mail to the siblings, but frustratingly received no reply. Much like the Rush Limbaugh family, the Gregors, I found upon further research, were/are very conservative and own public businesses, so speaking openly about extraterrestrial evidence or encounters is evidently just not acceptable.

.In my trip to Cape and researching the countryside, I could see that Kyle's descriptions of the PCS in a field near "Rock Island" fit well with still other clues that I had previously accumulated, now brought to mind. For instance, Linda L. Wallace described her mother coming home from college in May of 1941 and soon going to a picnic in Scott County. It was held on a flat hill overlooking sweeping farmland for miles around, making for a beautiful and memorable view. Linda's mom was informed during the party that the "little people" crash site happened not too far away, within this spectacular distant vista. With Kyle's clues I was able to see how this was possible. Just north of Chaffee and even tinier Rockview, Missouri, there is quite a steep climb of topography, a flat-topped farming area that had breathtaking views of the countryside – and the MO41 crash area. Linda Wallace had also listed within her e-book's grandmother "Judy" recollection that the UFO calamity happened on farmland not too far from the "Little River Drainage Ditch." That particular Mississippi River "diversion channel" was not too far away also. And this site was all near the country road that Kyle (and a second new source) specifically named. "Southwest of Cape," as yet another source for Linda Wallace had described. About a mile or so from the Gregor House's SCS. It was all coming together perfectly now but still out of my reach.

In all of my hunting around Cape Girardeau and Chaffee farm country, there were was an overwhelming amount of greenery that literally stopped me in my tracks. Crops, trees, shrubs, weeds, flowering plants... they were sprouting everywhere, blocking my view from my car and when on foot. I had no desire to trample this growth. Even if there *was* alien wreckage metal still in the ground somewhere – not a given - I surely could not access it during the warm and productive spring and summer months. *Winter, with all its bleak lack of growth, that was the best time to do a proper ground search*, I realized at last.

.Around this same time, a woman from Cape Girardeau posted some surprising statements on Facebook, declaring that she knew that wealthy and conservative *Southeast Missourian* newspaper owner/publisher Gary Rust once took an interest in searching for MO41 information some years ago. {I had e-mailed him about five years ago with questions about the crash, but he never got back to me.} According to the posting Mr. Rust dug into the Ryan S. Wood MUFON online report around 2001 regarding Ryan's initial search of the Cape area for debris. This included an October 1941 U.S. Geographical Survey aerial photo, snapped from an airplane, *of a section of Houck Woods near Bloomfield Road*, with its latitude and longitude lines listed. Ryan actually went to this intriguing site back around 2000 and did some metal detection and field work for his later MUFON report, but found nothing of substance. Of further frustration, I discovered that this locale is nowadays the new aforementioned Dalhousie golf/residential complex, carved out of 900 acres via Houck family descendants. The Facebook poster said her friends went up in an airplane to see where these Ryan Wood coordinates led to, they also noticed the country club was being constructed at the time, tearing up the land. "There was some noticeable scarring of the earth" and "some trampling" at the locality in the '41 survey images, Ryan wrote in his MUFON report, and of course this site is indeed near where Maury was now telling me about, not far from property Carl Armstrong had mentioned as well.

.Thanks to all of these clues, I began pondering the SCS and exploring Houck Woods and Bloomfield Road more and more. Then, Carl e-mailed me again in mid-March of 2016 with a new message that allowed his original source, a friend named "George" (pseudonym), to tell more about the enticing supposed 1946 peaceful landing saga. George wrote within this specific e-mail, then a surprise follow-up e-mail of his own. I was grateful to get more pertinent details, and they are as follows…

"My Uncle Howard relayed the story to me since he actually saw this event" back in 1946, George began. It seems Howard was excitedly notified by friends one afternoon about a foreign-looking spaceship that had landed in the Houck Woods area, so he went racing to the site. He saw there was a crowd "of around three hundred people there," eyeballing with great excitement the settled astonishing alien sight. "It was shiny, a disc-shaped craft, about thirty feet in diameter and about fifteen feet in height, with three or four beings around it," the uncle told George. "We observed it for about ten to fifteen minutes," presumably from a safe distance with the growing crowd of dumbfounded onlookers. The non-terrestrials in metallic-looking flight suits walked around in the distant green pasture, possibly searching for something, or maybe making mechanical repairs. After a while, they calmly stepped back inside their settled ship. It sat in that grassy field quietly for another ten minutes or so, then… suddenly lifted up off the ground, "by about twenty feet, making no noise." The stunning craft gleaming in the sun seemed to defy our laws of physics, hovering in place. Then, abruptly, the foreign disc shot upwards at a tremendous rate and soundlessly took off into the sunlit sky, gone from view. "My Uncle Howard said there were two uniformed Cape patrol officers there telling everyone to stay back during this, but didn't say how far from the ship they all were," George related further. This astonishing event was placed "sometime before the point in 1946 when my aunt and uncle were married."

I asked about MO41 memories. George replied that if the uncle was aware of the Cape Girardeau UFO crash he would have happily discussed it, but that he never mentioned that tragic cosmic affair. As for the nearby

Campster School – where someone like Herb Schaper *had* to have been working the phone furiously to inform others (in the days before cellphones, personal computers, and tablets) – it was in the vicinity of the landing occurrence but Uncle Howard "did not say how far past the school he was on Bloomfield Road." So again, I was left with no specifics, but very enticing allegations (plus one woman's memory that a herd of buffalo grazed in the same fields around "1946 or '47").

A few days later, George e-mailed again to say that he had spoken to his brother, who also recalled a conversation with their Uncle Howard about the extraordinary extraterrestrial landing event in a field "past Campster School." This pasture was "about a half to three-quarters of a mile" beyond the old schoolhouse, the brother had claimed. The year as the brother remember it was around 1946, or at least "after the war," which of course ended in early September of 1945. The number of the people watching the aliens walking about on the Cape Girardeau property was still described to me as "around three hundred," which seems pretty dubious, unless the school was having a public outdoor event where a pre-existing crowd could have been in place beforehand.

I noticed that Mr. Armstrong's friend did not agree with Carl's assertion that the MO41 affair's main event took place north of the city. In fact, the buddy "George" passed along statements that he had heard the 1941 crash happened on farmland just south of Bloomfield Road and Highway 74, just west of a secondary, smaller area airstrip, the old Consolidated Airport (mostly just a grass field landing strip in '41, where Rush Limbaugh Jr. had a great deal of pilot training). Well now that was a different crash site entirely from anyone else's claims! If it had only been located about a half-mile further south, this PCS claim would corroborate perfectly Kyle's recent recommendations, along with a few others' statements, happening at a farm field west and not far from Cape's more established airfield, not the less utilized aerial facility.

One allegation that I had never really paid much mind to previously was another supernatural rumor about Houck Woods and the Gregor House, but it bears mentioning here. These places are supposed to be "haunted." At least, that was an old rumor I had heard long ago and it was still to this day the reaction from a few people when chatting about this possible crash-landing story, and also found online, when perusing a *Topix* forum thread on the subject. For example, there were tales of ghostly apparitions and eerie noises from within the Gregor house, which was built in 1907. Nearby "Gregor Field" that was used for a new subdivision, this property was seriously alleged to have once been a Native American graveyard; it was later flashing occasional contemporary spectral visions, much like the plot for the old Steven Spielberg film, *"Poltergeist."* On top of all that, there was a whole surprising history of violent crime by desperados in Houck Woods' past, using the dark shadows and shade of the towering trees to plot, execute, and escape lawless misdeeds, including robbery and attempted murder. This atmosphere created still more strange and disturbing local lore. The cackling ghost nicknamed "Mad Lucy." A marching ghost Confederate Army. A headless horseman apparition. So-called wandering "spook lights." Eerie ghost stories and supernatural-sounding claims from this Cape area have thrived for many decades now. Thus, some citizens mentioned online that they won't even drive down Bloomfield Road at night, or a few during the day! It certainly made for a colorful past and present in this part of the city. {Thrown into this odd mix was the fact that the city was forced to sell off a part of the woods to a private citizen when a public park within it became rife with young people abusing drugs, alcohol, each other, and God knows what else.}

Was the old Houck/Gregor estate really where at least a secondary or partial segment of the MO41 incident came to a sudden rest? What would this metallic material consist of? How could so much come down in one spot, and a little bit more just fly off and crash-land a mile or more away? In speaking in person to journalist Linda Moulton-Howe in April 2016, at my first ever "UFO Convention" in Eureka Springs, Arkansas, I may have found a surprising answer.

"I have a source who is knowledgeable about the true nature of the Roswell crash, from 1947," Linda informed me over lunch. "He told me that the rumors of a "second crash" at the time were true, but that the government privately felt this was an "escape pod."" This alien module ejected from the plummeting spacecraft, she explained, and landed some miles away, in the undeveloped New Mexican desert. Wow! That was a mind-blowing suggestion for MO41! One that seems to fit now, at least in theory. A "Secondary Crash Site" that might well have been where a small "pilot escape pod" came to rest, whether it had any actual occupants is unknown. Perhaps all three ET astronauts died at the farm site where Reverend Huffman ventured and saw them… but possibly there were more in a smaller canister-like contraption that fell to earth near Houck Woods? Or it was empty? Or it held other life forms, or material within it that wasn't explainable? But just where *is* this SCS item from the Gregor's lawn? Or any photos or film of it? Turned in to Cape Girardeau cops right away in '41? Or to the Army, or the FBI, or the fire department, with little fuss in the jarring MO41 aftermath? As usual I had more questions than answers, and for once Kyle had no recommendations.

{I was quickly of the mind of the hit 1997 Harrison Ford movie, "*Air Force One*," where the U.S. president deliberately triggered the release of a strong metal "escape pod" from his world-famous airplane in flight, even though he was not in it, in order to fool terrorists on board into thinking that he had departed in the container. The actual American chief executive at the time, Bill Clinton, told the press he loved the movie, but that Air Force One had no actual escape module.}

Around this same time, I also noticed a brand new video surfaced on the internet, one showing a UFO hovering over – of all places – Rostov-on-Don, in Russia. The same area as the apparent April 1941 UFO crash on Zelyony Island! The resulting contemporary footage was uploaded the day after it was recorded, March 5th, 2016, and reminded me once again of the weird parallels between MO41 and the claimed Soviet ET crash affair, allegedly involving more than one extraterrestrial craft. The modern, somewhat shaky footage revealed a strange-shaped orangeish craft hovering in the night sky, recorded by a surprised Russian on the ground, a source who captured its movements as best he could while a second, white-colored object in the sky remained stationary overhead nearby. Two same-species spacecrafts? Or was this another rivalry, an ET "battle" over the Rostov River as in April 1941? It all left me with the notion reinforced that there may well have been at least two - maybe even *three* – Cape Girardeau area crash sites from "that night" so long ago. And yet I could not properly pinpoint a single one of them. It continued to plague, baffle, excite and entice me to find out more.

All of this might fit together even better today if researcher/author Ryan Wood's October 1941 aerial photographic survey site could be specifically tracked down and explored for evidence. Unfortunately Ryan e-mailed at this time to say that more in-depth and reliable '41 government aerial photography was being held in D.C.'s National Archives. And also that the new Dalhousie golf course on Bloomfield Road created so much excavation of the soil a decade ago for homes, streets, and golf facilities since his initial search... well, it wasn't likely remaining evidence could now be located.

Add to all of this the fact that that the Houck/Gregor woods, fields, and homes continue to be considered private properties and off-limits... as is the specific farm primary site... and that the old Consolidated Airfield was long gone, as were many 1940s homes, businesses, and barns... and that Campster School students and teachers were long since deceased... and that Kyle was fresh out of recommendations... Well, I had to admit defeat on this "quest for proof" trip to Cape as well. I had struck out yet again.

Thus the intriguing MO41 puzzle pieces remain – like our apparent alien visitors - still up in the air, very tantalizing and exciting... and yet mysterious and unresolved. Perhaps finding leftover wreckage wasn't meant to be. *It may never be concretely proven.* But at least I tried. I did my part. I dutifully recorded all of the surprising information surrounding the incredible crash-landing and its recovery, and its overall impact. I had looked around intensely, almost lost in a maze of green crops in the hot sun, sweaty and hungry and flustered. But I had come up empty.

I once again admitted defeat and drove back across Missouri with some amount of calm resignation. It was time to go home and study the clues again, and perhaps redouble my efforts for the next hunt for "gold." Then another thought hit me. *Maybe it is better off NOT being found.*

"What if the specific site *is* discovered? And then openly publicized for the world to see? Or at least, word leaks out? Knowing the state of today's human race, what a mess it would become! A nightmare, potentially, for the property owners. Farms are not just businesses, they are people's homes, their entire lives. Where they live and work and play every day." That was my mindset on the drive home.

To picture this scenario further and logically is to imagine the worst in human nature, frankly. For instance, you can't put up a wall to keep strangers out, it would cost a fortune and block out the sun. A barbed-wire fence around an entire farm would also be expensive and impractical. Everyone in the world would become fascinated by the specific crash location farm and want to go see it. Visitors would park on the property, get out and roam around, taking pictures and video footage without permission. They'd trespass while eating and drinking, and leave trash behind, maybe even go to the bathroom on the famous land. Some folks would probably arrive unannounced at all hours and start digging with shovels, uprooting crops and lawns, searching for their own proof. Or run metal detectors, radiation sensors, and scientific equipment, legitimate or not. Some would walk up to the farmhouse's front door, knock, and demand to know more about the famous land. Touristas would block traffic on these narrow country roads, try to put up exploitive souvenir stands and give tours, and make noise night and day. "The reactions of humanity would make life on that farm a living hell, really," I realized. *It just seemed for the best that even if I pinpointed the right impact spot, I should keep my big mouth shut.* Blabbing would trigger an avalanche, an unstoppable disaster for the land's privacy-seeking owners and area citizens who were used to the bucolic serenity of their rural community. And I might get the blowback, the simmering anger and resentment from any farm site owners and nearby outraged citizens, deeply affected by all of the negative repercussions.

Thank God I did not find the right farm. And unless it was handled very, *very* quietly and discreetly, I hope nobody else does, either. In so many ways, it's probably for the best that the MO41 impact site and residual evidence is *not* found.

When I got home I put aside my dreams of glory and began writing the next section of this book, slotting together mounting research data on another surprising, somewhat different, FDR-era flight catastrophe that seemed to uncannily connect at times with MO41…

.....SECTION III:

.. January 1942 – Hollywood - Aerial Accident #2

CHAPTER NINE

Carole Lombard's Flight From Hell – Part One

"A strange round yellow light that appeared to hang in the sky."

.Did MO41 events have something to do with the sudden death of superstar movie actress Carole Lombard in a January 1942 plane crash? Maybe not. In fact, such a suggestion at first seems ridiculous, but based upon further review, the similarities and synchronicities in the two stories seems astonishing. The time to contrast and compare the pair has come.

It turns out at least one or more "Unidentified Flying Objects" may have played a part in Lombard's tragic fate, but so did a startling number of circumstances and coincidences we've come to know within the MO41 storyline. Along the way there strangely lurked many dark omens and spooky signs of disaster, foreshadowing events to come. Carole Lombard Gable's untimely demise has been considered one of the most eerie and ironic, sudden and shocking celebrity deaths in the history of the American entertainment industry, and that was *before* learning now that alien visitors might well have been involved. The largely untold or unpublicized Lombard otherworldly drama ranks as the next "big thing" in UFO experiences after the April 1941 Cape Girardeau alien crash and speedy Army recovery, yet it has been almost completely overlooked since it went down – literally – over seven decades ago. Until now…

.As most old-timers know - and some of the younger generation may have heard or read - Carole Lombard was once amongst the biggest female motion picture superstars of the 1930s and early '40s, Hollywood's so-called "Golden Age" just before World War II. Hers was a household name. At her death, beautiful blonde Carole was the highest paid working woman in the country, "beloved by all America," as one writer described her. The curvaceous film and radio actress achieved her great fame and fortune partly due to her vivacious personality and talents, and partly because she was married to the incredibly handsome and admired movie star of the day, Clark Gable, the box office champ known to all as "The King of Hollywood." Quick-witted Carole was at least assuredly the popular reigning queen of so-called "screwball comedies," which were considered wacky comic films in those pre-television days.

.Named "Jane Alice Peters" at birth in 1908 - in Fort Wayne, Indiana – Carole's family moved to Los Angeles when she was five. A tomboyish tornado of energy, she soon landed roles in Hollywood movies as a child and again as a teenager, then plenty more as a young woman of maturing beauty, performing ability, sex appeal, considerable brains, and athletic skills. Today she might seem very "New Age," for Carole and her mother often hung out with and/or consulted psychics, astrologers, numerologists, and mystics. The two also believed in both the Christian faith and Baha'i, an Eastern religion that unusually allows for belief in life on other planets, all created by a benevolent God. "Know thou that every fixed star has its own planets, and every planet its own creatures, whose numbers no man can compute," one quote from a Baha'i prophet explains. As author Duane Troxel summed up: "Baha'i writings contain *many* statements that implicitly and explicitly point to existence of not only extraterrestrial life-forms but to extraterrestrial intelligence as well."

Perhaps to honor this progressive otherworldly understanding, Carole took to wearing special jewelry called "Skyrockets." These were unique matching clips that were shaped like red *discs or flying saucers*, with thin sparkling rays emanating from one side apiece. So eye-catching were these glittering diamond-and-ruby rocket ships, they were featured in a newspaper article of the time.

There were also many print articles during the 1930s on Lombard's unstoppable life-force, her irrepressible spirit. When learning to fly an airplane in 1935, for instance, a magazine article offered a story with artwork showing Carole's aircraft hitting the side of a mountain jutting up out of a western desert setting, the mountain "losing," a stunning slice of irony and foreshadowing as we shall see. A year or so later, when she was conjuring up ideas to promote her latest movie, Lombard urged her publicist to say that her plane was missing, and rumored to have possibly crashed in a rural setting. Instead, Lombard's private flight would land safely in an obscure locale so she could lay low for a day or two while lurid newspaper headlines would have the whole country asking about her whereabouts if alive, or if she was lying dead in unfound wreckage. {The plan was scrapped as too risky.}

After a seemingly long and lucrative career, Carole returned – sporting her "Skyrockets" - to her native Indiana in chilly January of 1942 to headline the first celebrity cross-country bond-selling tour to help support America's fledgling efforts in WWII. Obviously this took place just nine months after the MO41 crash just outside Cape

Girardeau, Missouri. {Cape is just a few miles north of Illmo, Missouri, whose sole movie theater was airing on the night of the April 12th UFO accident a Clark Gable picture (the classic "*Gone With The Wind*," in fact) while another nearby town's feature film that week was Carole Lombard's "*Vigil In The Night*."} On her way back home to Los Angeles (suburban Encino, really), thespian Lombard's airplane ride became what any person could rightfully call "the flight from hell." Before we get to that, we must go back in time a little over one year...

.In 1940, Carole had given her new hubby Clark a small Brownie box camera, to snap intimate pictures of their lives together. A kind of pocket camera, popular at the time, very much like the small Brownie-type camera that was whipped out by a newsman and utilized to photograph a dead ET at the MO41 crash scene. By late December of '40 things were going smoothly for Carole both as a movie star and as a busy housewife, despite the occasional dark premonition and/or feeling of doom. She stated a few times privately that she could not see herself growing old, and felt that someday she was going to "die young." To cheer up, Gable and Lombard took advantage of some time off when they traveled to Washington D.C. with their camera, for a sightseeing trip with most of the American government and other tourists out of town for the winter holidays. And naturally the world famous duo ended up at - where else? - the U.S. Capitol Building!

.It's unknown if during their tour of the revered D.C. structure the two popular stars were taken downstairs to the sub-basement level. But with no congress in session and few people around just days after Christmas, the two Hollywood V.I.P. tourists were free to roam the halls of congress nearly as they pleased. Of course, out front of the revered building flew a large U.S. flag - then with 48 stars - which would come back into play a year later.

.Next, Carole and Clark were escorted to and inside President Franklin Roosevelt's White House, to get a quick tour and meet with the First Family. The liberal, enthusiastic Lombard idolized Masonic FDR while the conservative Gable was a little more grounded but respectful. Roosevelt and Gable, polls showed, were not only the two most famous men in America over the past decade, but in the entire world. After Gable and Lombard chatted amiably with the president in the Oval Office, they sat in chairs and listened closely to one of his famous "fireside chats" for a national radio audience in another room of the White House. At that time, FDR warned the nation of the dangers of a world at war over totalitarianism creeping closer to American shores and business interests. During the broadcasted speech the two movie stars were seated next to none other than Cordell Hull, the solemn Secretary of State who once showed off MO41 bodies and hardware down under the Capitol Building to his visiting cousin, an Ohio pastor. Afterward the admired actors sipped drinks with the First Couple, discussing their showbiz experiences for a while. Carole suggested that if America was to get involved in the world war going on, movie icons could act as bond salesmen, special fund-raisers on tours around the country, and all agreed. The next day the Gables resumed their area tour, which included a trip to Mount Vernon, to learn more about Freemason George Washington and his unique home. Lombard loved this part of their sightseeing a great deal, but it had an extra special meaning for Gable. As perhaps did the Capitol Building visit, *and* the confab with FDR. Why? *Because Clark Gable was a Freemason.*

.It turns out Clark had joined a Masonic fraternity - Beverly Hills Lodge #528 - way back in 1933. He was evidently fairly serious about his secret society membership, maintaining his position within the secretive group that elevated him to Shriner status, which means like FDR he quietly attended the private club's meetings and closed events often and gave time and money to charity - especially for children - quite willingly. Gable had undoubtedly at some point undergone the ritual of being placed in a dark basement or sub-basement room, or at least was blindfolded for Masonic initiation. And this was three years before Clark first dated charitable Carole. Did Lombard fully grasp the secret society aspect of their sightseeing? We'll probably never fully know, but the coincidences don't stop there, they only multiply a year later, when Mrs. Gable left on another cross-country trip

.In December of 1941, a year after the D.C. tour, Clark Gable was appointed leader of the "Hollywood Victory Committee," a collection of movie production people dedicated to doing whatever they could to aid the American war effort after Pearl Harbor's devastating attack. Mostly this consisted of raising morale, funds, and cinematic awareness of the U.S. military's needs in fighting back against armed, deadly Axis Powers aggression. Mr. Gable's first act was to assign his loving wife the job of raising funds by way of selling war bonds in her home state of Indiana, as she suggested a year before. Sort of a "trial run" for other movie performers to follow, copy, and build upon in the months and years to come. Lombard was pleased to go on this very first tour, which was to be conducted strictly by train. FDR's Treasury Department told Hollywood handlers told Lombard and other movie stars in general they did *not* want any beloved celebrities to travel in the air for bond tours. Roosevelt himself always traveled by train, car, or boat, by that point in his presidency. In light of revelations now about the weird Missouri 1941 ET crash - and likely further "flying discs" or "foo fighter" sightings around the country - perhaps we can see why Roosevelt's administration was so nervous. {During that April 12th extraterrestrial event, Carole was in Hollywood rehearsing for a radio play she would star in the following night, and helping celebrate her eldest brother's birthday.}

.On Monday, January 12th, 1942, Carole Lombard Gable set out by railroad car from Los Angeles with her mother and an MGM Studios publicist named Otto Winkler, with plenty of luggage in tow. The trio first rode the train north, towards the state capitol of Sacramento, before turning east. FBI documents uncovered decades later stated that apparently on this very night, a strange bright object was sighted hovering in the California desert sky, just west of Las Vegas, Nevada. The odd, round UFO just hung there, without movement, in a generally recognized commercial flight airway. The incident was evidently not publicized. By then, Carole's train was already chugging along beyond the borders of both states, but this unusual sighting would prove somewhat linked to Lombard's later fate.

.The superstar's party rolled on to Utah, where Carole spoke at a train station rally and raised morale and awareness for buying war bonds. From there, the long railroad ride took her to Chicago, Illinois, where she gave a newspaper interview and then a few radio interviews at some local stations. Chicago was where Lombard's Democratic Party ruled, and thus Charlie Schwartz territory (see Bonus Chapter). It was also where General George Marshall held his Army Intelligence training school and the city university atom bomb lab was located. Where author Linda Wallace's father, a member of the MO41 recovery team, was now receiving special training. {Schwartz could conceivably have been part of a dignitary-filled local welcoming committee; Lombard also huddled with members of the Treasury Department at this stop.}

Despite repeated, stern orders to stay on the ground and take only the "choo-choo," as Lombard called it, Carole impulsively decided to hop a short flight from Chicago to Indianapolis. It would be quicker and less taxing on her this way. Press agent Winkler couldn't talk her out of it, although he desperately wanted and tried to. Why? Because his family revealed many years later that on the previous early Sunday morning a deeply rattled, sweaty Otto woke up from a terrifying nightmare. It was quite explicit and left him very shaken, just before he departed on the bond tour. According to the fine research of author Robert Matzen, in his excellent 2014 book *"Fireball,"* it was a vivid bad dream in which the veteran publicity man admitted later he saw himself dying in an awful airliner accident! If the special tour ever traveled by airplane, Otto ominously informed his startled wife before he left the house, "I won't be coming back."

.Lombard's mother, Elizabeth Peters, had a general great fear of flying, so she stayed with the train schedule to Indianapolis, by way of Fort Wayne, her old hometown. She expressed repeatedly her additional innate sense that the entire journey was very dangerous for the threesome. There were no tragic events taking place on the brief plane ride from Chicago to Indianapolis for the superstar actress and the MGM publicist. And that was a problem. It only gave Carole the impetus to ponder taking an airliner again, after finishing her bond-selling rallies in Indianapolis. While in Indy, she also helped raise the American flag that had been flying over the U.S. Capitol Building the previous year. Possibly even when the MO41 materials were apparently trucked in right past it and tucked into the building's sub-basement that previous springtime. She watched it go up the flagpole outside her home state's capitol building, then went inside for a rally. Carole spoke to a large crowd in the frigid cold and within the warm statehouse about galvanizing efforts to defeat the Axis Powers. Some miles north of the city, at Purdue University, modern MUFON sources claim at least two grad students were working at the time on adapting captured MO41 spacecraft technology into advanced transistor engineering.

Representatives from the college were on their way to see Lombard in person...

.That final Thursday evening, January 15th, Lombard led a huge rally in Indianapolis's tabernacle, appearing as the lead speaker and singer, alongside the governor, three military bands, a choir from Purdue University, and twelve thousand friendly faces. Carole sang; spoke passionately; posed for press and public photos; encouraged the sale of war bonds; hobnobbed with local politicos and military officers; and urged all to "Sacrifice, Save, and Serve." Everyone left feeling the night to be a mighty triumph of good spirits and astonishing fundraising totals, four times the expected goal. It might have been the highlight of popular and patriotic Lombard's entire personal life.

.For sure now, on a cold January night, Carole Lombard foolishly – in hindsight - ditched the rest of her train tour and impulsively decided to fly back to L.A. She and Otto argued a bit about this decision, so they flipped a coin. Lombard "won." She pushed Otto to buy three tickets for a Transcontinental and Western Airlines flight that had begun at LaGuardia Airport in New York City. It was a new and reliable airplane, considered topnotch technology for its day. Transcontinental Western Airlines Flight #3 then touched down briefly in Newark, New Jersey, then Pittsburgh, Pennsylvania, and twice in Ohio, all prior to Lombard's party boarding the late-arriving vessel at an Indianapolis airfield in the initial Friday hours. The silver, sleek TWA "Sky Club" landing site immediately before Indy, was none other than Dayton, Ohio. Likely Dayton Airfield, since it was a TWA hub, but this was situated very near Wright Field, where it is greatly suspected some MO41 crash materials ended up for examination and duplication, at some point. Wright was where the likes of Air Force leaders Hap Arnold and Nathan Twining often toiled in guarded, top secret facilities, some underground and others still under construction. Those in Dayton knew that Albuquerque, New Mexico's airport was a regular TWA and military aerial route stop. Sacks of Priority Mail and packages headed west were loaded onto Lombard's liner, in Dayton and other stops. Many young military cadets and fliers, along with mail and materials, were often sent by *commercial* flights - including Trip #3 - to destinations across the country in the early months of America's struggling war effort.

Just before boarding, Lombard suddenly told a nearby *Life* magazine photographer she had a genuine fear of flying, and had to have been questioning her wisdom in taking the flight, feeling such "a premonition of some kind," said the shutterbug later, recalling fearful Carole.

.Weighed down with more and more equipment along the way, the 21-seater plane in retrospect gradually grew overloaded as the day went along. In the early-hours of Friday morning it flew from Dayton to Indianapolis to St. Louis, Missouri. It was still dark outside as Carole's flight buzzed over Oliver Parks' PAC airfield in Cahokia, Illinois, near the Mississippi River, close to downtown St. Louis. Flight #3 instead touched down at larger, better equipped Lambert Field, one hundred miles to the north of the 1941 Missouri UFO crash site. Lambert was likely Oliver Parks' favorite airport, having trained often there, at least until he opened his own in Cahokia. Lambert was a TWA hub, just a few miles from businessman Stuart Symington's factory production of aircraft parts, and where the future Air Force Secretary and U.S. senator also hopped flights now and then. Additionally, Lambert wasn't too far from Stu's favorite Masonic lodge, where Cape Girardeau members would occasionally drive up and attend, like Rush Limbaugh, Sr., or visiting Kansas City area Masons, like Harry S Truman. In fact, just as today, many Cape Girardeau citizens traveled north to St. Louis to attend sports, cultural events, shopping centers, museums, parks, and more; it is like a second hometown to many in southeastern Missouri.

.Impatient Mrs. Gable and her fellow passengers were forced in St. Louis to wait out a strange foggy front that stubbornly refused to lift for almost two full hours. Eventually the shiny, mostly-aluminum TWA plane took off across Missouri for Kansas City, where it landed and experienced yet another delay. To kill some time, Lombard sent a telegram to reticent Clark Gable, working at MGM in Hollywood at the time. She urged him to join "this man's army." This was mildly strange: why bother to take the time and expense to message one's husband this way? She was just going to see him at dinnertime anyway, and a phone call would have been more personal. It was in a sense Lombard's dying wish, one that Gable later lived up to by joining the Army Air Force some months afterwards. But for now, it almost seemed as if tired Carole had a sense of foreboding again, like she knew somehow she was not going to make it home. For the rest of the flight she was said to have often sported a rather dour, dark expression, not at all her natural upbeat, lighthearted personality. Perhaps part of that resulted from a side trip before departing Hollywood for the tour. Carole dropped by unannounced to visit Gable on the set of his latest MGM film, only to find a buxom starlet sitting in his lap. Lombard left, quite rattled, said a friend, not saying a word to her handsy husband.

.Back in Indianapolis, before boarding, mom Elizabeth Peters had run a numbers count of the trip home, and didn't like what her numerology training told her. "16" was said to be a number representing *death* for air travel and it was by now January 16th. And "3" was a terribly unlucky number for these situations too, she somberly informed Carole and Otto. There were 3 in the Lombard flight party.

It was a DC-3 they were in, and Flight #3 to boot. The TWA (3 letters) vehicle was to arrive in Indianapolis at 3:00 a.m., with 3 people in each row. Carole was 33 and 3 months old. It was the third week of the new year. {Plus, the flight ended tragically about 33 miles from its last takeoff, in Vegas.} The star actress's fretful mother was actually overheard by people at the Indy airport warning her daughter, "Don't get on that plane!"

.As mentioned, even intuitive Lombard herself felt forewarning of early death; this was only reinforced when noted psychic Jeanne Dixon - she later claimed in a biography - bumped into Carole a few days before departure, at a Los Angeles hairstyling salon. Miss Dixon alleged she then "saw the sign of death over Carole," which was the image of a disembodied hand over Lombard's head. She supposedly warned the movie queen not to travel by air for the next several weeks, while Carole underwent this "danger period."

.During this overnight, a stagehand-friend of Lombard's dreamt something very strange and traumatic. He said later he saw a plane, a crash, and a mountain, with the letters "P-O-T-?-S-?" spelled above it, and awoke in a cold sweat too. What the two missing letters added up to in an ominous word of warning the friend stated he did not understand at the time.

Returning to the journey, TWA Flight #3 flew south to Wichita, Kansas, where there was another delay, and then on to Amarillo, Texas. More airport stops, more refueling, more mail, more passengers, more luggage, with some of those on board getting bumped at the next stop in New Mexico. As mentioned the Albuquerque airport was the home of adjacent Kirtland Army Airfield with satellite Los Alamos lab connections Sandia Labs and the Manzano storage facility all possible classified MO41 study sites, even if for only small parts of the materials, perhaps before

Flight #3's arrival, perhaps more in the years afterwards. All of these locales were perhaps now literally right within sight as Carole got off the plane at the airport!

.Priority Mail and cargo was exchanged, and some more Army fliers were added to the plane at this time as well, some having been trained at Kirtland, as part of the new "Air Ferrying Command." That was a special unit of Army pilots, vital to America's war effort. They often traveled to Los Angeles to take command of the new warplanes coming off factory floors in Southern California, and then fly them to their proper airbase destinations in North America to teach others how to properly handle them. It was a critical unit largely organized by that man "Hap" again: General Henry H. Arnold, traveling between Wright Field and Kirtland. Some of these completed, crucial aircrafts were from the Santa Monica headquarters of Douglass Aircraft, which was associated with Project RAND and Hap Arnold after the war, including a project regarding a "world-circling spaceship." On top of that, Arnold and his assistant Jo Chamberlin mentioned the Air Ferrying Command amidst private "foo fighter" or UFO investigation notes, found later in Hap's papers (a topic explored in Linda Wallace's e-book "*Covert Retrieval*"). And who was an influential Army air officer who would very quickly contact Clark Gable in the days after his wife's death? None other than Hap Arnold! The general wanted to induce the box office champ to enlist in his Air Force, and he eventually did so later in '42. {A rumor went around after the airliner tragedy that in the days *before* Lombard left Hollywood, Gable was away at an important D.C. conference with his fellow Freemason, General Arnold; this story was later revealed to be false, created by MGM in order to cover for Clark not being present when Carole left L.A. by train, following an ugly spat they had at home over his philandering with a sexy movie co-star.} It is also interesting to note that FDR aide Harry Hopkins –

likely quite knowledgeable about MO41 - was the one who was said to have originally urged *Gable* – not Lombard - to go on the bond-selling tour in the first place, but by train only. And that was to Ohio, Clark's birthplace, not too far from Wright Field. Gable passed, being deathly afraid of giving speeches before crowds, which tended to mob him and expect great theater whenever he spoke. Clark of course urged Carole to go in his place, to her own Midwestern birth-state, a decision that would haunt him for the rest of his days.

.While in Albuquerque, a new co-pilot filled out a flight plan that would take Lombard's TWA flight to Boulder City in southern Nevada. From there they'd fly over - or safely *around* - risky ridges of mountains that dotted the western landscape to come, in crossing over into Southern California. The new pilot - Wayne Williams, from St. Louis, Missouri, therefore a candidate for friendship with likely MO41 handler Oliver Parks - did not sign the flight plan and yet no one thought anything of it, despite the fact that the airliner was now hopelessly off schedule, running several hours behind time, crammed to capacity, and overloaded by acceptable weight standards. When exhausted Lombard was asked by officials to leave the flight in New Mexico, along with her mother and Otto Winkler, she crankily refused. The U.S. Army was trying to pack in still more AFC pilots, needed to ferry those new factory roll-outs in L.A. Carole's party was asked to give up their seats, but she balked, growing upset. Carole had to wait out a dull, tiresome plane transfer and delay in the Albuquerque airport a few months earlier and had no desire to repeat the experience. Travel-weary, she did something unheard of in her life. She pulled rank, threw an angry fit of sorts, and demanded to stay on the plane, claiming she was serving her country too, in her role as war bond fund-raiser. This cost her – and her mother and publicist – their lives.

.The commercial liner finally took off with Carole, mom, and Otto, for what should have been a Winslow, Arizona, refueling, but strong headwinds suddenly popped up. The unexpectedly fierce gusts made the cramped, overloaded flight need to land for still more fuel. This was originally supposed to take place at Boulder City, Nevada, but there was just one problem. The Boulder City airport had no landing lights. The various trip delays had pushed the schedule back so far that the veteran pilot and his younger, less experienced co-pilot had to make other arrangements. They'd settle the plane for refueling and engine oiling at McCarren Airport (now Nellis Air Force Base) in northern Las Vegas. *That* airfield had landing and takeoff lights. It was by then a dark and cold Friday night. Jet-lagged Carole, Elizabeth, and Otto loped off the plane – which was militarily guarded on the runway, it was so critical - and into the Vegas terminal for a short respite. Both pilots remaining on board were experienced in takeoffs from Las Vegas; the captain had just done one at night a week or so earlier. He knew the proper way to L.A. and surely would heed the special warning to all pilots on the danger area of the nearby mountain range, the ominous posters on that had been pinned up in the Vegas airport TWA pilot lounge for months. After a thirty minute delay, *finally* it was time for all passengers to re-board on the Vegas tarmac. Worn-out Lombard, still in her pink pantsuit and special UFO-like clips, was *at last* now to go home a hero, having raised on her own *more than two times* as much war bond money as expected, more than many Hollywood stars would later be able to produce from the excited public *combined*!

.At any rate, just after seven o'clock (Pacific Time) that frigid January 16th, 1942, the TWA aircraft managed to push up into the night sky, taking off for Burbank's airport, heading out a bit off course. Then smallish Las Vegas began to fade into the distance, much of it blacked out for possible aerial bombardment concerns. Additionally, two of three rural ground air route beacons to guide flights were not functioning. It was clear and still, nearly moonless, with "unlimited visibility and ceiling," according to eyewitnesses and weather reports. Lots of stars were out. For now the movie star was safely surrounded by fifteen Army pilots, and even Lombard herself knew how to fly a plane, having taken those piloting lessons some years before. Nearly the only ones on board who *didn't* know how to command an airplane were the stewardess and another female passenger, plus Elizabeth and Otto. And yet… the plane veered (or steered) even further off course in a short distance from Las Vegas.

.As the plane soared, the engines sounded even noisier, due to a new, altered-density fuel pumped in at McCarren Airport (where the Army had a gunnery school). This was done supposedly to make up for the heavier load aboard the flight and the higher altitude flight that was to come, thanks to the looming Spring Mountain chain on their way westward. The dreadful pre-flight fears by Carole, Elizabeth, *and* Otto all appeared to be totally without merit. Carole likely closed her eyes and tried to sleep, or at least daydream, thinking happy thoughts. But unfortunately, the nightmare for all on board was only beginning

.As the two fliers in the cockpit undoubtedly looked over their checklist of steps undertaken from takeoff, it should have become quite obvious the DC-3 wasn't flying at the proper elevation *or* direction. The experienced pilots *should* have known the planned proper magnetic course for Los Angeles, and any control panel readings that would have told them every procedure they were making was in great error. They were quite off the regular compass figures. There were the snow-capped mountains plainly visible right in front, but subsequent investigations later postulated that maybe the pilot was distracted by filling out paperwork following the Vegas departure. Perhaps the cockpit lights were on, it has been suggested, for Captain Williams to better see the clipboard list he needed to pencil in. Only one pilot should have been checking navigational charts, maps, radio contact numbers, gauges, and flight plans, which would necessitate having such a small light on. Once a helpful light was flicked on it would reflect in the glass windshields all around the flight deck. However it was usually a kind of tiny light traditionally hand-cupped by the pilot when scribbling clipboard notes and reading, to cautiously avoid just such a blinding situation.

Experts have stated over the years that it was unheard of for two veteran pilots to have "just forgotten" the inaccurate flight plan and to have been *seven full miles off course in fifteen minutes* in a short while without realizing their mistake. The two pilots' headphones should have immediately picked up a "radio directional beam" that would warn them they were heading way off line. The pilots also *had* to have seen the bright air beacon for pilots, the one that was still lit on the ground near Arden, Nevada, glaring upwards. Plus they had to have noticed the lights of the nearby city Goodsprings, and also the headlights of highway traffic on the ground below. *All strong, reliable clues that the airliner was definitely and dreadfully adrift.* What was going on? The two trusted pilots were *not* amazingly stupid and incompetent, naive and unaware, to be so continually off course and not realize it at some point. Things literally "went haywire" when apparently some sort of abrupt, calamitous electrical malfunction affected flight controls.

Aftermath investigations didn't find any burned wiring or sabotaged electrical mess within the DC-3 wreckage later on as much of the plane literally burned up, so it could easily have been masked. The cockpit itself was found to be totally demolished, its control panel unable to be examined, and almost all telltale records and paperwork went up in smoke, the airliner was so fully ruined. Due to the effects of crash fire and extreme damage against the cliff and mountainside, *there would be no sure answer by examiners on the scene as to possible power failures* during the flight's final horrific minutes. A careful, lengthy, and detailed scrutiny of the plane's remains later became complicated and simply wasn't fully done, due to the great destruction, gruesome carnage, cold weather, and almost urgent wartime need for closure by those investigators involved. Drawing firm conclusions simply from the wreckage was a slippery slope - literally - for anyone inspecting the case looking for rock-solid facts (in the days before the indestructible "black box").

. It hasn't been well reported over the decades, but... in those last mysterious minutes on board, an unusual sight might have captured the attention of the two pilots and some of the passengers sitting near the plane's windows behind them. Something stationary lit in the sky up ahead now round and bright, unwavering and just plain *weird.* The unidentified object in the sky was described as a round, bright amber light, lurking in place over the looming, snow-dusted Spring Mountain Range. "Reddish-yellow," as one witness specifically recalled later, found in an existing report. The Nevada night's visibility was nearly *limitless*, with no clouds or moon out, and some stars easily visible, but no star or planet was *this* big, *this* globular, *this* obvious, *this* close. Whatever it was, it was said to have flown into place and then just, well, *"parked"* in mid-air. Eerily, the UFO moved into position only "a few minutes before" the airliner arrived, recalled the main eyewitness later. This was apparently around the time the electrical operating power problem began.

.According to FBI reports *held in secret for over forty years* - released in 1985 with great censorship present - a handful of residents in the area had reported seeing "mysterious lights in the sky just above the peak," according to one modern online website's summary of the bizarre case. More shocking recorded FBI and Civil Aeronautics Board information on this eye-catching situation was *heavily redacted and buried for a long time*, with lines and whole paragraphs blacked out, the information obviously judged too explosive for an unprepared public to fully grasp, even in the 1980s.

.Released paperwork shows that on May 11th, 1942, FBI Director J. Edgar Hoover personally dictated a letter sent from his office to a Special Agent in Charge, out west, to take a closer, more comprehensive look at the UFO situation during the Lombard air crash. Strange, ominous FBI field reports had apparently been piling up for four months and worrying the director. Hoover was by then probably full of knowledge regarding the MO41 alien tragedy, despite the U.S. Army absconding all the pertinent materials and ordering silence. Thus Edgar was basically aware of the general scope of extraterrestrial flight technology and aerial abilities. "I'm instructing you to extend the investigation in this case to include complete inquiries into the nature and origin of the lights alleged to have been seen by several individuals," Hoover wrote a federal investigator that spring. We'll likely never know the full scope of the results of the FBI and Civil Aeronautics Board findings, but the remaining, declassified files give us clues

.In one censored report leaked decades later, a local rancher and eyewitness to the passing Lombard flight and the UFOs told of a galvanizing claim. Pressed to recall if the unusually bright object hovering in place was present prior to the airliner crash, the rancher chillingly confirmed it. The name of the most prominent mountain the orb or object was hovering over? Potosi! "P-O-T-O-S-I." For one man connected to Lombard, this was something to dream about, the stuff of nightmares, evidently.

.A Civil Aeronautics Administration investigator for the Lombard aerial tragedy wrote about the rancher who lived in the Mount Potosi area, backing up what the original disquieting report stated. The rancher had informed another man "of this light that was seen by him a few minutes before the plane crashed." The man recalled the UFO was "described to me as a light that was yellow and round in form and hung in the sky like a lantern." The C.A.A. man himself had seen that similar orb or lit object in the California desert sky earlier in the week, apparently the same Monday night Mrs. Gable left the state on her train trip headed east! Both mid-January night sky lights were noted to be "on the airway course" between Las Vegas and Los Angeles, an estimated "2000 feet above a ranch house" in the area. Another source placed the January 16th UFO to be about "1200 to 1500 above the contour of the low mountains." The rancher and his wife had first seen it while out driving, several minutes before the Lombard flight arrived. He also added emphatically: "It had no flickering to it," akin to "a light that was covered with a parchment." He later reinforced this amazing statement, saying "It didn't flicker or move in any way." It simply hovered over imposing Potosi (which is located on nearly the same global latitude line as through Cape Girardeau, Missouri).

.Certainly with this big round, unblinking *thing* in the sky - just sitting there and glowing brightly, unlike anything mankind could engineer - the various pilots and other people aboard the twin-engine TWA Sky Club would have been quite intrigued as they left Vegas airspace. There likely were only a scant number of citizens on the ground who *could* have noticed such a stationary light. Why? Because there was a blackout going on, following the December Pearl Harbor sneak attack. It was pretty dark on the ground. Citizens were indoors on a cold night, generally minding their own business. Many Americans were so afraid of being bombed by the Axis Powers at night, curtains were drawn and doors were shut tightly inside warm homes and businesses, or lights were just plain turned off in many cases. The higher the elevation and imposing the mountains, the more frigid and less populated the snowcapped range became. Curious, hardy people outdoors were few and far between.

.So why was there such a weird foreign light blaring so noticeably over the mountain range that night? There were no balloons or blimps assigned to the mountainous air route area, with no military bases around Potosi. There were no crude, noisy "auto-gyros" or "helicopters" around back then, not really. Whatever the one or more UFOs were, they had no business being there, lurking almost like tourists or time-travelers waiting to see an exciting but tragic, historic event in person, from a safe distance.

.And what a sight "they" would have viewed. *What took place next was the worst crash in United States air travel history*, at least to that point, according to investigators. Perhaps to this day, it remains one of the most destructive, horrifying, and seemingly inexplicable. At a fairly level position, the DC-3 smashed wing and then nose-first into a sheer rock facing of Mount Potosi, at over 200 miles per hour. Carole Lombard Gable and the 21 others on board were all killed instantly. The sleek plane was of course demolished. The physically shattered passengers and crew - their luggage and seats, food and blankets, personal effects and plans for the future - were all thrown violently into and *through* the collapsing cabin wall and fuselage, against the cliff at 8,500 feet up, and then down, down, down the rugged, unforgiving mountainside. The nasty fuel-soaked crash and crush exploded in the snow, igniting into a giant fireball, creating a huge glowing fire seen for miles around.

Ghoulish body and airplane parts and charred remains… twisted metal and smashed possessions… burned trees, cactus, and shrubs… oil and bloodstained rocks and dirt… and a scorched movie script were found by first responders and later follow-up visitors in the snowy, devastating aftermath. The aroma of burned human flesh and gasoline filled the frigid air. It literally looked and smelled like hell on earth. Beautiful Carole Lombard Gable was found decapitated, with an arm missing, her broken body burned to a gruesome crisp. Her pitiful, grisly remains were recognizable only by a patch of her bright blonde hair attached to the top of some scalp, plus her teeth later matched her old dental records. It was a horrible, yet quickly merciful way to die. The national (and often international) press made the story the number one headline for days, as deeply affected searchers struggled to reach the accident site, recover the bodies, and find answers to just what went so dreadfully wrong. No one could seemingly answer the critical question: *why?* Why couldn't this terrible tragedy have been averted?! Just a simple flick of the pilot's wrist would have maneuvered the controls to lift the DC-3 up over the looming snow-capped mountain peak.

Clark Gable – waiting in Burbank that Friday evening – was sickened and numb when informed and remained devastated for the rest of his life, falling back on his friends and Masonic brothers for emotional support. Lombard's publicist didn't believe the first news reports of the "missing" and then "downed" airliner, feeling sure it was Carole's old promotional stunt proposal, come to life. People close to Carole were utterly devastated upon hearing the news, and millions around the world were shocked and saddened. The dreadful details duly described in the press only made the stunning developments feel so much worse, deep down inside. Newsreels later showed moviegoers the very depressing and difficult task of local volunteers outside of Vegas trekking up in the snow to the proper mountain crash site on Saturday and Sunday, toiling with blankets and rope, pack horses and body bags, to bring the broken, bloody, and burnt corpses down the slippery slopes and extremely rocky, rugged terrain. The whole thing seemed so senseless and mystifying. Puzzling and enigmatic. *However...*

.Upon closer examination in hindsight, one could make a case that the "UFOs" that appeared seemingly out of nowhere above Mount Potosi didn't "just happen" to show up innocuously. It wasn't a coincidence, as if "innocent bystanders" blundered into a busy general air route for American vessels, both commercial and military. Instead, one could make a hypothetical case that these were intelligently guided non-terrestrial vehicles or light-emitting orbs that *deliberately* waited in a kind of "sky snare," to carefully entrap a key flight during the difficult early war era in post-MO41 America. That's where this heart-wrenching matter gets even more terrifying to contemplate...

.

CHAPTER TEN

Carole Lombard's Flight From Hell - Part Two

"The light was there during the crash, and then it was gone."

.A sudden, sickening aerial crash, into the side of a rock cliff, with a giant fireball. Passengers from on board the vessel, now suddenly dead on the ground. Flames and twisted metal aircraft shards landing in a big rural debris field. Uniformed U.S. Army pilots. A first response team featuring the local sheriff, the police, and concerned others, expecting dead and wounded victims needing urgent medical care on the scene. The news media sending reporters and cameramen, taking pictures of the tragedy. Hoover's FBI ordering his agents to investigate. A "UFO" that turned out to be a big part of the equation, and this startling fact being kept from the public. A very definite cover-up that was put into place, one that lasted for decades, finally being released through redacted and censored government documents to reveal aspects of the aging story. *Carole Lombard's final flight was in so many ways a spooky near-duplication of the Cape Girardeau UFO crash, nine months earlier.*

Since Mrs. Gable had recently rubbed shoulders with so many people and places that were a part of the upper reaches of MO41, the entire saga was spine-tingly familiar. For instance, Carole had even once met J. Edgar Hoover, at a Hollywood film studio, a few years before, and had her own FBI file. She was a supporter and friend of the president. She was open to the notion of the supernatural, aliens, and premonitions. Her aircraft hit the side of a rocky outcropping, just like the MO41 alien ship possibly slamming into "rock island" in the farm field outside of Cape Girardeau. Or was her flight "radiated" – accidentally or on purpose – by aliens, or even "*shot down*" like the alleged ET aerial battle above Rostov-on-Don (Zelyony, see Chapter Seven) in Russia?

.The true manner of the Lombard crash has remained a wild, ongoing, heart-wrenching mystery, even after the release of "*Fireball*" in early 2014. The startling Robert Matzen book strangely omitted any reference to the curious UFO activity, and oddly glossed over a key eyewitness description - a respected Nevada rancher - in describing what really took place just before the terrible end of the seemingly-cursed Transcontinental Western Airlines flight.. Fifty-two year old ranch owner Willard George - who was amongst those who saw the main UFO that evening and was considered credible by authorities - described to investigators precisely what took place just before the TWA tragedy. It was disturbing and shocking to witness, unforgettable, really. "I heard a terrific roar in the sky due south of me. I looked up and saw what appeared to be a large plane - I would judge about 1,500 feet above the ground. This would place the plane at about a 7,500 foot level." Obviously this was 1,000 feet or so too low, for dreaded Potosi rose 8,500 feet into the cold desert air. Mr. George's continued account makes one's blood chill even colder...

The doomed DC-3 "seemed to be revolving, from left to right in a dreaded "flat spin,"" the rancher explained, yet the plane's motors were still running. A flat spin for a large, sinking airplane certainly indicates a sudden lack of control and maneuverability. It is nearly the worst news possible for an airplane. Everyone within had to have been frightened out of their wits. But it actually grew worse. "It appeared like a disc revolving in the air, and gradually losing altitude," Willard recalled. It was obvious that "the pilot was trying to stabilize his plane, or level it off" at one point; "he was not banking." These are crystal clear *signs of an aircraft with sudden power failures as it neared the UFO area*. But how precisely could this have occurred?

.Willard George stated he could not see much of the actual plane at times, "but *the red and white lights which appeared in the sky*." Was he referring to the strange UFOs in the area? It is difficult to tell from his report statement, but the area native continued, discussing how "the plane appeared to revolve maybe twice and then all at once it went off to the south probably for ten seconds, then abruptly to the northwest at a ninety degree angle." Obviously this was not part of any flight plan or a pilot showing off, but another strong indicator that the power on board was briefly restored at times, then sadly, then failed again. Sickeningly, things went from bad to worse, for the next description made "the flight from hell" grow even hotter

."It went into dives, known perhaps as the movements of a porpoise, leaping in and out of the water." The TWA Sky Club was struggling to stay up, to stay alive. To maintain power and elevation, control and hope. The panicked passengers had to have been *screaming*, perhaps scared beyond rationality, and literally sick to their stomachs. Luggage, mail bags, and heavy Army backpacks were probably pressing up against passengers, or sliding down the aisles, along with all other loose objects, hot coffee, and anyone who wasn't in their seats. It is likely that airsick, traumatized passengers and crew were vomiting and possibly even losing consciousness, the ride was so wildly uneven and unstable now. It was a hellish rollercoaster in the sky, apparently observed by the UFO nearby. What a macabre, real life nightmare.

."These dives and climbs I would judge were at least two hundred feet and each time that one of these were made, the plane seemed to gain a little more altitude." Willard George was undoubtedly stunned as he stood in his hardscrabble Nevada front yard and watched the awful aerial circus. "After making about four or five of these dives, the plane flattened out again very close to the mountains and revolved in a "flat spin" once or twice again, losing altitude." No reliable power was available, with "the throttles appearing to be out of control."

.Utterly terrified, Carole, Elizabeth, and Otto had to have clung to their seats and each other for dear life, enduring the horrible feeling that all of their dark premonitions of disaster were now coming true, in spades. "The cabin of the plane appeared to have no lights in it," Willard mentioned noticing, confirming the basic lack of electricity during the blood-curdling plight in the wintertime sky. "At no time were the landing lights or any other lights lit on this plane, nor did I observe a green light."

."Then it took off directly southwest, gradually climbing, and then disappeared into the direction" of the looming mountain chain, beyond Mr. George's ground-level view. All aboard must have been breathing a tremendous sigh of relief at this point. Perhaps they'd get straightened out and get straight home after all, or at least find a place to make an acceptable emergency landing. Encouragingly, the rancher insisted that "the entire time the plane was going through these movements the motors were operating and were revolving at a very high speed," which resulted in "a terrific roaring sound." So while there was a pilot struggle to control the vessel the engines were often functioning at a very pumped level. But it is possible even the motors went out, too, sporadically. One other ground witness later declared: "I heard that motor for a minute, then I couldn't hear it, and then it would come on again." Again, obviously an electrical outage; it was like, said one man, "when the power goes on a bit, and off a bit." Another witness said he saw flames up to four feet in length shooting out of one engine but strangely not out of the other.

.Towards the end did the flight apparently did at least level out a bit, as investigators found from cliff markings it was struck at a fairly even impact, with no trees damaged directly underneath. One witness said shortly before the hideous end the plane seemed to be weirdly turning only "left, left, left" as it struggled to get on an even keel, and indeed it struck the rocks with the left wing first. Willard George added he also saw "the tail bobbing up and down" as it sailed out of his sight, near its finish. Veteran pilots interviewed by newspaper reporters afterwards said that there must have been something unusual and dramatic going on in the cockpit, whatever it was happening very quickly, for such odd, abrupt behavior and then an avoidable wreck to have occurred. At the end, the vessel was just too low, and was dashed and smashed to pieces. Then, just as strangely, the unexplained, foreign "yellow light" in the sky overhead suddenly took off, evidently having seen enough. Rancher Willard George also noted the departure of the "light like a lantern" that hung over the impact mountain. "It was there during the crash, and then it was gone." This hovering orb or object exited as quietly and mysteriously as it had arrived, evidently along with any others in the night sky nearby. *Whatever the UFOs were, they sure didn't help or save the doomed flight.* But one must somberly ask: did they actually *cause* the crash?

.Purposefully or coincidentally, *something, some external force* caused the flight's sporadic control and power outages. After all, the plane was mechanically sound all during its long cross-country journey, and was checked out at nearly every stop during the route. It was fully fueled and oiled while guarded by a soldier at the Las Vegas airport. The engines were later found to have been likely functioning at the time of the crash, but how well is certainly debatable. Its propeller blades were obviously damaged by the impact, as was everything else. What state of the mechanisms could be of great certainty in hindsight when the plane was so badly demolished? There was no radio transmission of distress from its last minutes, but if the pilots were struggling for control *and* there was often no electricity, they likely did not have had a workable radio to signal for help. "At no time was there any fire from the motors or the plane," Mr. George declared. If he was right, and there was no actual blaze on board, perhaps the UFO involved *did* somehow play a part. *The commercial liner was seemingly fine until it neared the strange lit object(s) in the sky. Then everything went to hell fast.*

.In the 1978 Steve Spielberg hit movie *"Close Encounters of the Third Kind,"* alien spaceships visiting various locations on earth inadvertently ended up causing manmade vehicles and even entire neighborhoods to lose power. Such electrical interference, short circuits, and power outages shown in the famous motion picture regarding sudden UFO appearances were based on *real life research, from actual documented cases*, many by respected UFO writer/researcher Jacques Vallee. Case studies of cars and mechanical objects suddenly going dead as higher-frequency ET technology hovered or passed nearby. *Could this be what took place on January 16th, 1942, UFOs killing the Lombard plane's power?* And *deliberately?* No one on the ground apparently reported any power failures, but the TWA wreck occurred up in the elevated atmosphere, in a very rural locale, where few folks were situated to be affected down below, and any mention of a temporary village power outage would have been obliterated in the press by coverage of the infamous aerial disaster.

."The plane appeared to me like a hawk that might be shot while soaring through the air," the Nevadan Mr. George stated, sending chills down one's spine again. *Shot down?* Was there an extraterrestrial vendetta here, one that deliberately and gravely affected - at times disabling - the DC-3 in mid-flight? An *intentional* brush with different, superior, and more complex alien technology? Or an outright *assault?*

Carole Lombard Gable's showbiz friend, famed director/actor Orson Welles – an FDR supporter who claimed to be related to Undersecretary of State Sumner Welles, a man likely knowledgeable of MO41 – swore quite seriously late in life that *his* inside government information on the TWA tragedy was that *it was indeed deliberately shot down by dark forces.* Orson added ominously: "The people who know it know it. It was greatly hushed up. The official story was that it ran into the mountain." {Unfortunately for his credibility, Welles speculated rather foolishly that pro-Nazi agents were assigned to the Spring Mountain Range airway and shot down Flight #3 as it neared, but there is no evidence for this, for instance no bullet holes noted in the fuselage recovered.}

.In her rather shocking 2011 best-selling book *"UFOs: Generals, Pilots, and Government Officials Go On the Record,"* author Leslie Kean compiled an impressive number of astonishing real life stories of fliers and military personnel who have admitted - some for the first time publicly - that alien crafts have buzzed manmade aircrafts and thus caused malfunctions, *such as power failures.* Engines and/or electrical applications in mid-flight have gone kaput, sometimes in minor ways, sometimes not; in some cases aircraft have managed to fly on, but often crippled, and in other cases they have not and crashes occurred. But all of this lesser-known, dangerous phenomena has been kept largely covered up until the more tell-all era of the last two decades' social culture. The misery-filled Lombard flight might just well be the saddest, most tragic result of all from this specific, hair-raising electromagnetic interference phenomenon. Yet we *still* don't know if such collisions of differing energy fields and technologies are carefully orchestrated by the advanced extraterrestrial airships.

.To hypothesize reasonably, extraterrestrial flying machines seem to possess or issue a different electromagnetic pulse and/or field, which in turn causes disabling and difficulties within overpowered cruder, manmade civilian and military aircrafts. Spark plugs, electrical wiring, radio incoming and outgoing waves, combustion engines, metallic and/or magnetic parts in every part of a TWA airliner these were all obvious suspects in hindsight for what could have been affected and malfunctioned, when clashing with the different electromagnetic operating systems of advanced alien technology, emanating outward with perhaps superior energies in the thin oxygen upper atmosphere all around. The two aerial vehicular approaches were simply operating on two different wavelengths, as the old saying goes.

.As we have seen elsewhere, German-born physicist Dr. Otto Krause was imported - just after World War II, apparently - to work with American scientists on very high-level government projects. Otto still labored for the United States government on classified projects through the coming decades. A photographer who also worked on such classified projects stated he met and spoke with Otto Krause repeatedly in the early 1960s. In 1962, the aging scientist told the young cameraman during late night card games that he knew well that recovered alien technology not only existed in U.S. hands, *but some of it came from a*

Missouri UFO crash. Otto also alleged seriously that non-terrestrial spaceships recovered and scrutinized were felt to have operated on magnetic principles, *and that often these working ET systems would result in power failures on earth, including manmade vehicles stalling or dying!* One such test of a recovered alien ship that was tinkered with and tested by government scientists in West Texas did not go well in the early 1960s, a story known by both men. The test craft was allegedly manned by three American pilots, sounding once again like a replica of the MO41 crashed disc. The main problem for this airship, Dr. Krause stated to the photographer, was that the earth's "magnetic lines" in West Texas were not really in alignment with the spaceship's magnetism. "The magnetic energy it generated was so great that anything it came close to" was overly magnetized and practically ruined, the photographer recalled hearing. Two or three entire towns in West Texas lost power as a result of this inadvertent misalignment. *Could this have been the exact cause in the sad 1942 Lombard TWA disaster?*

.{Furthermore, one must ask if there really are invisible "magnetic lines" that stretch across the planet, utilized by visiting ET scout vehicles, then is there a kind of alien "flight path" that stretches East-West across America and includes Cape Girardeau and Las Vegas along the way? There are on nearly the same latitudinal line. According to Otto Krause, recovered ET ships operated on magnetic principles and were designed that way due to the electromagnetic field or pull of Earth's atmosphere. They were evidently little scout ships created by advanced aliens to work in the *inner*, not *outer* atmosphere, say, beyond our lifeless, orbiting moon.}

.It's as if as soon as the TWA airliner left the runway at McCarren, the main UFO zipped down, into place, in the general airway route, over Mount Potosi. It aligned itself right in or near the general designated airplane flight path, the accepted aerial route between L.A. and Vegas. Possibly more than one weird round light was soon present in mid-air, possibly joining forces with the main amber entity, then they waited patiently. There was "unlimited visibility" that night, but whether the two professional pilots noticed the aerial anomalies is debatable, yet *it is certainly conceivable that the reason the TWA vessel headed off course from Vegas - or never recovered from its initial off-course start - was that the pilots purposely wanted to go check out the one or more strange lit objects in the sky ahead.* Perhaps the curious passengers wanted a closer view too. And it cost them their lives.

.Was this all a carefully-laid ET trap for the onrushing Lombard flight? Truly advanced extraterrestrials would almost *had* to know that their operating energy fields and high-tech magnetic propulsion systems would gravely affect any passing plane, including the cruder TWA Sky Club's power source. Possibly the UFOs *purposely* radiated a pulse field that would render the lower-tech manmade craft at least somewhat inoperative. The poor DC-3 had little chance of making it through the clever extraterrestrial snare unaltered. It limped along in great pain and peril, with drained power much too low to survive the mountainous countryside. Intelligent ETs might have known that such a crippled airplane *would* be sunk low, out of control, and not make it through the Spring Mountain Range alive. That's why the orbs or discs suddenly flitted from the gruesome death scene after Flight #3's impact: *mission accomplished.*

That's all a dark *theory,* anyway, on how it could have happened by deliberate actions.

.Was there someone or something on board the plane, perhaps loaded in Dayton, or Albuquerque, that interested or even *angered* an observant alien race? Was there a deliberate high frequency energy assault on the TWA aircraft as a kind of malicious "payback" for how America's citizens, government leaders, and/or military handled the crashed aliens and their wreckage in the MO41 case? We can only speculate and hypothesize since obviously information is lacking and redacted on some 1942 reports. It seems quite apparent that UFOs were purposely cut out of the public's understanding of the '42 equation/estimation. The dark truth within the Lombard crash might well have started a panic and also devastated the entire airline industry, and thus America's fragile economy and psyche during wartime. One thing is for sure, that those fifteen Army Air Corps pilots aboard the DC-3 were described at the time as "the cream of the crop." The most advanced and trusted fliers the American military could muster, under Hap Arnold's general supervision, and some were even under the TWA pilot's recent instruction. Were *they* the actual target? Did any of them have any involvement in the recovery of the April '41 extraterrestrial crash? Or was the target perhaps FDR-loving *Lombard,* due to her amazing fund-raising and anti-Axis awareness efforts? She was an amazing force of light and energy to all who knew or met her, and very publicly fighting for the American cause. Again, we'll likely never know.

.Thanks to author Matzen's fine research, we know that a full two years after the DC-3 disaster was probed by TWA corporate researchers, one of the company's executives issued a startling summary statement in an in-house letter. "There has never been any convincing evidence as to the exact cause" of the Lombard flight's strange end, privately *rejecting the official government-based "pilot error" conclusion.* "TWA does not purport to be able to explain how the accident happened, nor do we believe anyone else can," the remarkably candid statement summed up. Did Transcontinental Western Airlines execs know about the UFO angle of the bizarre tale? TWA certainly knew the *conventional* governmental answer was inaccurate but evidently could not speculate further. Neither could congressional and FBI investigators who began to compile the crash reports and UFO sightings for Director Hoover, for they were likely sworn to silence. We have to ask ourselves exactly *why*? The obvious answer was that the bottom line otherworldly truth of the tragic mystery was just "too hot to handle" for the American press and public back in '42 and for decades to come. And when some reports *were* grudgingly released, info had to be blacked out, for the painful truth was too explosive and upsetting to contemplate.

.In the last two decades, *"Fireball"* author Robert Matzen sought out the full, uncensored FBI report on Flight #3. After all, it had been a long, long time since the terrible crash, and Americans now live in a more open, tell-all society. *Yet he found the U.S. government's reaction scarily off-putting.* Robert first filed a Freedom of Information request, but this was denied, so he issued a follow-up appeal. This too was rejected. Finally a helpful FBI historian supposedly found some "hard copy" and slipped it into the mail to send to FBI headquarters in Washington D.C., to see if it could be forwarded to the author. Empty-handed Matzen was only told later that this mail was somehow dubiously "lost en route." Why all the red tape and rigmarole? *Obviously the cover-up on the stunning complete story continues to this day,* and now we know why, but is laced together here completely for the very first time.

.Precisely who else dug into the dreadful accident's cause back in 1942? Well there was as mentioned Hoover's FBI but perhaps their digging in the case wasn't evidently all that deep or satisfying, at least according to Army Air Force brass five years later. In the 1947 "White Hot Intelligence Estimate" by General Nathan Twining it is declared that "In the early months of 1942, up until the present, intrusions of unidentified aircraft have occasionally been documented, but there have been no serious investigations by the intelligence arm of the Government." Obviously the main "unidentified aircraft" cases reported seen in "early 1942" and considered an "intrusion" that was "documented" would have been the famous Lombard flight, possibly investigated also by General George Marshall's Army Intelligence (although his IPU had not been formed yet). Certainly sabotage was suspected but never proven by anyone at any time.

The stunning Lombard plane crash mystified everyone who took an interest in it. Transcontinental Western researched and wound up puzzled. Movie newsreel reports, national newspaper headlines, and radio story themes from reporters who dug into the crash were almost unanimous: it was a "baffling unsolved mystery." The powerful Metro Goldwyn Mayer film studio was amongst those who sent first responders, partly out of concern for their employee (Otto Winkler) and partly to help their biggest star (Clark Gable) receive closure on his beloved wife's enigmatic end. MGM had no answers. And since there was mail on board, the U.S. Postal Service quickly sent some representatives to the gruesome site and reviewed the matter as they gathered up surviving letters and packages in the snow. Additionally, Wright Aeronautics sent a representative up the mountain to check on their product's damaged engines, to see if company liability was possible. The Clark County, Nevada, sheriff's office, and the Las Vegas Police Department also took an active interest. Then there was the United States Congress; they investigated with data collected and assessed in - what else? - *the Capitol Building*, with staffers reviewing various censored reports and testimony in offices down below the surface level, possibly not far from where MO41 materials were once stashed. The federal government's Civil Aeronautics Board helped curious congress, the War Department, and the FBI research "the peculiar lights appearing in the vicinity where the airplane crashed," as one uncensored fed document stated. It mentioned the Senate's ongoing "Sub-Committee Investigating Airplane Accidents," *indicating that there had been other troubling U.S. aerial crashes in the aftermath of MO41.* Did they also involve UFOs? Or was the sub-committee's title just a cover for a fairly private, controlled congressional inquiry to the Cape Girardeau UFO recoveries down in the sub-basement? *For the senate to form a special group to look into such matters is a red flag that men in government were becoming seriously worried behind the scenes,* perhaps even prompted into action by a concerned, knowledgeable President Roosevelt. Were ETs vengeful after MO41 and taking it out occasionally on U.S. flights, one way or another? And what was so shocking and explosive that it was documented within the reports and then had to be blacked out before its eventual release after four decades of stalling?

Missouri Senator Harry S Truman could not take part in any senatorial investigations into civil aviation crashes going on in early '42 as he was still busy chairing his military oversight committee. But when he became president, Harry initiated just such an aerial crash investigatory group, just weeks *before* the Roswell UFO affair. In May and June of '47, many American airplanes were crashing - possibly as high as *sixty* military vessels! - and MO41-savy Truman had to take action, forming a blue ribbon committee to research the nettlesome topic. {Researcher Linda Moulton Howe has pieced together more data on this little-known part of American history, within her "*Earthfiles*" website and radio program; she says it is possible these enigmatic airplane disasters came on the heels of the American Air Force shooting down a UFO in the desert southwest that spring!}

Ensign John F. Kennedy was as stunned and saddened by the Lombard crash news as anyone, perhaps more so since he had always had a thing for gorgeous "blonde bombshells" from Hollywood. He would later go on to have torrid affairs with similar sexy actresses, like Jayne Mansfield, Angie Dickinson, and Marilyn Monroe. JFK during the time of the mid-January '42 tragedy had just been sent to Charleston, South Carolina, ostensibly for training in PT combat boats, but closer to the truth it was to get him away from juicy Washington secrets and blonde sexpot Inga Arvad. He was *still* surveilled and bugged by the FBI in Carolina, however, with J. Edgar Hoover remaining worried about what Kennedy was telling his lover (see Chapter Four).

The moviemaking community in Tinseltown reeled (no pun intended) in the aftermath of the depressing Carole Lombard calamity. Tributes poured in, but questions about the cause of the weird wreck remained. Celebrity actors, stagehands, producers, directors, and filmgoers alike mourned. The public did not realize that the C.A.B. duly issued a report that carefully cut out all mention of Willard George and UFOs, and the senate did as well. Perhaps it was just too frightening and foreign of a subject, kept muzzled for there was a war on, and national nerves were already frayed.

.Could there have been an early cover-up of the crash? Tellingly, a TWA station manager in Las Vegas, author Matzen discovered, called Burbank's TWA's office to report the crash some minutes after it was discovered, then asked what he should do about it. The Burbank company representatives had a quick, chilling response: *nothing*. Say nothing, do nothing. Release no public information. Don't even undertake a ground search for possible survivors, at least "not yet." It was all supposedly "under control." Incredibly, that was all the Vegas TWA office manager got, besides a click of the phone hanging up on him from Burbank. It was as if someone high up in TWA *knew* something critical – received via a government source? - and felt it was best not to even properly look into the matter for fear of what they might find in the minutes and hours after the accident. Or talk to the press or other TWA employees while a cover story was being hastily concocted. *Why do that over a simple and explainable accident?*

.Could the Roosevelt administration really have ordered a cover-up? As author Matzen noted, the passenger ship S.S. Normandie was sabotaged by pro-Nazi spies as it rested in New York City's harbor, ruined by fire just over three weeks after the Lombard crash. FDR's White House consistently denied the disaster investigation's later findings and publicly offered other ideas, in order to cloak the fact that the vessel was purposely destroyed by anti-American saboteurs. Could President Roosevelt have sent down word to others to do the same on the Lombard case? The president's quiet public reaction was to merely issue Clark Gable a telegram: "Mrs. Roosevelt and I are deeply distressed. Carole Lombard was our friend, our guest in happier times. She brought great joy to all who knew her and to millions who knew her only as a great artist. She gave unselfishly of her time and talent to serve her government in peace and war. She loved her country. She is and always will be a star, one that we shall never forget, nor cease to grateful to. Deepest sympathy, Franklin and Eleanor Roosevelt." Beyond that, the president had little to say, other than posthumously approving a medal for Carole as "the first woman to be killed in action in the defense of her country against the Axis powers." But was she killed in action via offense by *aliens?* It of course sounds outlandish and ridiculous at first. But then

.Days after the crash, Hollywood movie studios stopped production one mid-day for the playing of taps and two full minutes of silence and reflection, a completely unprecedented gesture. Americans from that era "would remember where they were when they heard the news," recalled one video documentary, decades later. Tribute to Lombard was paid by an Indiana senator on the floor in the United States Senate. The Roosevelt administration and U.S. Army offered to give a full military funeral to Carole, with all the pomp and circumstance they could muster, including a 21-gun salute, flag-draped coffins, and a caisson for a grand procession – precisely what President Roosevelt received three years later. Plans for a grand memorial to her in Hollywood were begun. However, Clark Gable turned them all down and simply honored Lombard's Last Will And Testament's request for a private and uncomplicated funeral service, and a quiet Forrest Lawn vault burial for the coffin graced with the charred remains of the great star. A wall crypt, and that would be it. There was a war raging, and perhaps further exploration and exploitation of Lombard and the others who died was frankly depressing and bad for the nation's overall morale, and potentially painful for the families involved. {Ironically, the cremated remains of the TWA flight's lead pilot were eventually interred not far from Lombard at Forrest Lawn.} Carole's final film – *"To Be or Not To Be"* – was delayed in its release but soon became a hit and a minor classic in cinema history, despite having to edit out the scene where Lombard asks aboard an aircraft, "What could happen on a plane?" Yet thanks to the many, many traumatic headlines and tragedies of WWII, the '42 airliner disaster began to fade from public memory.

.Back in Cape Girardeau, Missouri, the local January 17th, 1942 newspaper screamed the headline of Lombard's shocking death, and the 15 pilots on board, like all other news outlets in the country. There were also articles that day on, or mentions of, some of our MO41 cast of characters, including Reverend William Huffman, Mayor

W. Hinkle Statler, auto dealer Fred Groves, and Cape police officers. As a fitting conclusion to the way the two tragic air accidents seem mildly intertwined, two years later, in the Los Angeles harbor area, two uniquely-named ships were released separately within a few months' span into the Pacific Ocean, to aid in America's war effort. One that January of 1944 was entitled *The S.S. Carole Lombard*. The other, around this time, incredibly, was *The S.S. Cape Girardeau*.

.{In a strange twist of fate, a few rather bizarre, loosely-related news stories popped up in the 2000s. They specified that famous pilot and aviation industry baron Howard Hughes once viewed in the 1940s the wreckage of alien materials, plus the dead ET occupants of those crafts. One 2009 source was a man named "Bob" who called in to "*Coast to Coast A.M.*," the overnight radio show. Bob claimed live on the air to be a military man who was breaking privacy codes by admitting he had inherited old 16mm footage of Mr. Hughes – who was once Carole Lombard's boyfriend, in the 1920s – inspecting some metallic UFO wreckage and small ET bodies. In the old black-and-white film, Hughes scrutinized the alien crash recoveries alongside Dwight Eisenhower (before he became president). A second story involved the daughter of an aviation employee of Howard Hughes stating the famous billionaire boss told him in a late 1940s closed-door meeting that he had recently been shown in an air force hangar the recoveries of a crash-landed spaceship and alien bodies that appeared to be like "dwarves" wearing "form-fitting space suits," which again could be MO41. Still another report, from 2015, declared that some photographic stills and slides were recently found in Arizona showing small dead alien bodies from a crashed starship. These still-tightly-controlled 1940s' Kodachrome snapshots were apparently taken and developed by a desert southwest geologist named Bernard A. Ray, discovered in a box in his

Sedona home's attic. Other subjects within this startling photo collection – apparently shown separately - include future president Dwight Eisenhower *and actor Clark Gable!*}

.In the end, all that widowed superstar Gable had left from Lombard's final flight possessions were pieces of her two special jewelry clips, worn on her clothing during the trip. The dazzling disc-like "Skyrockets. What little that was left of the unique items were found in the snow and gore on the Nevada mountainside, then later placed in a locket which Clark Gable wore around his neck for much of the rest of his life (perhaps occasionally along with his Masonic jewelry). The pair of gorgeous clips – featured in a newspaper article from October 19th, 1941 – once seemed like shiny miniature spaceships, emanating rays, incredibly. Now they were crashed and crushed too. They had been close to Carole Lombard's heart, and for decades afterwards close to Gable's, figuratively and literally. The heartbreaking crash recoveries couldn't have been more ironic, all things considered. They came from the stars, in more ways than one, and fell to earth to rest in pieces.

BONUS CHAPTER

FDR-JFK: Corpses & Coffins, Cover-ups & Conspiracies

"There was even more intrigue than that!"

The deaths of American presidents Roosevelt and Kennedy were in many ways weirdly comparable. Both Democrats died suddenly while in office, leaving behind very famous and beloved First Ladies who outlived them by decades. Both liberals were old Navy men who were treated in life and in death at Bethesda Naval Hospital. Both lay in repose in the White House East Room, caskets kept shut. And both were eventually interred with the help of Gawler's Funeral Home in Washington. And both men were buried in public services that did not feature Masonic ceremonies.

Wait! This seemingly can't be. When President John F. Kennedy was brutally murdered in November of 1963, his nationally-televised funeral naturally did not include any Freemason's rites, indicating he clearly wasn't a member of that fraternity. But President Franklin D. Roosevelt *was* a member, a very devoted member, and yet he also was not given Freemason ceremonies at his services either. *That is because Masons do not allow it for members who take their own lives*, which FDR apparently did on April 12th, 1945, the 4-year anniversary of what could be called "MO41

Day." Rather hastily arranged cover-ups – aided by the Secret Service - kept the painful truth hidden regarding these two presidential deaths, "for the good of the nation," it could be claimed, in both stunning cases.

As relayed in *"MO41, The Bombshell Before Roswell,"* internet forums after the turn of the 21st century have featured fascinating public posters who have written about their once-hidden family knowledge of Roosevelt's suicide-by-gunshot, hushed up fairly effectively for sixty years until cyberspace contributions broke the dam of official falsehoods. Some examples with connections to the Kennedy assassination – and possibly to MO41 - were brought out on a website's candid forum near the sixtieth anniversary of Franklin Roosevelt's sudden demise, helping to reveal some shocking secrets and mysterious wrinkles finally ironed out for the first time herein…

One online forum contributor named Curtis Carter claimed that his personal physician once caught him reading the book *"Best Evidence,"* by author David Lifton. This groundbreaking early '80s bestseller (and later documentary film) dealt with the many discrepancies and mysteries surrounding President Kennedy's body; his bronze Dallas casket (empty?); and his hushed 1963 autopsy at Bethesda Naval Hospital, just outside the District of Columbia. At that very controlled event it appeared – and was carefully noted in an FBI report - that JFK's corpse had undergone a secret surgical procedure to remove bullet fragments in his brain, if not much of the brain matter itself as well. And also to widen the frontal neck wound to make it appear an exit wound, all *before* the official Bethesda autopsy began. This surgical process removed key evidence *and* obfuscated bullet entry wounds from different directions, via more than one assailant's rifle, covering up a troubling Kennedy murder conspiracy in Dallas. These facts all quickly reminded Mr. Carter's physician of the wild, dark truth within the old FDR saga, via a private conversation the doctor said he once had with the late President Roosevelt's "attending pathologist." {Bearing in mind there *was* no pathologist, officially, upon FDR's death in Warm Springs, Georgia.}

Franklin Roosevelt being a former Navy Under-Secretary who had been treated dozens of times at Bethesda Hospital in the past... one would naturally guess that this specific medical center would have been the prime choice for a very covert operation on Roosevelt's embalmed remains, especially when one considers FDR's private health records and doctors were all in place there. Additionally, another forum's poster claimed he first heard of Roosevelt's suicidal act long ago from a source in Bethesda Naval Hospital, apparently someone who worked there. A different online forum's source wrote: "I worked for a man in the 1980s who claimed to have been friends with a Marine who was on guard when FDR died. According to the Marine guard FDR committed suicide with a shot to the head. He thought the reason was because in his final days the pain he was enduring was insufferable, he knew he was dying and simply expedited the process." A Marine in those days would have been under the command of the U.S. Navy, which some other internet forum sources stated put out an early radio bulletin to sailors that FDR had just died of a gunshot suicide in Georgia, until the story was quickly changed to "cerebral hemorrhage."

The idea of a secret military-controlled FDR cranial autopsy at Bethesda, observed by the Secret Service, while the president's always-closed casket sat undisturbed in the White House East Room this is where we slide into a fascinating labyrinth of presidential death facts and theories that wind around and around shocking real-life covert conspiracy charges...

.Secret Service Agent Floyd M. Boring (1915-2008) stated in an interview he was on duty "outside the window" when Franklin Delano Roosevelt abruptly died in his "Little White House" vacation cottage. The next day, Boring said, he accompanied the late president's casket on the train north to Washington. It seems clear that this attractive Georgia coffin was closely guarded by military men and Secret Service guards all the way from Warm Springs to Washington, via a slow train ride. From the D.C. train station, in sight of the public, the press, the cabinet, and the new president, the expensive casket was taken through the city streets in a somber, soldier-saturated procession. The container rested on the back of a horse-drawn carriage and was taken past the Capitol Building, to the White House, and placed in the East Room, surrounded at all times by security. But… *was it empty?* No one was allowed to open the casket at any time during this trip, and only once in the East Room, when Mrs. Roosevelt had the room emptied and guards turn away when she took one last look at her dead husband. FDR's casket was later unceremoniously removed from the executive mansion, taken across Washington to the train station, and placed back on board for the rail trip north to Hyde Park, New York. There, the coffin was set on the ground next to a corresponding grave, and a second service was undertaken with family, friends, dignitaries, and much security all around. *No one in the Roosevelt family was allowed to open the closed casket and view the body at any time, despite the fact embalmed and preserved FDR should have been most presentable.*

Flash forward to eighteen years later, when Agent Floyd M. Boring helped plan "security" for President John Fitzgerald Kennedy's trip to Dealey Plaza. *Officially*, Boring didn't go on the Texas trip with JFK. Floyd said he stayed home in D.C. that day, but personally inspected the slain leader's limousine after it was flown back to D.C. and driven back inside the White House garage on the night of November

22nd, 1963. Agent Boring much later revealed in an interview he found some JFK skull/brain fragments as well as bullet fragments in the already cleaned target car – hard evidence that would have been needed for a court trial - and was joined in this unrequested late night inspection effort by Agent Paul Paterni (1907-1984), who also worked for the Secret Service during the FDR years.

.Paul Paterni was literally a spy, having also been during the Great Depression a Roosevelt Secret Service guard *and* a concurrent member of the OSS, the forerunner of the CIA headed by William Donovan, who according to an FDR memo coordinated information about MO41. It was common but covert procedure, then and now, for American spy agencies to secretly plant their own people within other government branches, to extract inside information, much of it very secret and sensitive. It seems pretty assured that FDR was being spied on by the FBI's Hoover, and also by the OSS's Donovan, and perhaps still others unknown, via some of his own Secret Service agents, acting as moles. If so, they may well have known about the amazing MO41 affair and sent word around on it to their old superiors. Floyd Boring and Paul Paterni may well have known quite a bit about MO41 without ever having seen it in person, or any photos or film of the Cape Girardeau recoveries. Trusted agent Mike Reilly admitted in his autobiography that he "kept a little bit of my ear open" for conversations going on in the president's offices.

.In a further intriguing twist, digitalized 1963 photos clearly show Agent Boring *in* Dallas on November 22nd, 1963 - *identified decades later by fellow S.S. agents* - unlike his being at home that day, which he had always claimed. *Why lie?* And why was he in Dallas of all places when not officially assigned to the Texas trip? Of all the things he could have done in Lone Star State, Boring suddenly popped up at Love Field, the Dallas airport where

Kennedy's casket was driven to, via an ambulance-hearse from Parkland Hospital. Boring was photographed helping to carry the heavy bronze presidential coffin up and into Air Force One, as reported by Secret Service author/expert Vince Palamara in late 2014. There was a five minute lull as all others waited on the tarmac as the Secret Service "secured the casket to the plane," to keep it from sliding around during the flight. In this interlude, the coffin could easily have been opened, the body removed, placed in a grey body bag, and hidden somewhere within the large airplane. In fact, the aft site where the casket was placed featured a large closet right nearby. It could conceivably have even held a shipping casket, but either way, any corpse (in a bag) placed inside this closet could have been locked tight for the flight and kept its shocking secret. Or the body could have been taken down below, into the luggage compartment, off limits to almost all personnel.

Agent Floyd Boring is also seen in the photos and footage taken that evening at the other end of the tragic trip, when the president's heavy Dallas casket was removed from AF1 at Andrews Air Force Base near D.C. and placed in the grey naval ambulance. This means *Boring helped guard JFK's casket on the flight home to D.C., eerily just like FDR's coffin by train in 1945, and it's possible both were actually empty at one point, while the body was secretly smuggled to Bethesda Hospital to have a bullet removed from the president's brain, in both cases. Is that why murdered Kennedy needed careful guarding by someone in the know, with experience in such subterfuge matters, like Agent Boring, who previously helped handle Roosevelt's macabre bodysnatching?*

.Doubtlessly it's very suspicious and strange that F. M. Boring performed the same exact duty in both presidential deaths. But it makes more sense if the considerable evidence mounting over the decades for a highly-placed domestic conspiracy to murder JFK is true, and Boring knew in advance that Kennedy was to be killed. First, President Kennedy's deceased body needed to be safeguarded from any close inspection, since this would have visibly shown multiple assailants firing from different directions, not just one assassin, firing from behind, leaving behind one "patsy" (Lee Oswald) to go to jail. That was the firm plan and official cover story before and after the shots were fired, assassination conspiracy experts have agreed for many years. And second, the casket would have to be quickly but quietly emptied, to rush Kennedy's body – kept zipped up inside a grey body bag - to the Bethesda Naval Hospital morgue for its cranial inspection/surgery, *just like FDR*. And yet the heavy bronze Texas coffin had to be kept guarded at all times to be sure the secret subterfuge was not discovered. Yes, this all sounds like a wild James Bond movie plot, yet it is *possible* this is precisely what took place and had to be kept from the American public for many years.

Despite threats to JFK's life, he was provided a terrible lack of Secret Service, police, and army protection in Dallas; Kennedy was suddenly left wide open to shooters in unguarded Dealey Plaza. As mentioned, his main Dallas motorcade planner for this pathetic and outrageous lack of security was as mentioned none other than Agent Boring. And guess who took nearly the exact same open-car motorcade route (only in reverse) through Dallas with *genuine* Secret Service and police protection some twenty-seven years earlier? President Franklin D. Roosevelt!

"Coincidences" in the FDR and JFK death cases don't stop there. Roosevelt's White House S.S. Detail chief James Rowley (1908-1992) stated he was on the grounds of Warm Springs' "Little White House" and was urged to rush back to the president's cottage that day, after word spread of the sudden death. Rowley ran fast and entered the simple building too late, but observed everything amid the grief and disbelief. James Rowley likely had great fondness for F. D. Roosevelt; it was this president who hired James to become head of "presidential protection" in 1939, keeping him close by in D.C. and in Warm Springs. It might have been James' job on April 12th, 1945, to have found a door key...

One online poster stated that his father's elderly friend was a portrait painter present on the final day for Roosevelt. This source – likely either Elizabeth Shoumatoff (1888-1980) or her artistic aide - learned that the disabled president had told his small entourage in the cottage that April 12th, 1945, "to go eat in the kitchen" while he was wheeled back to his bedroom, telling others he was going to "to take a nap." The bedroom door was shut behind Roosevelt, to give him requested privacy. Just a bit later, the gunshot was heard, and this account is backed up when another forum's contributing poster claimed that Secret Service guards rushed in only to find "Roosevelt's door locked." {Likely *both* bedroom doors, one to the hall and one to the rear outside "sun deck."} When the anxious guards managed to get one door opened – with a key? or brute force? - and hurry inside, it was said that they found the commander-in-chief near death of his self-inflicted gunshot wound.

We can say with more certainty now that a fabrication was put together by the elite Roosevelt group to say that the great leader simply had a stroke at his desk in the living room and was carried back to his bed and died there later, when in fact we know now he committed suicide while seated alone in his wheelchair inside the locked bedroom, a .45 caliber pistol likely nearby when found. This sudden, violent injury triggered the cerebral hemorrhage. It seems obvious that a comatose Franklin Roosevelt was gently picked up by his cardiologist and valet and set on his bed, and undressed there, where he expired hours later without regaining any consciousness or uttering a word. A veil of secrecy dropped during that afternoon as a cover story was concocted and the White House and Mrs. Roosevelt were called and notified.

The inner FDR circle now had a big problem: how to get the bullet removed from the president's cranium and then repair the damage in order to offer an open casket funeral, as family members, friends, the public, and the press would expect with a death that was supposedly by "natural causes," like a cerebral stroke. As stated in medical textbooks, a gunshot in the skull, making contact with the flesh, can release trapped gases once held within the layer of skin, scalp, and underlying bone. This in turn can cause a burst or tear in the surrounding tissue, creating even a star-shaped puncture with discoloration all around it. This mess would need cleaning and covering up, in more ways than one. The bullet *must* be removed, and the body *had* to be worked on, and in great privacy, Eleanor Roosevelt decided. Therefore, it needed to be separated from its official coffin and taken stealthily to Bethesda's hospital, where military officials could ordered to perform tasks and then ordered (or threatened) to keep their mouths shut about it later, or else.

In later interviews, 1963 Secret Service boss James Joseph Rowley said he also helped escort the closed presidential casket home on the funeral train from Georgia in 1945 and didn't resume White House duties until Roosevelt's corpse was firmly in the ground in New York. And eighteen years later this supposedly "*ex*"-FBI man *also* helped coordinate Kennedy's trip to Texas, while officially staying home in Washington D.C. By '63, Rowley was Chief of the Secret Service *and* a friend to Vice President Lyndon Johnson, FDR's favorite congressman who spent much time in the executive mansion during the Great Depression, observing his hero Franklin Roosevelt in action. Some researchers have stated with unearthed new facts that LBJ knew of the plot to assassinate JFK and even urged it done, and also assisted in the cover-up as best he could, to keep it under wraps at least during his own presidency. There are entire books detailing these issues so they won't be disseminated further here. But if Johnson knew, did Rowley and Boring? And other Secret Service guards? They were all in on the advance Dallas motorcade planning and their actions afterwards indicate they also hushed up certain sensitive matters that could have revealed a conspiracy.

This is not to say there was an enormous Secret Service plot to murder their commander-in-chief; no, that seems to have been mostly a mafia operation, probably with a few rogue intelligence agents. But it was a heinous plot that V.P. Johnson probably knew was developing and may have passed along information to both his D.C. next door neighbor Mr. Hoover and also to Mr. Rowley in advance, so that they could order their men to take part in pulling back protection for the president in Dealey Plaza without these agents really knowing what was truly going to happen to Kennedy. And then for Rowley to order his most loyal men to swap out the dead body on Air Force One to get it faster to its Bethesda morgue inspection and cover-up surgery. To do so would not necessarily have made these agents knowing accessories to murder, but simply following orders, somewhat based on an FDR suicide aftermath template.

Books have detailed meticulous research in showing that J. Edgar Hoover hated and spied on JFK, and secondly knew all about the many monitored and reported mob organized plots to assassinate Kennedy when he was to ride in a motorcade in the American south. And once again, Rowley used to work for Hoover and may have been a mole for the FBI within the Secret Service, and also was a friend to

Johnson, who promoted and praised him in the JFK murder aftermath, instead of firing him for incompetence. And that Rowley relied on his old friend Boring to help pull off some of this and keep it from the American public, just like they did in 1945.

More facts possibly link the three spine-tingling cases (FDR, JFK, and MO41). According to Mr. Rowley's recorded interview for the Truman Library, James knew Office of Strategic Services head William Donovan so well he routinely called him "Wild Bill" and met with him overseas during WWII, and likely with Paul Paterni as well. Rowley was also assigned to regularly protect President Roosevelt back in 1941, making him very possibly close by in the White House when MO41 went down that April Saturday night, and hovering near the high level Oval Office meetings the following week, when FDR might possibly have gone "motoring" with agents to see the wreckage for himself (see Chapter Two). In 1963, Paterni was now Rowley's Secret Service Deputy Chief, perhaps his most trusted underling. The many connections and their pasts are dizzying indeed. It is still speculative, but... *Rowley and Paterni could well have known all about the results of the Cape Girardeau outer space crash recovery as the year 1941 progressed.* They certainly would also have protectively stuck to Franklin Roosevelt like glue in any perceived ET viewing scenario, wherever the physical evidence was stashed in D.C. (under the Capitol?). Recall that even more so than other presidents, ill and immobile FDR had to be assisted physically and helped at all times. {Floyd Boring was not an agent on duty in 1941, but was hired not long thereafter and could have been briefed on the Missouri UFO crash matter during his tenure.}

Additionally, President Roosevelt dictated the special Oval Office "Double Top Secret" MO41 memorandums in '42 and '44 (and likely others not yet leaked) which had to be escorted from the White House across town by *someone* very trusted. He also most logically *verbally* discussed MO41 matters in his Oval Office and likely on his private yacht and at his other homes, and still other places. FDR's most trusted agent, Mike Reilly, admitted in his autobiography that he "kept a little bit of my ear open" for juicy conversations going on in the disabled president's offices and other sites. Likely all agents were informed to listen carefully for any information that might be of importance to the Treasury Department and Secret Service intelligence-gathering personnel – or any other agency they were secretly reporting back to.

What is more, FDR's office and/or private quarters' telephone might have been tapped, as well. Spies were everywhere, most of them domestic and keen for any top secret juicy classified information and projects for U.S. agencies. And frankly, much the same could be said for the White House years of President John F. Kennedy. Electronic bugging became even *more* popular with devious businessmen, spies, and politicians in the 1960s, and even JFK bugged his own White House telephone and had transcripts made of his taped calls.

{Speaking of the Treasury Department, which of course oversaw the Secret Service, its cabinet secretary, Henry Morganthau, Jr., arrived by train in the rural Georgia area from Washington the day before Roosevelt's suicide. Supposedly Morganthau was on his way to Florida, but he made sure to take a side trip to Warm Springs, where he huddled with FDR on the evening of April 11th. What the two men discussed is unknown, but at dinner that night eyewitness Shoumatoff later noted a strange "encompassing tension" between the two powerful men, longtime neighbors and childhood friends from their days back in New York. Whether Morganthau actually left the Georgia community the next day is unknown, but three facts *are* certain: that all Secret Service guards were stationed *outside* the president's cottage on the afternoon of his death; T-men and other government agents often carried .45 caliber pistols; and that just months after Roosevelt's funeral Secretary Morganthau abruptly resigned his post, the first of FDR's cabinet to quit. He soon published a controversial book that he claimed he received permission to issue on the night of his April 11th, 1945, meeting with the president. Henry's son Robert was to go on to become President Kennedy's pick for U.S. Attorney in New York, and eventually hired JFK, Jr., as an assistant.}

In returning to some revealing online forum information boards from the year 2000 going forward, one source in 2009 stated that he knew of an older man whose father worked at the funeral home in Washington that handled Roosevelt's body. In fact, the "elderly gentleman" stated that "when he was twelve," his family actually resided at the funeral home. This would have been "Gawler's," which was located then at 1700 Pennsylvania Avenue, just down the street from the White House; their personnel handled both FDR *and* JFK in death. The "elderly gent" had asked the forum poster why he thought President Roosevelt's casket was always kept closed, "when he died of natural causes?" The answer: "Because my father didn't know how to hide a bullet wound!"

The online source assured all that "the Secret Service and the FBI had visited the funeral home and made everyone swear under threat of death" not to discuss with others the true nature of their sensitive work on Roosevelt's body. The posting's author stated that he researched the facts and found through inspecting old 1945 records that indeed his friend and his mortician-father lived precisely where he had said and worked at the specific D.C. funeral home at the given address. Still, that doesn't mean the allegement is true, of course, but it is intriguing for sure. Could the mortician have worked on FDR – trying to patch his cranial bullet wound - in a private room within Gawler's? Or, much more likely, in Bethesda Hospital's morgue? That's where autopsy equipment and personnel were routinely available (and men were able to be sworn/threatened to silence), and when morticians could work in a peaceful, controlled environment when the medical team finished their task.

Research shows at least two Gawler's employees were also present during the similar Kennedy Bethesda autopsy procedures, noted by others later. All 1963 medical, military, and mortuary personnel were ordered *not* to speak or write of what they saw and heard, keeping the matter tamped down for decades, until private investigations by intrepid writers began piecing together the truth as the century passed. {For more inside data on this stunning JFK body-switching, casket-lugging, wound-shaping episode, see the meticulous website *"What Happened To JFK's Body? A Cover-up on the Fly?"*} But even reporters at the scene of the JFK casket removal from Air Force One spoke live on television – viewable now on *YouTube* – noted during the coverage "an Army helicopter has landed" and that "it is our understanding here that the body will be flown by helicopter, possibly to Bethesda Naval Hospital." It was this quick body-to-the-chopper subterfuge on the far dark side of the plane, away from reporters, that brought Kennedy's corpse swiftly to Bethesda's helicopter landing pad, and from their into a Gawler's black hearse, for the short ride to the morgue dock nearby. Additionally, White House Communications Department audiotapes released decades after the '63 tragedy reveal the Secret Service man in charge there ordering Air Force One's agents: "You accompany the body aboard the helicopter." Not the *casket*, and not by climbing into an *ambulance*.

The forum contributor Curtis Carter stated that in 1982 his "early sixties" doctor-friend told him the attending pathologist stated he *finally* succeeded in removing FDR's slug, but evidently we can surmise that he left the head wound so unacceptably obvious that an open casket was still out of the question, mortuary work or not. Thus the East Room ceremony for the late F. D. Roosevelt went on as scheduled with the coffin kept firmly closed (as did the Hyde Park service). T-men/SS agents Boring and Rowley were around to make sure the covert "switcheroo" operation was a quiet success that April of '45, and were rewarded handsomely when they did much the same in November of '63, with neither man facing legal scrutiny or punishment for their actions or failure to protect either of the two late presidents. {Rowley was made Chief/Director for more than ten years, while Boring was named Inspector.}

It's very intriguing to note that one week before he left Washington for Georgia on a train, President Roosevelt was driven to – of all places - Bethesda Naval Hospital. FDR had been treated or tested at Bethesda Hospital a whopping 29 times (at least) from 1941 to 1944 alone; the staff knew him well and they kept his voluminous medical records under lock and key. Ostensibly in late March of '45 he went to visit ill Cordell Hull, and then meet his old mistress, Lucy Mercer, whom he hosted at the White House the next day, likely planning their (final) rendezvous in Warm Springs in a few weeks. Strangely, Franklin's old romantic affair with Lucy was rekindled just after MO41 went down; she even began signing in to the White House log book as a low-key guest ("Mrs. Johnson") as of June 5th, 1941. It seems quite possible FDR confided in her some secrets, including the UFO crash, but this is speculation.

In backtracking a bit, we must recall that there *was* for a fact a startling 5:45-9:15 a.m. gap on April 13th down in

Warm Springs, Georgia, between the time the Spring Hill mortuary group finished their work on FDR's body and the point at which the presidential casket was formally and publicly taken from "The Little White House" and placed in the back of a mortuary hearse in the front driveway. Then it was driven slowly, under heavy guard, to the town's train station, in a procession before a weeping public. A Georgia mortician who wrote a summarizing report of his group's work said "the government" took over the body during this three-hour dawn timeframe. *Could this have been when the body of FDR was removed from its casket?* If so, it was likely done at the direction of a bereaved Eleanor Roosevelt by two or more trusted Secret Service guards, who could have placed the thin cadaver in a different container or body-bag in order to smuggle it to Washington for its critical skull autopsy and bullet removal. There would have been plenty of time within this "government gap" for obedient agents and aides to have rounded up a large trunk or simple shipping casket, and then a sheet or blanket to wrap FDR's corpse in, to carefully place it inside the new container, in order to quietly sneak it out of to a waiting vehicle, possibly when it was still dark outside. The "box" was carefully placed in a car's trunk or back seat. From there, it could have been driven by a loyal aide and S.S. agent to an airport, such as the one at nearby Fort Benning, Georgia, where the military airplane that brought Eleanor and her party down from D.C. was likely still sitting on the runway, all fueled up and ready to go. This would have swiftly and secretly brought the body to Washington, and to Gawler's and/or Bethesda's morgue, a full day or more before the official casket arrived on the train for the public to somberly view. While this scenario is admittedly purely speculative, it is at least plausible. Especially when considering another online forum posting, one that identifies an actual name…

Describing someone involved as "high in Illinois government," an internet forum author named Virginia Jarrow in 2012 referenced a family friend in Chicago named "Charles Schwartz" who later confessed that he was in Warm Springs and helped FDR mistress Lucy Mercer – and presumably the portrait painter and her aide, Robbins - hurry out of town, which took place within an hour of Roosevelt's abrupt demise. Virginia claimed that Charlie also told her mother (who worked for him) how he personally "saw that Roosevelt died of a gunshot" wound. Moreover and more revealing, Virginia said online, *Mr. Schwartz "was chosen to remove the body to Washington D.C."*

Perhaps Charles Schwartz physically helped pull up FDR's cadaver from its casket and place it in another container, but apparently with more certainty he quietly rushed it up the East Coast to Washington for the private bullet removal from the skull. If this is true, *the ceremonial Georgia casket was indeed empty*, the entire time it was taken from the cottage, guarded on the train north to D.C., paraded through the streets, and given a solemn, brief service at the White House. Perhaps being a part of bare-knuckle Chicago politics evidently gave Charlie Schwartz the experience and maturity to handle the touchy FDR cover-up situation. While anyone can write any sort of scenario on the internet, Virginia Jarrow gave her real name and that of the helpful person involved in the FDR death cover-up, and overall her allegations seem to fit known facts.

In a chilling 2014 coda to the '12 forum allegation, Jarrow stated that her mother discovered Charlie Schwartz near death in a wrecked car in Chicago, in "an attempt on his life because he knew too much." Virginia's mother and uncle rushed broken Charlie to the hospital to save his life, and while he did recover frightened Mr. Schwartz never spoke to them again, very frightened. His life and career were obviously in jeopardy, as perhaps was Virginia's mother, who was then supposedly harassed and shuttled about to less meaningful jobs within Illinois government, in Springfield, the state capitol. Later when back in troublesome Chicago "she resigned under duress" and left the state entirely, according to internet poster Jarrow. Certainly this indicates that it became known that Charlie had told his loyal employee too much, for her to be demoted and harried so, if true.

Online research shows a married "Charles E. Schwartz" lived on Park Avenue in Chicago in 1940, and would have been the age of thirty-seven in the spring of 1945. A second candidate, "Charles Phineas Schwartz, Sr." was fifty-nine (with a twentyish son named Charlie, Jr., in 1945); he was involved in Chicago politics as a lawyer and dedicated alumnus from the University of Chicago, the site of secret atomic bomb laboratory. This Charles worked for the Selective Service Commission in WWII, Illinois political action committees, and *was an FDR supporter who kept correspondences from the late president in his personal papers*. As an active Jewish fundraiser and civil rights attorney, Charles P. Schwartz, Sr., had even developed a friendship with FDR's Secretary of the Interior, Harold Ickes, also a Chicago native who attended University of Chicago. A third candidate, "Charles K. Schwartz" is simply listed in *"The Political Graveyard"* website as a "Cook County, Illinois, Democrat and Delegate to the Democratic National Convention {held in Chicago} in 1940, presumed dead and burial location unknown." Either of these three possible candidates would had to have known some pretty deep, dark secrets about Roosevelt to have been threatened - and nearly murdered - although other factors admittedly could have been involved, but the third candidate seems to be the most likely choice. What possible reason would they have, to have been in Warm Springs, Georgia, at the time of the president's final, fatal decision?

One thing is for sure: FDR greatly valued and courted Chicago politicos, and was once nearly shot, ironically, when an assassin instead wounded Chicago's powerful mayor, Anton Cermak, standing next to his open car when both men were visiting Miami in early 1933. Hospitalized Mayor Cermak later died of his gunshot injuries just two days after FDR's inauguration. Chicago's mayor in 1945 was Democrat Ed Kelly, who was "an often consulted advisor" to President Roosevelt, according to an online biography. Outside of solidly pro-FDR New York City, Chicago was the next largest and most influential U.S. city and the Democrats courted it often with party conventions held there. Cook County, Illinois, politics often meant corrupt "machine" insiders dealing dictatorially with the rank and file through hardball "ward-heelers." Meanwhile history shows that bloody organized crime and violence had long been a major problem in Chicago. Sam Giancana, a national mafia figure of tremendous ruthlessness, was a Chicago-based contact of JFK's, an early supporter who soon grew deeply disenchanted with the burgeoning Kennedy administration's "War on Organized Crime." Many investigators have pinpointed Giancana and his mob influence in the murder of JFK, and possibly also in the sudden, suspicious deaths of some of the people "who knew too much" in the aftermath.

In her only reply on this author's inquiries on what is now known about the FDR covered-up suicide and secret autopsy saga, octogenarian Virginia Jarrow wrote briefly but most enticingly in 2016 about what she learned from her mother (and thus Charlie Schwartz): "There was even more intrigue than that!" And much can likely be said of the JFK murder and secret autopsy cover-up as well.

The dark side of the Roosevelt death data must sound very familiar to those who have investigated the various mysteries and apparent conspiracies surrounding the '63 murder of President Kennedy. Many JFK assassination eyewitnesses were harassed and attacked. Some turned up abruptly dead, many by very dubious, frightening circumstances. When one looks into the detailed and impressive research of JFK conspiracy authors Vincent Palamara, Doug Horne, David Lifton, and others, there was much the same subterfuge and trickery going on with the very same Secret Service agents guarding assassinated John F. Kennedy's body and/or casket once it was flown on Air Force One to D.C. and then driven to the Bethesda Hospital morgue in November of '63. At least one key military hospital eyewitness seriously alleged it was a black hearse – apparently from Gawler's – that delivered JFK's body to Bethesda's morgue in a grey body bag inside "a pinkish-grey shipping casket," a full *twenty minutes before* the now-famous grey Navy ambulance that slowly transported the (empty) Dallas coffin and grieving First Lady, along with Attorney General Robert Kennedy and two Secret Service men from Andrews Air Force Base.

Webpages and a few books have chronicled at least some of this fascinating body-napping chicanery so well that further details will not be given here. Neither will the subject of whether JFK was murdered as he was about to inform the public about the truth regarding extraterrestrial visitation, a serious charge better left to other authors and venues. But it seems that in both life and death, a great aura of mystery and intrigue surrounded both Franklin Delano Roosevelt and John Fitzgerald Kennedy. Many questions arise as to their inside knowledge and secretive actions behind the scenes on many issues, especially regarding the matter of aliens observing us on earth. Did MO41 influence in any way, even small ways, either man's death?

So many of those questions are seemingly answered when you conclude that perhaps as early as late 1941, Jack Kennedy found out about the three alien bodies and their crashed spaceship culled from a Cape Girardeau farm field. And that Franklin Roosevelt found out right away. It remains reasonable and feasible, and fits with the jigsaw pieces already in place. It makes a spine-tingling case even more stunning, the implications and complications therein.

Post Script

I wish at this point to pass along the names of seemingly obscure men, all likely deceased, that were probably related to the MO41 saga, directly or indirectly. They are worth mentioning as some of them may well have *seen and handled* the Cape Girardeau farm's ET recoveries and helped import them to a Sikeston, Missouri, airfield on Saturday, April 12th (and perhaps 13th). And others in this group of Army fliers may well have learned the shocking truth before their time in the Missouri Institute of Aeronautics ended that spring, through rumors or reports, or even just peeking into boxes. According to *The Sikeston Herald* newspaper from April 24th, 1941, this was the class of cadets – associated with the affiliated Parks Air College - from the Army's 309th Flying Training Detachment that had been in pilot training and were to be shipped out "the next day" to their next assignment in San Angelo, Texas (along with their leader, Captain C. B. Root).:

George Abel, Lee E. Baker, Richard Baldwin, George F. Bechtel, John W. Berry, Edwin S. Bracher, Sherman W. Broka, Willis H. Brooks, Harry R. Bulmer, Ed W. Carpenter, Fred P. Cesnik, Ed G. Cook, Nathaniel T. Cornell, Harold A. Cunningham, Robert E. Daley, Waltemar E. Dombrowsky, Robert L. Dunham, Robert L. Elwel, William S. Evans, Albert R. Fingerman, Willis F. Flick, Edward J. Gabor, Virgil C. Greer, Richard D. Giles, Matthew Glossinger, Jack E. Grapevine, Rockford V. Gray, Delvert E. Hamilton, Mahlon B. Hammond, William R. Heck, Robert T. Henning, Howard A. Henderson, Ed G.

Hoffman, Charles W. Hughes, James E. Hunter, James E. Huntington, Elbert W. Hyde, Alex G. Kolinsky, Ed P. Kreimer, Joe E. Lamphere, Robert W. Lennox, Weston M. Lennox, William V. Litvin, Robert Luebbe, William A. Marsh, Harold A. Martin, Robert A. Matre, Fred A. Mayfield, Alan P. Michaels, Maurice J. Murray, Robert J. Neal, John A. Vanderpoel, Francis R. Warner, and James B. Whitten.

Another April 1941 Sikeston newspaper article also mentions A. C. Miller, R. F. Stemen, Myron Cole, H. E. Miller, Fred Olds, John G. Shriner, A. W. Howard, and Richard Beavens. And let's not forget Ben B. Schade, James P. Wallace, Ralph Rockwood, and Captain Charles B. Root.

If anyone knows anything relating to MO41 via these aviators who were taking the various primary courses while serving their country honorably in the Army Air Corps back in the day, perhaps they can either contact me via the publishers of this book. Or at the special Facebook page "Cape Girardeau's 1941 UFO Crash, America's First."

Of all of the aforementioned young men, the most likely "in the know" would be Jack Grapevine as he was listed by the news article as the unit's Intelligence Officer, and that would make him the most likely candidate for having participated in and/or keeping the lid on such a top secret affair. Finding surviving relatives and friends of these departed souls nowadays would be most difficult and beyond my capabilities as a writer. But some of these Army trainees might have left behind information on the greatest story in American history, if not all of human history?

My friends, it will now take some more seasoned and well-connected investigators with greater power and patience to acquire further inside MO41 information. I humbly hand the case over to anyone with the necessary curiosity, open-mindedness, and connections to dig further for proof. This will require genuine investigatory ability, financial backing, and inside sources to uncover more data on this aging but still fascinating, historic saga. After issuing these ten chapters and the following bonus section and source notes, I'm all tapped out, as mentioned earlier. I have no further data to share. If the reader wishes to continue the investigation, that's great, but please remember patience and open-mindedness are important assets to possess and utilize. With the original "*MO41, The Bombshell Before Roswell*," and this sequel, "*3 Presidents, 2 Accidents*," to guide you, you should be on the right track to guide you to possible fame and fortune. Or perhaps only more frustration and fruitlessness. I wish you good luck and God speed. - - - PBS

3 PRESIDENTS, 2 ACCIDENTS

More MO41 UFO Crash Data and Surprises

Chapter Source Notes & Trivia

SECTION I:

CHAPTER ONE – The Rusty Blevins saga arrived via Facebook, in May 2016. The friendly source led off by informing me that my data for MO41 was "spot on" minus the detail of Rusty being a farmhand, not the farm *owner*, who called for help on the night of the accident. The source was to go back to his grandmother – Rusty's friend late in life – who told this online helper the crash details, apparently a few years before Blevins passed away, or so I was told. They declined to say what Rusty's real name was and I will respect that decision; it indicates he might have living relatives in the Cape Girardeau area. . . . Blevins' story fits in with what "AllSouls" wrote a few years ago in *Topix,* that his *grandparents* "owned and farmed the land where the crash occurred" but he never said that the married pair saw the UFO hit the soil, or that they called the fire department, or were even home at the time. They were also said to be very nervous and scared about repeating the tale, meaning the Army talked sternly to them too about blabbing on what took place on their land. . . .

Paul Blake Smith

White House Saturday and Sunday activities are found in the FDR presidential digitized database. "Easter Monday" information from internet sources, and a front page article found in the 4/15/41 *Southeast Missourian* newspaper. . . . The lowdown on Stimson and Marshall's plan to create the all new "Army Air Force" was culled from *Wikipedia* and Linda Wallace online articles. The Marshall memo to Stimson is shown as mentioned at the digitized document database within the "George C. Marshall Foundation Database," a helpful website. The text mentions that Harry Hopkins organized the White House afternoon meeting to discuss war-related topics, but even if that were true it doesn't mean that this was *all* that was discussed, or at least mentioned in the hand-delivered GCM memo. Marshall admitted to Stimson, "The discussion with the President was of a general nature," which *still* could well be an inclusion of MO41, possibly without even mentioning it by name. Also, a letter has surfaced dated Monday, 4/14/41, from Marshall to his friend Douglas MacArthur, covering the issue of handling retirements of Army officers and their return to duty, but this was clearly typed up at his office by a secretary and had nothing to do with the Missouri events. It could have been typed after sitting around as mere notes for days or even weeks . . . Annie Cannon's life and death described in her *Wikipedia* page. . . . The remarkable 5/27/41 FDR radio and newsreel address would have needed careful construction over the course of weeks, so Marshall might well have been in on that planning in late April and much of May 1941. The critical speech was delivered along with an official emergency proclamation for that date, with wording that may have alarmed some citizens who didn't realize we as a nation were that close to or vulnerable to some sort of assault - by any outside forces. . . . Data on GCM's 4/12/41 directive on air defense came from the web page, *"The Army Air Forces in World War II: Men and Planes."* Chapter 2, page 71. Edited by W.F. Craven and J.L. Cate. The original text added: "New air support commands in the summer of 1941" were notably stepped up. In other words, more aggressive patrols of America's skies by armed planes, and plans to create more civil and military defense warning sirens and systems. . . . Info on FDR's remarkable "triskaidekaphobia" comes from biographies and a 10/5/2000 article in *"Update"* magazine, by Neil Thomas, Volume 20, #3. This can be found online at udel.edu/PR. . . . *"Franklin D. Roosevelt, Day by Day: A Project of the Pare Lorenz Center at the FDR Presidential Library"* is the online source for perusing the late president's daily records. Most of the FDR logs center around his activities recorded by secretaries, plus the White House usher's diary, a stenographer's diary, and perhaps even household staff, especially for visitors to the Oval Office, who were recorded in the appointment book by an aide or social secretary. "Errors can occur in data entry," the site is careful to note, thus some leeway is required in exact times of certain meetings with Roosevelt. The archivist at the FDR Presidential Library e-mailed to say that they have no records of any sound recordings created by FDR and his White House staff from 1941, sadly, nor any White House or Oval office telephone records, not even for the White House switchboard. . . . The digitized records show FDR receiving Canada's Prime Minister at the White House for tea for nearly an hour late Wednesday 4/16/41. . . . Mackenzie King's fondness for spiritualism is found within a number of webpages on him, along with *Wikipedia* on his history. He was a devout Christian, Freemason, and lonely bachelor who had lost many relatives in a short span of years, causing him to treasure his dogs greatly, and also his lady friends who enjoyed testing mediums and séances with him. All of this is fodder for howling skeptics and critics online today, calling him a "lunatic." . . . King was also a friend to President Truman and the two men signed a special document for a Calgary Masonic Lodge's event, records show. . . . Eleanor Roosevelt's famous *"My Day"* diaries can be accessed online at gwu.edu/erpapers; she is unlikely to have been briefed on MO41, not in a "need to know" situation. In March of 1950, Mrs. R hosted the NBC talk show, where she discussed issues of the day and interviewed two commercial airline pilots who recently saw a "flying saucer" that impressed them - and her, via a newspaper report. Eleanor tellingly said on the air about unidentified flying objects as her unusual interview wound down: " I never remember hearing before, and I will say I've been a little skeptical before, I thought people were seeing things." This does not absolutely mean "E.R." did not learn of MO41 but was referencing various citizens' reports of various UFOs in the skies in the late 1940s and 1950, yet still the phrase "*I never remember hearing before*" indicates a lack of knowledge of alien visitation matters. The entire UFO subject was "certainly very interesting" she concluded on the broadcast, before moving on to other topics. Information on this show comes from presidentialufo.com, where webmaster/writer Grant Cameron cited "UFO historian Barry Greenwood" for bringing forward an actual NBC transcript of the Eleanor-pilots interview. . . . It may not relate to MO41 news, but Eleanor Roosevelt's confidante, Joseph Lash, was recorded as having arrived at the White House Sunday morning on 4/13/41, at 12:40 a.m. This was probably the general appointed time it was originally conceived that the First Lady would arrive home by plane, the flight of which of course was cancelled. . . . Coincidence or not?: FBI agent Henry Boone quit the agency just two months after MO41 and joined George Marshall's Army Counter Intelligence Corps. Thomas Cantwheel joined the CIA the following year, to help recover and hush up UFO crashes. According to historicalgmen.com, Boone was joined by two other FBI men in an intelligence group called "The Pond," likely sending Hoover inside data from within GCM's CIC. . . . According to the helpful *Missourian*, less than two weeks after the crash, there was another confab of local lawmen.

St. Louis FBI agent Norris - not Cape Girardeau Agent
Jones, interestingly - traveled to a Sikeston meeting of
"Missouri Peace Officers" that featured Cape Girardeau
County Sheriff Ruben Schade. Fellow officials from both
the Missouri police and highway patrol and the Federal
Bureau of Investigation all gathered in the seemingly
obscure small town where the PAC/MIA - including Sheriff
Schade's brother Ben - was situated. Ex-Sheriff J. Fred
Hartle was said to be there, too. Crime-fighting efforts were
ostensibly discussed at the closed-door confab. But was
that all? It would have been the perfect time to coordinate
information on witnesses to the crash and how they were
reacting in their communities at both ends of the stick, in
Cape Girardeau and in Sikeston. . . . Was Hartle at the
MO41 scene as well, and now called in to help discuss any
loose ends in the ET recovery case while meeting with
others in the know? And what kind of "work" was J. F.
Hartle doing at the MIA school? It turns out that the "dirt"
on Hartle was that conditions were extremely windy that
spring, and loads of valuable soil from all the nearby area
farms were ending up getting spread across the Sikeston
airport's mostly grass runways, endangering landings and
takeoffs. According some local history Linda Wallace dug
up, "30,000 yards of top soil at a two inch depth" was
deposited "on the home field" at a cost of $15,000 to
remove that April and May. *The Missourian* stated
elsewhere that Hartle was the main man in charge of MIA
"dirt removal."

CHAPTER TWO - Details of FDR's December 1941 trip
to the Capitol, and his ramp access there was derived from
the pages of *"Pearl Harbor,"* by Steven Gillon. . . . The
story of the U.S. atomic bomb program can be found in
various sites online, and in books, such as 2012's *"The
Untold History of the United States,"* by Oliver Stone and

Peter Kuznick. . . . A two-part ABC-TV "20/20" in 1991 reported on how the American military had its own sneak attack plan for bombing Japanese targets *before* any war was declared in December of '41. A lone surviving member of FDR's administration was interviewed on camera to acknowledge that this emergency proposal was valid, quite top secret, and very sketchy at best. It was discussed in private military circles for some time, and first formulated on paper in July of that year. The dicey plan was for American pilots and planes to join forces with the "Flying Tigers," the U.S.-backed fighter planes that operated out of Asia. Under the guise of a "Chinese assault," the false flag air operation would undertake aerial attacks on specific sites in Japan and later claim "no direct American involvement." This desperate scheme was of course never undertaken, and was merely a contingency plan drawn up for Roosevelt in case the Japanese military began assaulting United States properties, either overseas or at home, or give obvious overtones that they were on the verge of doing so. Such military maneuvering on both sides, leading up to Pearl Harbor - and warfare elsewhere on the planet - would have been most entertaining for visiting aliens, observing without getting involved. . . . A Tennessee native, Cordell Hull's curious resting place in D.C. can be found within FindaGrave.com; he knew he was sick with tuberculosis for many years, and since it is an incurable disease he likely had this specific tomb picked out for decades in advance. . . . The mentioned letter from General Marshall that spelled out days before leaving his companions for the camp inspection tour - "Colonel Ward and two pilots" is found in GCM's digitized online database records. . . . An April 1941 newspaper report claimed that GCM attended the 4/11/41 funeral for Texas Senator Morris Sheppard, but this cannot be so. It was held in Texarkana, Texas, near the Arkansas border. Sheppard died on 4/9/41 in D.C. but he was given a royal sendoff since he was Chairman of Senate Military Affairs. According to the news story in *The*

Sikeston Herald, a Sikeston native (Captain Wade L. Shankle of Fort Leavenworth's 35th Army Division) handled the military-police aspect of the services, with a startling convoy of 65 trucks driving from Leavenworth to Texarkana to take part. "The men stated it was the largest funeral they had ever seen" and Marshall was said to be "a Guard of Honor," but he was actually not too far away, busy inspecting Army forts in mid-Texas that day. . . . Fun fact: Exactly twenty years after MO41, on 4/12/61, the first man to go into space, and then orbit the earth - Yuri Gagarin - accomplished his dangerous mission safely for the Russian space program. Gagarin ejected from his spacecraft after the goal was achieved and floated down to Soviet soil, while the ship crash-landed. Presumably, the April dating for this cosmonaut's historic space flight is coincidental, but who knows? The Soviet Union had countless spies in Western nations from the 1920s (to this very day), many riddling FDR's administration. These "red moles" sent back information for their communist brethren; Stalin and his GRU spy-masters might well have learned of the MO41 affair and his eventual successor, Nitika Kruschev could have arranged this orbital mission on this day on purpose. Or it's mere happenstance. . . . What was learned at *some* point by nuclear scientists in mid-1941 was that only 5 to 10 kilograms (about 11 to 22 pounds) of pure uranium were needed for an atom bomb, not the whopping *500 tons* as originally believed. What brought about this breakthrough understanding on micro-levels of uranium and how they could be utilized properly in controlled fission? What small but workable technology was discovered and tested to prove this was the successful path to hurry down in the rush to create the a-bomb? Perhaps MO41's recovery propulsion system... or... just regular lab research, possibly done by British scientists in the so-called "Maud Report" Bush read 10/3/41. Possibly we'll never know for certain. . . . Trivia: in 1897 several UFO sightings in central Illinois were reported in the news for April 12th, strangely enough. In one case, a human-like person emerged from a peacefully landed, elongated craft, and made mechanical repairs, allegedly. Many more American states reported odd sightings over the years on this specific date, including a 1973 southeastern Missouri glowing orb. For more, see ufoinfo.com, "On This Day." . . . The mentioned famous world leaders and their wives and staffers, military advisors, and reporters settled in for WWII Quebec conferences in August of 1943, and again in September of 1944, with bachelor Mackenzie King as the congenial host. It is said he moved around to the various parties and made sure they had everything they needed for a fulfilling and pleasant stay in his beloved Quebec. Air Force General Hap Arnold and G. C. Marshall also attended these well-guarded meetings alongside FDR, notably. *If* extraterrestrial visitation was to be privately discussed, these were the perfect men to undertake the issue and keep it from the public. Also, at the '43 meeting, a formal "Quebec Agreement" was agreed to and signed, allowing for the merging of two atom bomb projects to create combined policies via a committee led by Dr. Bush and Secretary of War Stimson, two familiar names within the MO41 governmental examination.

CHAPTER THREE - Info on Freemasons can be found within books and online sites, some presented by Masons themselves. This includes their ties to FDR, HST, George Washington, members of congress, astronauts, and J. Edgar Hoover. Historical/biographical books helped only a little, as being a Freemason is often so secretive that such authors don't have much information to present. . . . Cape Girardeau's Masonic past can be found online, too, in their own world wide website. Their Broadway & Spanish Street "Masonic temple" hosted a long-planned, largely women's special dinner on Monday, 4/14/41, and then their usual

Tuesday evening male/female "Order of the Eastern Star" affair, even advertised as such in the local newspaper, for "Eastern Star Offices at Mason Temple, at 6:30." The men's private lodge meeting would take place later in the month, on Sprigg Street. . . . There is an unconfirmed belief that First Lady Eleanor Roosevelt was a member of "Eastern Star." . . . Rush H. Limbaugh Sr. was the highest-degree Mason in Cape. According to his biography he was a member of "Cape Council #20, Kriptic Masons." He achieved his thirty-second degree Masonic honors, however, in St. Louis, at their "Wilson Chapter Royal Arch Masons, Scottish Rite Lodge." Could Stu Symington and Forrest Donnell have also attended that lodge, at least at times? Certainly possible. RHL I's son Stephen became a fellow lawyer and Mason; he wrote an e-mail and a letter to me in 2013 to confirm his father's top status with the Freemason organization, and wrote me again in 2014 to mention his brother, Rush II, was not a Freemason. . . . Rush III's description of his father's love of aviation is from *"The Rush Limbaugh Show"* website, under "Archives" of previous radio show remarks, from 2/12/09. . . . RHL I's connection to F. C. Donnell was further strengthened when he was named a "colonel" within the governor's staff, 1942-1945. . . . RHL II was a major in the Army Air Force who "flew P-51s in the China-Burma theatre," according to his famous son, during World War II, then discharged honorably. {This sounds close to, if not part of, the aforementioned "Flying Tigers."} Rush II remained a member of the American Legion and the Veterans of Foreign Wars after he resettled in Cape Girardeau following WWII. . . . One of RHL I's fellow Freemasons in Cape was another radio source, Oscar Hirsch. He owned and operated Cape's first radio station, KFVS, and a decade later turned that into the town's first television station by the same call letters. As an older man, Oscar may well have employed young and inexperienced Rush III as a radio deejay for a while, perhaps out of friendship with his fellow Mason Rush I. It's interesting to know that KFVS radio had a mobile transmitting truck in the Great Depression, and conceivably have shown up with a news reporter and a microphone at the MO41 scene, only to have been shut down by the Army if so. So far that enticing notion is only a fuzzy possibility. . . . Sheriff Ruben R. Schade (a staunch conservative) rubbed shoulders with RHL I just days after MO41. Ruben officially served formal notice to Rush that he was accepted as a representative of Governor Donnell at the local level for the controversial gubernatorial recount session, according to *The Southeast Missourian* for Tuesday, 4/15/41. I suspect R. R. Schade was a Freemason, likely mostly at the Jackson #6 Lodge, but cannot prove it. Ruben's predecessor, Sheriff Hartle, was a Democrat and apparently a Mason. . . . Garland Fronabarger was apparently *not* a Cape Freemason, according to his son John, speaking to me by phone in the spring of 2013. . . . Rush Limbaugh Sr. was the Commencement Keynote Speaker at my high school graduation in the 1980s. His law firm today is run by a grandson and others who make sure to advertise they are "serving Cape Girardeau and Sikeston," reaffirming ties to that city about an hour's drive south of Cape. . . . One possible kin to the Rush Limbaugh family - and a possible MO41 source - was a barber in Scott County, James R. Limbaugh (another "Rush"?). Then fifty-three years old, according to a stat in an online viewable 1940 U.S. Census form, James lived and worked near the suspected heart of the MO41 crash area, in his modest hometown of Chaffee, Missouri. Owning a "private shop" to cut and style men's hair in a small town like Chaffee made him privy to plenty of local information, undoubtedly. He was also an integral part of his Chaffee church, directing a choir program there on the evening of Easter Sunday, 4/13/41, according to the *Missourian,* days later. (Rush Jr. was also a church choir director). So well thought of, James was elected the president of the local Rotary Club within two weeks of

MO41. . . . Another possible relative was William Rush Limbaugh. A virtual namesake, WRL lived a simple life tending to crops and cattle (often in Scott County, apparently) before he retired in the 1970s, passing away in Chaffee without next-generation heirs in May of '74. William had a wife but no children - sort of. He married Wilma Bridges at age twenty in 1933, the same year his son was born, and was then given away to be raised by another couple. Thus he has no kin to interview. Both RHL I and WRL were born in Bollinger County, Missouri. WRL was listed in the 1930 U.S. Census as a "cattle feeder." He was almost 33 at the time of the MO41 incident, and died 33 years later, in Chaffee General Hospital, according to his newspaper obituary. Whether William knew the MO41 facts is still unknown; his two former wives are also dead and so is the son he gave away to a foster family, so their trail goes cold. Overall, however, William - who was an Army corporal in World War II - would be a great candidate for a connection to the now-world famous namesake if he had been farming in the Chaffee area in '41. . . . In 1981 my non-Masonic father moved into a house on a street in midtown Cape, right next door to Rush Jr.'s former home, where Rush III, the famous broadcaster grew up. {Both Rush Sr. and Rush Jr. died in the 1990s.} Down the next street lived another possible MO41 player, retired Cape Girardeau Fire Chief, Carl Lewis, but he passed away shortly after my dad settled in. My father lived at this Cape house until his death in early 2009. . . Apparently Phillip Steck was employed by the city of Cape as a Fire Commissioner in the early '40s, and likely knew the truth about MO41 as well; the Steck family lived near my dad also. . . . Cape Girardeau firemen did not just sit around and loaf at "Firehouse #1" downtown, "back in the day." According to one source who at times visited a relative who worked there, Cape fire personnel would be put to work cleaning and fixing the truck and fire department vehicles, the station itself, and city Christmas decorations, which they'd then put up and take down at holiday time. The firemen would also fix and/or make toys for Christmas charities and even built a pond and landscaped garden next to the building, to relax at in the cool evening shade. A marker and flag pole from 1944 honoring those firemen who put time and hard work into the garden can still be seen there today. On the evening of Saturday, 4/12/41, if they were not out on a call, some Cape firemen were likely in the garage of the firehouse working on fixing the bent fender of the "hook & ladder" vehicle after its noontime accident. . . . Former Cape Girardeau policeman and (chief in the 1950s) Fritz Schneider was so serious about his Freemason status he guided his wife into becoming a member of "Eastern Star." Fritz and his spouse are buried side-by-side with a Masonic-symbol tombstone in a Cape cemetery. . . . The story of "J.W." and Masons using the lowest floors of a lodge... and also of UFO sightings over the U.S. Capitol, from the 1940s onward... has been covered within two books by author Robert Stanley, from Unicus Press (see unicus.com). . . . In the old days, Rush III was best known as a young Cape radio deejay nicknamed "Rusty Saw" and earned extra money as my Little League umpire in 1973 & '74. I tried to reach Rush through his EIB Network radio website, but he did not respond, and he did not reply to Ryan S. Wood's earlier attempts to reach him for opinions on MO41. I doubt that he will ever openly discuss the event. It was Ryan who learned of the brief Rush III quote on the airwaves from 2006, around the time he had mailed the famous broadcaster a copy of "*Majik: Eyes Only.*" . . . By all accounts, RHL I was a longtime Mason, a fine attorney, governmental rep, and quite devout in his Christian faith and Centenary Church membership, a towering and respected figure still in Cape Girardeau. In summing up his existence late in life, Rush Sr. would only tell a biographer "I have had a very large number of interesting things {happen} over the time that I have lived" (mostly in Cape Girardeau). He added, "I have been very happy and {yet} disappointed with a lot of things that have occurred." Somewhat intriguing, but so vague as to apply to most anything. Stephen N. Limbaugh, son of RHL I, wrote me an e-mail in March 2014 to say that his brother Rush II first became fascinated by aviation when he saw a stunt pilot fly his plane under Cape Girardeau's two-lane bridge over the Mississippi River. This publicized barnstorming event took place in 1935, yet elderly Stephen also clearly recalled for me: "Your grandfather witnessed this feat too." . . . In October of 1945 Harry Truman returned to Missouri as U.S. president, to the small boot-heel town of Carruthersville. Truman attended a legionnaire's conference, being a veteran of World War I. According to articles at the time in *The Southeast Missourian*, the new president also took time to interact with a friendly contingent from Cape Girardeau, including 1941's mayor, Wiley Hinkle Statler, and they promptly invited him to a Cape Freemason Lodge meeting! Mr. L. G. Stovall extended the invite; he "knew Harry Truman from Masonic activities" a news article claimed. HST met RHL II and the Cape reps (photographed for the papers), then he gave a privately-held interview with G. D. Fronabarger in a room at "The Majestic Hotel" - pure coincidence, "Majestic Twelve" fans - but who knows if the two spoke about matters related to MO41. Fronabarger had met Truman some years earlier, when Harry came to Cape to campaign; Garland said HST would visit with Fronabarger's neighbors and the gruff newspaperman would stop by for a smoke and a chat. In that one October '45 day's visit to slow-paced Carruthersville, former Army Captain Truman firmly established himself as a Legionnaire; a Freemason; a Baptist; a friend to Cape Girardeans possibly involved in MO41; and a pal to newspapermen Fronabarger (even discussing his boss, Harry's pal Fred Naeter). The trip to southeast Missouri was a conspiracy-lover's dream! Yet evidently Truman did not stray at this time north to either the MO41 crash site or to Cape Girardeau, nor even to

Sikeston, where he also used to campaign for the senate. According to researcher Linda L. Wallace, HST at those times (1934 & 1940) stayed at Sikeston's Marshall Hotel, his accommodations paid for by local political supporters with ties to the Parks Air College. Thus we have no proof but a possible mild connection between Oliver L. Parks and Harry S Truman, two proud Missourians. . . . What *may* have been a bit more conspiratorial was the ex-president's trip to Cape Girardeau in October of 1962. During the Cuban Missile Crisis, Harry gave a speech for Democratic Party candidates at a rally in town, but beforehand stopped in at the offices of *The Southeast Missourian*, according to photos and articles. Harry took owner/publisher Fred Naeter into his office after posing for pictures and closed the door. What the two men discussed remains unknown, but it is certainly possible they needed the secrecy to go over some details from MO41, which Naeter may well have squelched from publication, perhaps under duress, twenty-one years earlier. What else would be so private and critical to converse about, with both men's aides and local dignitaries left waiting outside for over an hour? I wrote to proud elderly Mason Stephen Limbaugh about the odd closed-door meeting but he was baffled as to its secret content. He referred my letter to a woman in Cape who is known as a local history buff but she too was unaware. It should be noted that Fred Naeter traveled to Washington to meet President Truman in the White House and also met with HST in Mexico City during his presidency, according to a 2012 *Missourian* blog summing up the unusual relationship. . . . HST got along well with the president of Mexico when both were in the highest position of power. Harry became the first American president to visit Mexico's capitol, perhaps since both men were Freemasons. One recent UFO book's authors point out that this unprecedented summit of two Masonic presidents took place 3/3-5/47 and that "some researchers feel that the topic of UFOs" was discussed at that time. If so, then the April

'41 crash might well have come up since there had been no Roswell crash, which happened four months later. . . . Freemason George Washington seemed to have his own "thing" with the month of April, oddly. He helmed the Army in 1776 in April, then helped guide Congress to ratify initial peace treaties to end the Revolutionary War in April of 1783, but lost a narrow vote the following April on another treaty. In 1789 Washington was voted by a committee to be the first U.S. president around April 12th and was informed of this at a ceremony two days later. He inaugurated on April 30th. . . . Cape's Sheriff Schade got engaged to his sweetheart, Maxine Seabaugh, and this was announced at a formal party described in *The Southeast Missourian* on 3/17/41. Mrs. Bee Limbaugh (Rush I's wife) attended the party, as did young Mrs. Ben B. Schade! This strongly indicates that Ruben and Ben were pretty close, along with their lady-loves. Maxine's mother's maiden name was Limbaugh, and she also participated in the engagement get-together, on West Main Street. I suspect that Bee was also an "Eastern Star" member. . . . Missouri's other U.S. senator in 1941, Bennett C. Clark, was not very liked or appreciated by the Roosevelt administration and probably learned little or nothing about MO41, at least from them. However, Clark got along well with Harry Truman and might have gleaned information from him as the years went by, although there is no proof of this. . . . UFO researchers have been debating the authenticity of another shocking HST quote supposedly given to the press and public on the presence of alien technology. Allegedly on 4/4/50 Truman told reporters with firmness: "I can assure you that "flying saucers," given they exist, are not constructed by any power on earth." This is another most knowing statement, is it not? The only qualifier or backtracking within the alleged quote is *"given they exist,"* as if the president was trying to duck being responsible for a whole slew of further questions on the subject. However, writers and researchers found it difficult to definitely trace, confirm, and accept this particular alleged Truman quote, with some pundits believing he never issued it, and others believing Harry delivered it as a silly aside to reporters as he gave a White House press conference that day. In the end, the quote may be real, but the timing and placing of it are simply not accurate; records show Truman was relaxing from a deep sea fishing trip in south Florida on 4/4/50. If the quotation is factual and actual, then we must ask how Harry could state these matters so confidently? *Time* magazine came out on 4/17/50 with a printed remark from Harry's press secretary who stated that the president "knows nothing about the saucers." Why bother with this comment, unless it was actually quite true that Harry told at least one member of the press the original April 4th "any power on earth" statement, or something close to it? And it was not Harry who issued the retraction, or denial, but his press spokesman, while the president remained publicly mum. Another time when asked about UFOs, Truman supposedly grinned and simply started repeating an old poem: "I've never seen a purple cow..." No one had actually asked him if he had *seen* an unidentified alien craft, but that was how he carefully answered while avoiding any serious discussion of the topic. Certainly the MO41 recoveries were in a sense not "unidentified." They were identifiably and demonstrably extraterrestrial in origin. . . . In 1941 House Minority Leader, Joe Martin of Massachusetts was a conservative isolationist Republican who had no love for FDR and his policies, and was not a Freemason, so if there *was* something wild stored down under the Capitol, he likely didn't get a pass to go see it. . . . The Senate Majority Leader for 1941, Alben Barkley of Kentucky, was also apparently not a Freemason and was bypassed by FDR as a potential veep in the 1940 and '44 election campaigns. It's iffy he knew the "sub-basement secret" too, although he became so well thought of as a Democrat and a man of the people, President Truman selected him as the new VP in 1948. . . . As president HST relied on fellow Missourian and Mason General Omar Bradley of the Army, and it is possible this respected military leader also learned the MO41 secret as well. . . . The 1941 Senate Minority Leader, Charles McNary of Oregon, was also not a Freemason. . . . General Doug MacArthur's remarks on UFOs are rather well known on the internet, but frankly somewhat overblown. Careful research - such as at Snopes.com - shows when quoted directly on the matter, in a speech to West Point cadets in May of 1962, the aging, retired MacArthur was merely talking in somewhat general terms about future possibilities for ET threats. Most likely he meant *hundreds of years in the future* would man face "an interplanetary war" requiring a "united human race and the sinister forces of planetary galaxies." His similar 1955 remarks were simply noted by a friend - the mayor of an Italian city - who listened to them and issued later to the press his own filtered summary, and again, MacArthur supposedly only spoke of unspecified futuristic situations involving hostile "people of other planets." . . . Author Knell's 2006 story of his father working for MacArthur and learning about the secret UFO report can be found on some UFO websites, such as Paranormalnewscentral.com, or JimMarrs.com. . . . Why George C. Marshall rode around in 1941 in an airplane with the Capitol Building logo yet evidently with no inscription or explanation seems very strange, even if it had nothing to do with MO41, which he could of course not talk about. If the photo of him next to his personal plane is from Friday, 4/11/41 - showing GCM arriving at Louisiana's Fort Beauregard, the day before the UFO crash - then it is more mysterious than if it is from GCM's later-in-'41 Beauregard trip. . . . U.S. Air Force General Robert Landry admitted in the 1980s that at Harry Truman's request he looked into UFO matters and reported back to the president regularly on the topic, starting in 1948. This fact can be found in numerous UFO books, but is explained rather nicely and succinctly within Grant Cameron's presidential UFO website. . . . In 2016 a Cape Girardeau Freemason proudly told me Harry Truman's name is clearly written in registering with (and in) the city's Masonic log book, on numerous occasions. . . . Senator HST once handwrote a letter to a government bigwig and fellow Mason; the one-page message was sent from Cape Girardeau, noted by Harry atop the letter on 11/27/40, just months before the crash. Remarkably, it was scribbled on stationary that was emblazoned with the Freemasons' logo and masthead of the *"Grand Lodge of Missouri, Ancient Free and Accepted Masons."* Imprinted under this was Harry's official work address: *"Harry S Truman / Grand Master / 240 Senate Office Building / Washington D.C."* This rare autographed letter can be seen to this day at universityarchives.com of Westport, Connecticut. {The archives website notes that HST's last duties as Grand Master of Missouri's Freemason society was to preside over a meeting in a St. Louis lodge on 9/30-31/41.} What precisely Truman was doing in Cape *after* his recent re-election to the senate weeks earlier is still a mystery, but that he had a reputable Masonic friend in mind could indicate Harry had attended a Freemason meeting at the Cape lodge and/or temple while in town. Cape needed a new post office and courthouse in those days and Mr. Truman *might* have been inspecting the situation for himself, as a concerned senator who could help allocate government funds for the project. Years later my father collected a few letters from Senator Truman to the Cape Girardeau City Attorney's office, some from the spring/summer of 1941, about that rather costly governmental issue. . . . A 5/13/16 article via *"Rare"* news service by Matt Painter described a 9-11 terrorism report mentioned it was once kept in "a vault deep beneath the Capitol Building," which was discussed not long thereafter on *"60 Minutes,"* which showed its actual double doors in a congressional hallway. . . . An excellent source for Masonic symbols in our nation's money designs comes from a

History Channel special, *"The Great Seal,"* delving into President Roosevelt, Vice President Wallace, and others who were privately invested in the 1930s' project being tied to Freemasonry. This topic can be found as well within books and webpages, as usual, some of them getting carried away with foolish "evil" conspiracy theories. . . . The subject of the Masonic fondness for a building's northeast cornerstone came from the original television series episode of *"Brad Meltzer's Decoded,"* on the History Channel, airing first in December 2010. . . . Information on Stu Symington comes from *Wikipedia*, online articles, and some mentions in a few books; he died in 1988 a very respected Missouri elder statesman and wealthy businessman. In February of '57, Masonic Symington welcomed Senator J. F. Kennedy to Springfield, Missouri, for the Shrine Mosque "Jefferson Dinner" where JFK was the keynote speaker (as re-reported in a 2/23/14 photo in *The Springfield News Leader*). . . . A digitized photograph of an October 1948 St. Louis University homecoming alumni dinner at the St. Louis Chase Hotel features Oliver L. Parks seated next to Air Force Secretary Symington, found within SLU online library files. . . . This hotel was where Cape mayor W. H. Statler was feted with other Missouri mayors on Monday night, 4/14/41, and then attended a baseball Opening Day game on Tuesday afternoon. After he got back home his wife was hospitalized, all this according to small paragraphs in *The Southeast Missourian*. . . . Strangely, President Dwight Eisenhower ordered all government and public buildings to lower their flags to half-staff in honor of George Marshall when he died in October of 1959 - *except* the Capitol Building's! Why was this federal structure, of all places, not permitted to honor the great man? . . . Info on fortuneteller Jeane Dixon and her FDR encounters comes from the online articles on her, under the headline "Psychic in the White House," within forteantimes.com. And also from the top paperback bestseller of the 1960s, by

author/columnist Ruth Montgomery, *"A Gift of Prophecy."*
It is additionally claimed therein that Jeane accurately once
told Senator Truman he would someday be president, and
informed Sam Rayburn that he would someday lose his
Speaker's position but get it back and remain very
powerful, which happened. . . . Research on Professor
Truzzi's findings on FDR and astrology comes from an
online *New York Times* article by Steven V. Roberts. . . .
Data on the two Mississippi congressmen who died in June
of 1941 comes from *"The Political Graveyard"* website on
Freemasons, along with *Wikipedia*. . . . As an addendum,
there are three more sudden, mysterious deaths of 1941
Missouri politicians to report. First, Mr. Charles H.
Richeson of Potosi (some miles north of Cape Girardeau)
died on 6/29/41; he was a Democratic Party operative in
Missouri and buried in Potosi's New Masonic Cemetery.
Second, Mr. Edward D. Hays, a Republican from Cape
Girardeau, former U.S. Representative on Capitol Hill (and
a lawyer-friend of Rush Limbaugh I); he died in Bethesda
near D.C. on 7/25/41, his Masonic membership unknown.
And third, another former U.S. congressman (from St.
Louis), Henry F. Niedringhaus, Republican, died on 8/3/41
and definitely was a Freemason. . . . LBJ and Symington
grilling Van Bush on the U.S. space program was culled
from *"LBJ, Architect of American Ambition,"* by Randall B.
Woods, 2006. . . . Info on Walt Disney is found online, and
within the Nick Redfern book *"Secret History:
Conspiracies from Ancient Aliens to the New World
Order,"* 2015, Visible Ink Press. My maternal Masonic
grandfather grew up in Kansas City and would occasionally
see a young Walt Disney sketching figures while relaxing
in a barber shop, or delivery newspapers in the community.

CHAPTER FOUR - The claim that in late '41 JFK was a
White House liaison comes from the 1988 Ted Schwarz

book, "*The Peter Lawford Story*," page 94. To date I have not been able to find confirmation on this, however a few contemporary books state that "a naval lieutenant" delivered on 12/6/41 to the White House a 13-part decoded diplomatic message by the Japanese, the night before Pearl Harbor, straight from ONI. Was this JFK? . . . There could be still another source that informed Congressman Kennedy in mid-1947 about the shocking alien nature of the Roswell incident: fellow Massachusetts politico Sherman Miles, *former top aide and confidante to George C. Marshall*. As GCM's "Assistant Chief of Staff" in '41 Miles almost *had* to know about the Cape Girardeau UFO crash, right from the beginning, and if he knew that JFK was aware of MO41 too they *could* have discussed Roswell's secrets as well. However, Miles was an older man, a strict Army intel officer, and a staunch conservative Republican in July of '47. He served only in the Massachusetts House, not in the U.S. House. It seems unlikely he'd openly share such a huge classified secret to young, ONI, liberal Democrat Kennedy. . . Sid Souers data comes from *Wikipedia* and MajesticDocuments.com, plus Symington's recorded interview with the Harry S Truman Presidential Library online page. Souers spent years in business working first south of Cape Girardeau (in Memphis) and north (in St. Louis), so he may well have traveled to or through that city. . . . Info on Lyndon Johnson stems similarly from online and book research. Interestingly, LBJ announced on the steps of the White House in April of 1941 his intention to run for the U.S. senate seat suddenly opened up in Texas. . . . The ONI history website article mentioned seems to indicate that Admiral Wilkinson purposely killed himself, but his *Wikipedia* page summary states that he valiantly managed to save his wife in the Elizabeth River before tragically drowning, apparently showing Ted *accidently* drove off the ferry. What his mindset was at the time of the incident is anyone's guess. . . . Some chapter data comes from Richard

Dolan in his 2001 article taken from his 2002 book, "*UFOs and the National Security State: Chronology of a Cover-up, 1941 to 1973.*" . . . John F. Kennedy facts come from biographies, online information like Wikipedia, and video presentations (some on YouTube), and TV shows, like a 2013 four-hour retrospective PBS special on his life. . . . For more on JFK and Don Menzel, read Larry Holcombe's fine 2015 book that I consulted: "*The Presidents and UFOs,*" or go online to digest mysteriousuniverse.com and its excellent 2016 Micah Hanks article "*The Art of Denial: The Secret Lives of Those Who Smear Saucers.*" . . . Information and actual photographs by Robert Knudsen of JFK greeting Masons at the White House are from the John F. Kennedy Presidential Library and Museum digital archives. JFK is also seen in a pair of existing pictures in September of '62, attending a Masonic lodge opening by handling a telegraph key. . . . The video of President Kennedy's April '61 Philadelphia hotel speech to newspaper editors, on the subject of secret societies and openness in government, can be found on *YouTube* and various online sites. . . . Data on a German source notifying a Cape Girardeau author of German "flying discs" in 1941 onward came from page 251 of "*Project Identification,*" by Dr. Harley Rutledge, 1981. One ship was said to have been 150 feet across, which flew on 2/14/45 at about 1, 250 miles per hour, 7.5 miles above the earth, supposedly. . . . Buzz Aldrin returned the Masonic moon artifacts to the Grand Lodge of Texas, where he attended meetings. He stated he carried a special silk Masonic flag to the moon. Today it rests in the District of Columbia Masonic museum, along with other interesting and revealing historical items. . . . Did JFK have a UFO sighting of his own as president? I don't know, but according to researcher Timothy Cooper, the answer could well be *yes.* "I have it from a very reliable source that JFK did fly out to an air force base to personally watch an unidentified bogie" - or alien spacecraft buzzing about - "track from an aircraft under tight security," Cooper claims. . . . Some researchers feel the so-called CIA "Burn Memo" proves that the UFO investigation group "Majestic Twelve" moved to liquidate JFK. That he was asking too many questions about ET matters the secretive group had been working on in private for decades, and that perhaps JFK was also interested in privately sharing these shocking facts with at least the Soviet government, or even possibly the American people. For more, see majesticdocuments.com.

SECTION II:

CHAPTER FIVE - I once visited the owner whose family has controlled the former Huffman-owned property on North Main Street in Cape since 1960, a few blocks up from the Red Star Baptist facilities. The property owner surprised me by replying she recalled the names "William and Floy Huffman" from the home's deed papers, yet had never heard of the MO41 story before. She allowed me to photograph two pages of the land ownership pages . . . The Ford Groves auto dealership in downtown Cape - now Nip Kelley's construction headquarters - was located at 42 N. Sprigg Street. Today the Ford dealership has relocated to 1501 N. Kings Highway in Cape, which was built and opened in the 1980s. Fred A. Groves was amongst the earliest vehicle dealers in Cape Girardeau. He took over the downtown Ford agency in 1916, after working for two years at another auto lot, having arrived in town from Farmington, Missouri, at a young age, according to an article in *The Southeast Missourian.* Now long deceased, Fred became a respected, successful businessman and leading citizen, his dealership also responsible not just for sales but repairs of various vehicles, new or used. . . . General Leslie Groves personal info was provided by

Wikipedia and a few other online pages, but I have not been able to establish whether he was related to Fred Groves. Helpful info on Leslie's application for joining "The Sons of the American Revolution" was provided by kindly Sharon Sanders, archivist of the Cape newspaper. . . . The Ford Groves improvised manufacturing plant was first established as fact in a *Missourian* news article entitled *"Parts Made In Cape Aided In Routing Japs,"* 8/11/45. There was no byline, but it seems almost assuredly written by G. D. Fronabarger. The author knowingly described the factory as a "closely-guarded military manufacturing secret" for the "Groves Corporation, a war-born Cape Girardeau firm." This seems to indicate that Fred (or someone close to him) came up with the resistors idea as a patriotic American aiding the war effort, and the Ford Motor Company had approved of the production program in order for him to gain the government contract for the manufacturing. The newspaper article does not make clear exactly *who* came up with the invention, why, and how. Even the local employees in the plant did not know the exact nature, impact, and details of the resistors and its covert project variations they were working on during WWII. However, returning Cape Girardeau area citizens who were wartime Army and Navy personnel, the article claimed, stopped by the plant on occasion to congratulate its management on the successful little items that were mass-produced in aiding the war effort, so it wasn't a complete secret. Not in military circles, anyway. A likely candidate for an example of a factory visitor would have been 1941's mayor of Cape, Wiley Hinkle Statler, who had patriotically entered the Navy following Pearl Harbor and won a Purple Heart after getting injured in combat. "Hink" came back to Cape early in '45 and eventually met with Vice President Truman in a Chicago hotel that spring, for some reason. Mr. Statler also met President Truman later that year when Harry visited southeast Missouri, as mentioned. What could they have been discussing in private? I tried repeatedly to contact Hinkle Statler's surviving daughters in 2013 and '14, and they did not respond in any way. . . . One newspaper-listed boost to the Ford Groves resistors enterprise was Fred's associates "Wesley Block & Co. of New York City." These were apparently sales representatives who supplied "field engineering service," whatever that was. . . . There were a few other converted factories during WWII in the Cape area, such as an electrical product plant that won a war production contract. Yet another was the Red Star Shoe Company very near the Mississippi River and Rev. Huffman's Tabernacle. The factory had turned to creating combat boots for American troops to wear. The preacher was likely familiar with this war effort production, before he moved away in mid-'43. . . . The organized Cape community meeting structure located on 17 Sprigg Street (room "A" for members) housed the Freemasons and other groups, right next door to Ford Groves, according to the 1942 Cape City Directory. . . . There were two Sikeston mechanics - brothers Milam and Ernest Limbaugh - who hailed from a Limbaugh family that owned a farm in Scott County, but it was located *south* of Sikeston, not north, far from the suspected crash site, according to a 1941 *Southeast Missourian* article and some further research. . . . In the summer of 2013 I approached Missouri's current lieutenant governor, Peter Kinder, and asked him about MO41, knowing full well he hailed from Cape Girardeau. He said he knew nothing about it.

CHAPTER SIX - The Chaffee Public Library was a help in research and one librarian there provided information on a few older local citizens who knew of the old days, but overall nothing too new was discovered from this source, yet thanks overall are in order. . . . Cape Girardeau fireman Quintin Williams did indeed quit the town's fire force on

Tuesday, 4/15/41, for some unknown reason. Williams was also head of Cape Girardeau's "Young Democrats Club," and as a fireman likely knew my grandfather, Randolph P. Smith, a local Democrat and former City Attorney who was often speaking to men in the fire/police HQ. . . . The Cape automobile-fire truck accident on Saturday at noon, 4/12/41, as mentioned in the paper, involved Earl Jones as one of the firemen and the two tailing cops in a squad car were CGPD Sergeant Leo B. Hill and patrolman William S. Wickham. Could any of these three have still been on duty that evening when the crash call came in? Perhaps if the grass fire response occurred at noon, by seven or eight o'clock of the MO41 report these three men were now off duty. But firemen Jones - who fell off the back of the fire engine in the minor traffic accident - might well have been recuperating in the upstairs living quarters of the firehouse when the call came in 4/14/41. . . . According to Chaffee research, the town had a mayoral problem in the spring of 1941. Their regular Chaffee mayor, Oscar T. Honey, was away in military service. He was replaced with an "acting mayor," L. D. Lankford. The city council and other leaders were having to appoint all new officials that April, including a new fire chief. The town's marshal was said to be C. A. Goddard, but none of these people were apparently very experienced or knowledgeable in their new positions at the time of the crash, so it's questionable if they went to the MO41 event. I discovered Mayor Honey's grave while checking on a Chaffee cemetery in October 2014; he died in the 1990s. . . . The story of Dr. H. Rutledge's astronomy class comes from the pages of his '81 book "Project Identification" and includes info that a source told him about a relative who was part of an aeronautical engineer-employing unit that supposedly operated near the Arkansas-Missouri border, possibly underground, to monitor UFO traffic in the Midwest. Also included was the name "Huffman" in his contacts, although it is unlikely these two sources were related to Rev.

William Huffman or his family, originators of the MO41 crash tale. One man – Mr. Robert Snider – told Rutledge that the U.S. Navy – which had an office in the Cape airport during the war, *operated a plane that flew on the hour north-to-south over the area, keeping an eye out for unusual aerial phenomenon. . . .* Amusing trivia: the creators of the newspaper comic strip *"Buck Rogers in the 25th Century"* wrote the White House in March of 1944 to ask if they could include President Roosevelt in a strip where Buck goes to another planet and finds an alien's machine that reveals time travel. In going back in time on Earth, it was set to display good and evil in the 1940s, with FDR to be depicted as "good" and Germany's Hitler and Japan's Tojo as "evil." The White House approved, but no one seems able to find a copy of the cartoon to this day, evidently. Amusingly, the *Buck Rogers* creative team included in their letter a special membership card for Franklin D. Roosevelt, to identify himself as a member of the "Rocket Rangers" and thus expect "every courtesy to be extended to him upon whatever planet he may happen to land."

CHAPTER SEVEN – I am most grateful to Cape's kindly Carl Armstrong for this chapter! . . . The original e-mailed information from Carl arrived via a Cape Girardeau newspaper source, helpfully forwarding it to me. Carl had been urging the newspaper to produce an article on MO41 for its sister publication *"The Best Years,"* which is targeted for senior citizens. I then contacted Carl and asked him for elaboration. . . . Information on the Graflex Speed Graphic camera can be found within *Wikipedia* and *Camerapedia*. . . . Carl still feels the MO41 crash took place near County Park in northern Cape. It's interesting that a street was constructed some years ago out of some old farm property near County Park and dubbed "Limbaugh Lane." Not far away, Rush Limbaugh III's brother, Cape Girardeau attorney David Limbaugh, built and maintains an upscale home on another street. Herb Schaper supposedly claimed that the MO41 crash happened in this general area, and Carl e-mailed me some 1931 parcel maps of the vicinity. . . . One might argue that World War II simply necessitated the special need for Ohio's Wright Field to break down and back-engineer recovered enemy jet planes retrieved from Axis Powers nations, but what possible "foreign" metals and "unfathomable" designs could have required such a pricey, intricate new underground analyzation set-up run by metallurgical experts? After all, many Axis Powers planes were basically copied off of American designs, and made from metals that the U.S. knew all about, if not even provided at one time. And the secret new Wright high-tech facility didn't even open until *after* Germany and Italy *had already surrendered* to the Allies. . . . The scoop on Wright-Patterson's "FTD" alien images for the October 1988 TV special comes from NOUFORS.com, the online site for Northern Ontario UFO Research & Study. The ET graphics supposedly came from a source named "Curtis Brubaker," given to "Seligman Productions" for their live broadcast. Brubaker in turn claimed *he* got them from an unnamed inside source at W-P FTD. Government-controlled ET examinations, biological studies, and informed medical speculation at W-P allegedly showed that the beings had such a larger-than-human brain apiece that its intelligence produced an IQ estimated to be at least two hundred, akin to an Albert Einstein. . . . The 1997 Corso and Birnes book was taken so seriously that the History Channel produced an hour-long special called *"UFO Files: The Day After Roswell,"* originally airing in June, 2007. . . . It is worth noting that UFO authors Don Schmitt & Tom Carey criticize and dismiss reverse-engineering claims by Phil Corso in the pages of their 2013 book, *"Inside the Real Area 51: The Secret History of Wright-Patterson."* My feeling is that there could well be truth - and honest mistakes – in *all* of these authors' claims, simply because the alien spacecraft metals and technology were likely spread out at *various* labs and bases for a wider range of opinions and breakthroughs in understanding their origin, rather than America "hiding all of its eggs in one basket," so to speak. Not every source or base for the materials knew what other sources and bases were up to. . . . "*Hangar 1*" is the nickname of MUFON's dossier center, where they keep their accumulated UFO reports. They worked with the History Channel (History2) to produce the March 2014 "Alien Technology" Season One program which mentions repeatedly the MO41 affair and how they feel it led to great advances in the field of tiny transistors used to make electronics, and thus is found in so many products in today's world. Yet the show was woefully short of any sort of proof or evidence, and later veered into some wild territory, discussing Nazi UFO claims, and that of Iran and its modern technology. . . . Ryan S. Wood is somewhat skeptical of the Purdue University grad student story, on their alleged scrutiny and reverse engineering of the MO41 materials for modern science and technology breakthroughs. "I doubt that Purdue was given "parts" to look at," he informed me by e-mail, perhaps "only guided suggestions of where to research *maybe*." Ryan added that he knew this as "my own father (Dr. Robert Wood) was involved in this TV program" - the background explorations - "and he has done some research around the origin of the transistor." . . . A location dot on a map aired on the "*Hangar 1*" show oddly indicated a UFO crash site *west* and somewhat south of the city of Cape, a little north of the "outside-Chaffee" area near the Cape and Scott County borders. It's possible the program's graphics department just slapped a red dot outside the city on a map for entertainment's sake, without any inside knowledge. I wrote to MUFON to ask about this but received no reply. . . . Data on the Zelyony Island UFO crash comes from rusartnet.com and rbth.com, plus a website I once viewed that for the life of me I can't seem to locate now, greatly frustrating me. Perhaps it has been removed from cyberspace. . . . *YouTube* videos on "Skinny Bob" abound, some misidentifying him as a "Roswell crash discovery." It was clearly Russian footage, nothing to do with Roswell. There was supposedly a snafu for the Russians back in the early '40s, however, when the alien visitors discovered they were being covertly recorded, quite against treaty stipulations, and got upset. The secret alien-KGB agreement was revised, perhaps under orders of Joseph Stalin. All-too-brief clips of ETs in the leaked footage show their crashed spaceship laying cracked apart in a desert-like setting, a dead alien body in the sand, and then an eerie medical procedure performed by human doctors, holding an apparent tiny, baby-like ET. Creepy! Almost nothing is known of the apparent "culprit" or "hero" who originally placed the footage on *YouTube*. The "Skinny Bob" video source's given screen name is "Ivan0135," thus a Russian-sounding originator, promising more footage to come, but since then nothing. The source uploaded the dramatic videos to *YouTube* the day he joined, records indicate. Did "Ivan0135" deliberately wait until the seventieth anniversary of the day after the strange southeast Missouri incident to post the imagery? Or was this a mere coincidence? . . . Australian writer Tony Brunt once noted a fascinating story that stretches all the way to Russia. In 1948, a top Russian scientist was supposedly called in by Joseph Stalin to view UFO documents that the Soviet Union had largely copied or stolen from American files, thanks mostly to the amazingly vast web of communist spies within the American nuclear weapons program based out of New Mexico. The Russian scientist allegedly told a friend later that documents from American governmental sources that he was allowed to read *indicated that in the 1940s the FDR and HST administrations had knowledge that recovered "non-terrestrial aerodynes" were from advanced alien intelligence, races here observing our planet*. Supposedly select American scientists were called away from their atomic bomb research to give their opinions at Los Alamos facilities on the stunning army-recovered alien hardware and their propulsion systems. This again confirms the fragmented information on this National Lab and the Sandia Lab data; both sites point to crashed/recovered ET ships secretly being inspected at length, including MO41. It also shows Stalin wanted the upper hand on UFO/ET matters, atomic weapons technological tie-ins or not. . . . Additional note: a 1947 report mentioned "the Missouri recovery of 1941" and its "neutronic propulsion device," which was utilized in the atom bomb to help win WWII, and research shows a special "Neutronic Reactor" was patented on 12/19/44 – just what lab scientists like Van Bush were working on, with Soviet spies all around the program.

CHAPTER EIGHT – "Kyle" was most helpful and I am indebted to him for this chapter. Thanks, my Masonic friend! . . . Info provided on Groves and Graves; the Army Corps of Engineers; the War Department; and the Pentagon can be found online, especially within *Wikipedia* and other online articles, such as the 1965 interview transcript within manhattanvoices.org, where Leslie mentions repeatedly working with Van Bush and FDR. . . . Linda Moulton Howe discovered that within four days of the Army's 7/11/47 Roswell UFO crash recovery process, a special law enforcement conference was arranged in a nearby city, announced in the local papers. Hoover's "FBI Special Agent in Charge" of this desert southwest area was helping to arrange "coordination of law enforcement officers" in the area for an unexplained reason, which we can reasonably guess now was related to the gathering of otherworldly information and talkative eyewitnesses. In the

MO41 case, there were already seasonal meetings of "Southeast Missouri Law Enforcement" group, a regular confab that *The Sikeston Herald* noted on 4/17/41 was inexplicably being "advanced several days ahead," and would now include the head of the FBI's St. Louis field office. The decision undertaken to hurry this Sikeston-based meeting along was obviously made within a day or two of the 4/12/14 crash and its Sikeston army recovery, and again, it appears that Hoover's representatives were helping to coordinate the timing of the conference and likely its subject matters. Cape Sheriff Ruben Schade was to be there, Cape's newspaper reported. Ruben would have been not far from his brother Ben, working within the Sikeston MIA's airport office. Whether the U.S. Army – via the Missouri Institute of Aeronautics in Sikeston and their MO41 retrieval team, or through other representatives – was to be present at the springtime law confab is unknown, but is certainly suspected. According to the *Missourian*, less than two weeks after the crash, there was *another* confab of local big-shots. St. Louis FBI agent Norris - not Cape Girardeau Agent Jones, interestingly - traveled to a Sikeston meeting of "Missouri Peace Officers" that featured Sheriff Schade. Fellow officials from both the Missouri police and highway patrol and the Federal Bureau of Investigation all gathered in the seemingly obscure small town, ex-Sheriff Hartle too. Hartle worked at the MIA in Sikeston. It would have been the perfect time to coordinate information on witnesses to the crash and how they were reacting in their communities at both ends of the stick, in Cape Girardeau and in Sikeston. . . . The alleged daytime 1946 alien landing event had supposedly played out "in a field near Campster School." If it was on the western side of Bloomfield Road and Houck Woods, then this would have been the aforementioned farmland owned by the Schwab family. Carl Armstrong wrote to me to say that he had contacted Kenny Schwab who was attending high school "by 1949" and that Ken knew nothing about any extraterrestrial events. That rather seemed to put a damper on the site being Schwab's Farm. On the other, eastern side of Bloomfield Road from Campster sat the somewhat open space dubbed "Gregor's Field," which was later sold and developed as a subdivision, evidently with approval of the Gregor family. And this is the same *general* area that Kyle insisted the SCS occurred on, but to be clear "Gregor's Field" was *not* a part of the lawn around the Gregor house. . . . Several questions came to mind on the alleged 1946 peaceful UFO landing. For instance, the Campster schoolhouse and its parking lot were small, as mentioned previously, and if relatives and friends were called, they had to either rush out on foot from their nearby homes (there weren't that many in the area in those days) or from across town in their cars. Where did they all park once they arrived? Bloomfield Road was narrow and dotted with many trees, some right up near the pavement, but of course there were undeveloped lots and farm fields to utilize. In fact, the Schwab Farm near Campster had plenty of open space along the road, as seen today on satellite map imagery. Educator Herb Schaper had apparently moved on as teacher at Campster by '46, which would explain why he knew of and spoke about MO41, but not the alleged landing event. . . . Many questions arise if a group of inoffensive ETs truly came down as described and drew a crowd of onlookers. Did the FBI or U.S. Army get called in at some point? Did anyone bring their camera and take some photos, and if so were they confiscated? Did a newsman like Garland Fronabarger show up likewise? How about any evidence left behind? Were there footprints, or landing gear pad prints, or radiation signs? Metallic or chemical debris left behind in the field? Could any of it be left there to this day? Did the landed ETs speak, or carry around weapons or gear of any kind? *Were they given orders to retrieve the MO41 crash materials, no matter how many witnesses there were?* . . . In doing some checking, I inspected the first *Southeast Missourian* after the Saturday night alien crash, the Monday afternoon 4/14/41 edition. It featured a society column that mentioned that "Mr. and Mrs. Ben Schwab" in Cape Girardeau had hosted an Easter Sunday meal at their home, which featured young "Robert Schwab, enlistee in the Air Corps training at Sikeston." Huh! The '46 alien landing event might have taken place on or near "the Schwab Farm" near Campster; was Ben Schwab the owner of this farm property, or related to the owners? One problem is that these could have been different "Schwab" residents of Cape, totally unrelated to the Schwab Farm owners. And that Robert Schwab may have been a houseguest all Passover/Easter weekend, and therefore may have known nothing about the Sikeston PAC/MIA crew that absconded with the ET goods on Saturday night. A check of the 1942 Cape city phone directory did not result in listings for Ben or Robert Schwab, strangely. . . . Another fact from *Southeast Missourian* articles from that 1941 spring is that the Campster School sometimes held "Campster Club" special events that drew people to the school and its grounds. This could have been a factor in producing a good-sized gathering of people already on the site, set up outdoors, with cops already in place, helping to direct traffic in 1946. . . . All during the fascinating 1940s global warfare era *Missourian* reporter/photographer G. D. Fronabarger kept writing for the local daily paper and snapping his Graflex pictures, some of which I learned were aerial, some of obscure rural small communities south of Cape, the very places described by many as existing close to the mysterious MO41 crash scene. . . . To Ryan Wood's father, retired engineer Dr. Robert Wood, PhD, the focus of crashes like MO41 are the paper trail, the leaked government documents that expose the amazing, advanced technology recovered and examined under tight security restrictions. In a 2008 interview, Robert told Linda Moulton Howe: "I believe it was the Army that retrieved the Cape Girardeau, Missouri, crash. So all these {other} agencies began snapping away to get control of the technologies." That was the main American governmental approach in the 1940s: what made up the hardware, and what made it run so well, better than our aeronautical machinery, and how to duplicate and exploit it. "They didn't care about the public," Dr. Wood added aptly. Disclosure was likely never a real possibility, only exploitation. Find out more through Ryan's website majesticdocuments.com. . . . Information on Houck Woods' colorful history comes from knowledgeable Cape native and paranormal researcher Michael Huntington. . . . Cape resident Randy Barnhouse once worked for famous underwater treasure diver Mel Fisher and is eager to search for MO41 metals in the ground with his metal detection equipment. . . . Carl Armstrong's helpful relative e-mailed me again in March 2016 with some supportive data about Herb Schaper, the Campster School, and its yearly "Play Day" public event featured in *The Southeast Missourian*, when none other than Garland Fronabarger showed up to take photos for the local newspaper of the organized fun, published on 4/11/58. Hmmm, "Frony" snapping photos... of a Campster crowd in a nearby grassy field... printed up on nearly the exact 17th anniversary of the MO41 event (missing by a day). More weird, wild synchronicity!

SECTION III:

CHAPTER NINE - Some data comes from my years of personal research on Lombard and was augmented by 2014's excellent *"Fireball."*. . . Carole's father, Frederick Peters, stayed behind in the Midwest (Indiana), much like Reverend Huffman's wife, Floy Peters and her kin (Missouri). It's certainly conceivable that there could be a Peters genealogical connection somewhere along the line. .

. . Baha'i Faith info stems from bahai-library.com. . . . Lombard's private interest in mysticism and the meaning of life is shown in the books by her bedside at the time of her death: "*The Prophet*" by Kahlil Gibran, and "*The Cloud of Unknowing*," which is a fourteenth century essay on union with God. . . . Mention of Carole's stop in Chicago reminds me that Naval Ensign Jack Kennedy was assigned to a ten-week military training program there in the summer of '42, supposedly to help prepare him for warfare at sea. . . . Some info on the lit objects over Mt. Potosi comes from a 2002 website centered around "*Fate*," authored by Oklahoma-based news-digger Kyle J. Wood. I wrote to him in February of 2003 and asked if he had any further information on the UFO situation from January '42. Kyle replied that in his opinion "there was no explanation ever given to resolve mysterious light in the sky issue." He felt that 1942 investigators briefly had the notion that it was possible someone "misdirected" an airway beacon to fool the pilots into flying in the wrong direction, but that it became quite apparent there was never any truth whatsoever to the theory. . . . Fellow Missourian Kyle claims he found a source that witnessed the airliner passing by in the distance that night, a pilot who felt he was able to see Flight #3's cockpit lights on and only one pilot in that flight deck. Author Matzen completely discounts that allegation. Mr. Wood stated his theory in an "E" Channel program, "*Mysteries and Scandals*" on Lombard's end. In that episode Kyle submitted the TWA pilot was thrown further away in the debris field from the co-pilot and cockpit in the aftermath and was therefore located in the cabin of the airplane, perhaps talking to Lombard, when the vessel crashed. Matzen scoffed and dismissed this entire theory, saying there was never any passing plane in the area able to see the doomed DC-3. . . . Even a Hollywood fan magazine article on Clark Gable (published in April '42) discussed Lombard consulting "a fortuneteller" just before departing on the bond tour. This psychic allegedly warned her to "keep out of planes in 1942. There is danger in them for you." This person might well have been Jeane Dixon. The *Photoplay* article can be found at DearMrGable.com. . . . In a very unusual story passed along in a 2014 paranormal book by Tim Swartz (who interviewed me on his podcast), a California-based pastor, Dr. Frank Stranges, declared he sometimes received messages from extraterrestrial entities. One of the insights aliens supposedly related to Stranges was that President Roosevelt had some sort of otherworldly encounter in late 1941. And beyond that the ETs claimed *FDR shot himself in 1945!* "Not even individuals in the U.S. high command knew" about the suicide, and "never saw the open coffin," Stranges is quoted as assuring. Precisely what I have been saying in *"MO41"* and herein. {What UFO or ET "encounter" Roosevelt supposedly had was not clear, but it allegedly occurred on 12/3/41.} Swartz's book also mentions a premonition in a dream that FDR is claimed to have once experienced regarding an airplane disaster, which was averted when action was taken, supposedly for everyone's safety at Washington D.C.'s airport. . . . After all the portents, one must wonder *"Why didn't Carole listen to the warnings of doom and stay out of airplanes?"* Apparently *love* – for her cheating husband – spurred her to ignore the premonitions of death, to hurry as fast as she could back to Hollywood and keep spouse Gable away from his co-star lusty Lana Turner. Carole felt her marriage was in trouble. Plus, she wanted to attend a screening of her latest film *"To Be Or Not To Be"* coming up in L.A. soon. The title couldn't be more ironic or apt.

CHAPTER TEN - Once again, material from *The Southeast Missourian* online archives was helpful with this chapter, including the 1/17/42 digitized issue. . . . I contacted author Leslie Kean, the UFO researcher whose

New York Times bestseller is mentioned herein. She said she was not familiar with the Lombard crash case, but found it interesting. She added that it is still impossible to say with certainty whether *deliberate* intent is the cause of UFO "radiation" crippling manmade aircrafts. . . . I consulted with aviation history buff Doug Scroggins in March of 2003, calling him to discuss the TWA Lombard accident outside Vegas from 1942. Doug operated a business that tracked down and recorded airplane accident sites, entitled *"Lost Birds."* He stated that flames shooting out of an airplane's engines should normally be present at "up to two feet in length." I recalled that one witness on the ground said he felt such flames from the one engine were up to four feet in length, while the other engine trailing flame was not noted. This could be a substantial difference indicating mechanical trouble. Doug declared proudly he'd been to the Lombard crash site "one hundred times" and could make the trip "in about fifteen minutes" up Mt. Potosi, not in the three hours it took his friend. Others who have been up to the scene have sadly trashed the place, illegally swiping "souvenirs" from the wreckage while leaving behind garbage, a very pathetic statement on today's selfish opportunism and exploitation of celebrity, even deceased ones. Scroggins leans towards the "pilot error" theory, and while I disagree, more can be found within his website, lostbirds.com where Doug repeats a '42 news story statement that some sort of event "happened inside that cockpit and happened so fast that the pilot could not" do anything about it. On that I certainly concur. . . . It means nothing, really, but a young John F. Kennedy went to Stanford University in late 1940/early 1941, and at times flew down to L.A., visiting some Hollywood studios where he met Clark Gable. Whether JFK ever met Lombard is not known, but certainly Carole worked for his father, Joe Kennedy, Sr., the head of Pathe Studios years before '42. . . . Orson Welles' radio version of H. G. Welles' *"The War of the Worlds"* was a nationwide story in 1938; the alleged (but untrue) audience "panic" for this broadcast was allegedly invoked over the years as a big reason why the U.S. government would aggressively hush up evidence of alien visitation via Army recoveries. Lombard was once tentatively scheduled to make a movie with Welles as her director, but the project never got off the ground. Instead, Welles went on to make his cinematic masterpiece, "*Citizen Kane*," which came out within days of MO41. Orson claimed there were "big-time physicists" on board her Flight #3, which is an interesting detail; the DC-3 seated 21 but only 19 were officially logged board, so at least 2 passengers in theory *could* have been scientists whose names were kept off the books in the hushed aftermath. See more at Hollywood-elsewhere.com. . . . In late October of '41, there were three airliner accidents, killing all onboard, and a week earlier an Army plane in Michigan. These and other aerial accidents may have led to the senate forming a senate sub-committee to investigate. Was MO41 included in this near-private research? . . . A secret report from 1960 was leaked just a few years ago, regarding a governmental "Subcommittee of National Investigations Committee on Aerial Phenomenon." NICAP had been quietly looking into cases of manmade aircraft being zapped by UFO-created superior energy waves. The 25-page document was entitled "Electro-Magnetic Effects Associated with Unidentified Flying Objects," and can be found online with many other recovered UFO documents in Ryan Wood's excellent Majesticdocuments.com. The information shows that the power-impaired TWA aerial accident was hardly unique, and that the U.S. government took the ongoing interference problem very seriously behind the scenes, for decades after '42. *UFOs gravely affecting human aircrafts might still be going on today.* . . . Backup information on Otto Krause's knowledge of a 1941 UFO crash's magnetic propulsion device comes from a source interviewed within the helpful website UFOmind.com. It uses the pseudonym "Alfred" for the same source Linda Moulton Howe utilized (with background info) on her own website. I also consulted the 1995 web page posting entitled "The Naked Truth From Open Sources," within "*The Groom Lake Desert Rat*," in that site, under "The Story of Alfred." . . . I have the complete Civil Aeronautics Board final report on the TWA calamity, printed out from exploringearth.com. The U.S. congress likely relied on C.A.B.'s findings when investigating the crash, but to me it is incomplete, ignoring the "lights in the sky" witnesses, and the Willard George testimony. Today we have more data and can form a clearer picture, despite government redaction. . . . The *S.S. Cape Girardeau* was supposedly a name first hit upon by a secretary working in an office within the shipyards of a coastal California community during World War II, according to a *Southeast Missourian* article on the eye-catching title. But it had to have been approved by those very high up in the Navy, and/or the War Department, and perhaps by the president himself? . . . In addition to the rumors of Howard Hughes being asked by the U.S. military to get involved in examining and duplicated downed UFO technology via modern research like Bill Knell's webpage "*Did Howard Hughes View a Captured UFO and its Occupants?*" from 2008, there's also the matter of ex-Army intelligence officer Thomas Cantwheel. He stated in his late 1990s typed letter to a researcher that the MO41 materials were copied and infused into a U.S. Air Force secret project to create a new circular flying craft that could be supplied with atomic weapons. "Materials used in the construction {were} by the Hughes Aircraft Company." . . . Also mildly helpful in exploring facts about Lombard's nightmarish finish were two biographies: "*Clark Gable*," published by Warren Harris, Harmony Books, 2002; and "*Long Live the King*," by Lyn Tornabene, G. P. Putnam & Sons, 1976. . . . Another source was the Arts & Entertainment Channel's "*Biography*" about Lombard, plus a few websites here and there. . . . Clark Gable visited the

White House only once more, in 1958. He had no appointment but was received warmly in the Oval Office by President Eisenhower, whom he met a few times during WWII in Europe. "Ike" cabled Gable after his November 1960 heart attack, just days before the actor died peacefully in a hospital bed. He was buried in a Forrest Lawn crypt right next to Carole Lombard. . . . In mid-1941, Gable and Lombard regaled director Alfred Hitchcock - who was renting their old house - with the story of a shrunken, burned head that was buried in the back yard. It seems this authentic South American tribal decapitation victim's skull was bad luck if mistreated, perhaps cursed. The two stars had thrown it out of a window of their car a few years earlier, then went back to look for it, with the aid of two passing policemen. The couple found it in an L.A. ravine and took it home, where Lombard had it placed in a special small coffin and gave it a lighthearted "funeral" on her property. Was there a curse? After her flight crashed Carole Lombard's own head was found lopped off, burned badly, and was later placed in a coffin and buried quietly in L.A.

BONUS CHAPTER – The lowdown on Secret Service Agent Boring comes from his oral interview published by the TrumanLibrary.org, and also via the book and online research of author Vince Palamara. Similarly on Agent Paterni, who was not with FDR in April 1945. Also in November '63, Agent Jackson Krill (19??-2000) served FDR and was also a part of the agency's JFK assassination response, instructing fellow agents to publicly keep their mouths shut afterwards. Krill also served as a spy in William Donovan's OSS (later the CIA) and in U.S. Naval Intelligence, and could well have found out about MO41 from both sources. Agent Gerald Behn (1916-1993) served both FDR and JFK as well and deserves closer scrutiny on his actions in responding to both presidents' deaths and the same can be said for agents Bill Greer and Roy Kellerman in the JFK case. . . . Agent Michael F. Reilly's book was published by Simon & Schuster in 1947, aptly entitled *"Reilly of the White House."* . . . Rowley's oral interview is also found online via the Truman Library and their website. Rowley said he chatted with Donovan on FDR's yacht in the Potomac, where top secret subjects could be spoken of quite openly, with no eavesdropping possible. Rowley was with the FBI in 1936, then transferred to the Secret Service in '38. Rowley was promoted in '46 and worked his way steadily up to overall chief in '61 - rewards for keeping quiet? Also with Rowley and Boring at Warm Springs was then-White House S.S. Chief Mike Reilly. Rowley stated there were about 15 total agents stationed at the White House in the Roosevelt/Truman years, working in three shifts, 24/7, often near the Oval Office and the upstairs private quarters (where FDR had a phobia about closing his bedroom door, his voice very audible in the halls). Thus such S.S. agents were easily able to overhear certain conversations, even top secret ones. . . . Trivia: just a few days before FDR's 4/12/45 death, Eleanor Roosevelt was in Washington, asking an aide to contact congressmen to do something about southeast Missouri sharecroppers who had been kicked out of their homes. She had tried to help them six years earlier. Some of the farm workers were from the Sikeston area, perhaps even near the airport MO41 holding site. . . . A source of info on the JFK assassination was Sergeant Robert Vinson, who was on an airplane with possibly connected personnel on 11/22/63, but the day before was seated "in a basement office of the Capitol Building," of all places. According to author James Douglass and his 2008 book *"JFK and the Unspeakable,"* this special underground Capitol room was considered an office for the official liaison between the Pentagon and Congress. Vinson said he overheard an Army officer warn over the phone how ill-advised it was for JFK to visit Dallas on 11/22/63. Any Capitol sub-basement room that might have held MO41 *might* also have been associated with a nearby U.S. Army or Navy liaison office to the U.S. congress, back in April 1941. . . . . A June 2016 *"60 Minutes"* report showed a hallway's wooden double doors and stated that behind them rested "a vault in the U.S. Capitol," indicating that *if* the MO41 materials were taken to this very room, the wide-opened twin doors likely could have handled an incoming spaceship cut up in sections, as has been alleged by Reverend Holt. A black plaque or framed directory was fixed to a wall to the immediate right, in this rare CBS footage. The doors were not opened for the camera, indicating the room was still secret and off-limits territory to the media and the public. . . . Information on Kennedy and the PT-109 widow and child comes from the pages of *"PT 109"* by William Doyle, in 2015. . . . The online "D.C. mortician-friend" story comes from the website *"Lies Your Teacher Taught You."* . . . The online source who "worked for man who befriended a Marine" story comes from wiki.answers.com. . . . I wrote to Virginia Jarrow in May of 2016 and received only a brief reply, so I wrote her back with a much more lengthy description of my FDR suicide research and some questions, but she did not respond. . . . One 1945 Illinois U.S. senator was Republican Charles Brooks (who lost his next re-election, in '48), and the other was Democrat Scott Lucas, who as an FDR backer became "party whip" in '46 and Senate Majority Leader in '48. Illinois' governor in 1945 was Dwight Green, in power during MO41 and named by Jarrow as someone who refused to meet with her mother regarding her harassment. . . . The Spring Hill mortician's handwritten notes were provided online by the digital library Scribd.com and its 2009 interested FDR health contributor, Dr. Steven Lomazow. There is no way of knowing if the original '45 notes had been heavily influenced by the Roosevelt inner circle or Secret Service, however. . . . Through Facebook in 2015 I asked JFK's accused assassin's mistress – Judyth Baker – if she had any insight into Lee Harvey Oswald and UFOs, and she replied affirmatively. LHO and Baker discussed ET visitation "because we were both intensely interested in science fiction so of course we discussed UFOs and believed the government was hiding the truth." Supposedly Oswald the Marine was an agent in the Office of Naval Intelligence and trained for a period in North Carolina; Kennedy was also an agent for ONI and trained for a period in South Carolina; both may well have found out during their intel service time more than hints of what the government knew behind the scenes on UFOs. . . . Bill Holden info was found in a number of online UFO websites and a book or two, stemming from his June 2007 interview on speaking to JFK on AF1 while flying to Germany. Supposedly, steward Holden placed two German newspapers in front of the president, since they featured prominent articles with actual photographs of UFOs. . . . In the spring of 1968, JFK's brother, Senator Robert Kennedy, arrived at an outdoor campaign rally in my hometown, and according to witnesses blurted out to the crowd, "I've always wanted to come to Cape Girardeau!" By his side was space-orbiting astronaut John Glenn, who earned his pilot's license after much training in the spring of 1941. Whether either famous man was aware of MO41 is unknown, but... *interesting synchronicity*: it was 4/25/68, just after the 27th anniversary of the UFO crash, which I believe largely took place near the very airport the twosome landed at and departed from that sunny day. Sadly, Bobby Kennedy had only six weeks to live.

3 PRESIDENTS, 2 ACCIDENTS:

More MO41 UFO Crash Data and Surprises

BIBLIOGRAPHY

First, I again utilized the same resources as in the first "*MO41*" book:

"*Above Top Secret: The Worldwide UFO Cover-up*," by Timothy Good, 1988, Morrow

"*Alien Agenda*," by Jim Marrs, 1997, Harper-Collins Publishers

"*Alien Contact: Top-Secret UFO Files Revealed*," by Timothy Good, 1991, Quill

"*Alien Mysteries, Conspiracies, and Cover-Ups*," by Kevin Randle, 2013, Visible Ink Press

"*Covert Retrieval: Urban Legend or Hidden History?*" 2013, by Linda L. Wallace

"*The Day After Roswell*," by Phillip Corso & William J. Birnes, 1997, Pocket Books

"*The Irregulars: Roald Dahl and the British Spy Ring in Wartime America*," by Jennet Conant, 2008, Simon & Schuster

"*It Didn't Start With Roswell: 50 Years of Amazing UFO Crashes, Close Encounters, and Cover-ups*," by Phillip Rife, 2001, Writers Club Press, an imprint of iUniverse.com, Inc.

"*The Lost Symbol*," by Dan Brown, 2009, Doubleday Publishing

"*Majic: Eyes Only*," by Ryan S. Wood, 2005, Wood Enterprises

"*Need To Know: UFOs, the Military, and Intelligence*," by Timothy Good, 2007, Pegasus Books

"*No Ordinary Time*," by Doris Kearns Goodwin, 1994, Simon & Schuster

"*Oppenheimer and the American Century*," by David C. Cassidy, 2005, Pi Press

"*Pearl Harbor: FDR Leads the Nation Into War*," by Steven M. Gillon, 2011, Basic Books

"*Rendezvous With Destiny*," by Michael Fullilove, 2013, Penguin Press

"*Rush Hudson Limbaugh*," by George Suggs, 2003, SEMO U. Press

"*Sage-ing While Age-Ing*," by Shirley MacLaine, 2007, Atria Books

"*Those Angry Days*," by Lynne Olson, 2013, Random House

"*Truman*," by David McCullough, 1992, Simon & Schuster

"*UFO Crash/Retrievals: The Inner Sanctum, Status Report VI*," by Leonard Stringfield, 1991

"*UFOs: Myths, Conspiracies, and Realities*," by John Alexander, 2011, Thomas Dunn Books

"*What If*," by Shirley MacLaine, 2013, Atria Books

Plus, I also utilized these other books:

"*America's Strange and Supernatural History*," by Tim Swartz, 2014, Inner Light/Global Communications

"*Best Evidence*," by David Lifton, 1980, re-published by Signet in 1992

"*Covert Encounters in Washington D.C.*," by Robert M. Stanley, 2011, Unicus Press

"*FDR and Lucy: Lovers and Friends*," by Resa Willis, 2004, by Rutledge, Taylor, and Francis Group

"*Fireball: Carole Lombard and the Mystery of Flight 3*," 2014, by Robert Matzen, GoodKnight Books.

"*Jack Kennedy: The Education of a Statesman*," by Barbara Leaming, 2006, W.W. Norton & Company

"*JFK and the Unspeakable*," by James W. Douglass, 2008, Touchstone Books/Simon & Schuster

"*The Presidents and UFOs: A Secret History from FDR to Obama*," by Larry Holcombe, 2015, St. Martin's Press

"*Project Identification*," by Dr. Harley Rutledge, PhD, 1981, Prentice-Hall, Inc.

"*PT 109: An American Epic of War, Survival, and the Destiny of John F. Kennedy*," William Doyle, 2015, William Morrow Books

"*The Roosevelts: An Intimate History*," by Geoffrey Ward and Ken Burns, 2014, Alfred Knopf

"*Survivor's Guilt*," by Vincent Palamara, 2013, Trine Day LLC

"*The Untold History of the United States, Volume 1*" by Oliver Stone and Peter Kuznick, 2012, Simon and Schuster

"*Wild Bill Donovan*," by Douglas Waller, 2011, FP/Simon & Schuster

Photo Session

1. Harry S Truman meets with President Roosevelt, in August of 1944. They shooed away reporters and talked in private about something critical that has never been revealed. All HST would say later was that FDR warned him to stay out of the air for the fall campaign, during their meeting just outside the White House.

2. HST with President-elect Eisenhower, in November 1952. They shooed away reporters and talked in private about something critical that has never been revealed. The two met in the Oval Office in the White House, despite great tensions between them.

3. HST meets with President Kennedy, in January of 1961. They shooed away reporters and talked in private about something critical that has never been revealed. Truman "just happened" to be JFK's first Oval Office guest in the White House.

4. HST meets with President Johnson, in November of 1963. They shooed away reporters and talked in private about something critical that has never been revealed. Truman met with LBJ in the White House, just after he became president, when JFK was buried.

5. HST meets with President Nixon, in March of 1969. They shooed away reporters and talked in private about something critical that has never been revealed. Truman was elderly when Nixon took office, and didn't care for him, but the new president flew to Missouri for this meeting two months after being sworn in, the topic was so important.

6. FDR and his fellow Freemasons meet in the Oval Office.

7. HST as a Freemason.

8. JFK in Germany, with Secretary of the Navy Forrestal and Commodore Henry Schade.

9. Carole Lombard posing on, of all things, the wheel of an airplane, a few years before her tragic airliner death.

10. Foreshadowing magazine article title on Lombard, her airplane, and a desert mountain crash, from 1935.

Printed in Great Britain
by Amazon